MERCHANTS OF ART

Jacques Seligmann (1858–1923)
Portrait by Joaquin Sorolla y Bastida, 1911.

GERMAIN SELIGMAN

MERCHANTS OF ART: 1880-1960

Eighty Years of Professional Collecting

APPLETON-CENTURY-CROFTS, INC.

NEW YORK

Grateful acknowledgment is made to the publishers for permission to quote material appearing on the following pages:

Page 23, extract from Frederick Lewis Allen's *The Big Change* (New York: Harper & Brothers).

Pages 37–38, extract from Marquis de Castellane's *How I Discovered America* (New York: Alfred A. Knopf, Inc.).

In loving devotion this book

is dedicated to my father,

Jacques Seligmann.

Acknowledgments

Several years ago when the idea of writing a book about my father and the collectors of his time was still germinating, a conversation with the late Francis Henry Taylor, then Director of the Metropolitan Museum, spurred the thought into action. His monumental study of art collecting in an earlier time, *The Taste of Angels,* had just been published, and he was acutely aware of the value of first-hand accounts by those who had actually participated in the events about which he wrote. If, therefore, these recollections of my father, the firm which he founded some eighty years ago, and the collectors who have crossed its threshold prove to be of value to the art historian and of interest to the layman, their thanks, and mine, are due Mr. Taylor for his encouragement.

Unfortunately, the earlier pages are not as comprehensive as they might have been, for most of the records of the Paris firm were destroyed during World War II, and the records of the New York firm prior to 1911 are meager. Thus a great deal has perforce been written from memory, which fortunately serves well for events which took place in one's early years, reinforced by invaluable help from the many friends who have so generously placed their own records at my disposal.

Foremost among these, again, I have to thank the late Francis Henry Taylor and the members of the Metropolitan Museum staff, especially Albert Ten Eyck Gardner, then Archivist, for his unfailing patience and kindness; the late Theodore Y. Hobby, keeper of the Altman Collection, whose knowledge of that great period of collecting was most precious to me; Elizabeth Gardner whose knowledge of all the great paintings in the museum has saved me much time in research; and James J. Rorimer, the Museum's present Director for assistance in straightening out the ramifications of the Morgan Collection.

My especial thanks go to Frederick B. Adams, Jr., of the Morgan Library for giving so freely of his time and for his patience in answering the many questions I put to him. Miss Felice Stampfle and Mrs. Francena Harris were no less generous and cooperative.

Franklin M. Biebel, Director of the Frick Collection, went to no end of trouble to throw light on problems presented to him. As for the Frick Art Reference Library, I wonder how many books on art would ever be written were it not for Mrs. Henry W. Howell, Jr., and her able staff.

The late Dr. W. R. Valentiner, whose tenure at the Metropolitan Museum coincided with the most active years of Jacques Seligmann in the United States, was kind enough to assist me with reminiscences and data.

My grateful thanks are also extended to all the museum officials and private collectors who so generously allowed me to reproduce works from their collections and who supplied missing information.

Assistance was given no less willingly by European friends and I deeply regret that these words appear too late to reach the eyes of two of them— Carle Dreyfus, late Curator at the Musée du Louvre, and Dr. Leo Planiscig, formerly of the Vienna Kunsthistorisches Museum. Men of profound knowledge and great personal charm, both were friends of many years standing whose passing I mourn.

Among others whose kindness I most appreciate are Mr. and Mrs. Gaston Brière, Professor Louis Réau, and André Blum, as well as certain private collectors who prefer not to be mentioned by name.

My thanks also are due to Robert Cecil, Assistant Keeper of the Wallace Collection in London, for assistance and encouragement in the difficult task of reconstructing the Paris section of that fabulous collection.

One of my best sources of information has been my associate, Mrs. Theresa D. Parker, who came to the firm in 1924 to do two weeks' work and has remained at my side for more than thirty years. Her vigilant eyes and ears have given her an insight into and an understanding of events which had escaped me, and she has recalled to me others which I had forgotten completely. Betty Morrison and Martha Barton Robertson, also of the firm, have been of the greatest help.

And, of course, Ethlyne, my wife, has been constantly at my elbow to bring order and method into the heterogeneous accumulation of names and events. It is truly as much her book as it is mine.

Last, but by no means least, my undying gratitude is due to Mima, Mrs. George F. Porter, for the peace and serenity which surrounded us at Les Mas, where much of this was written, and for the patience and enthusiasm she displayed as captive audience.

G. S.
Les Mas
Ojai, California, 1959

Contents

CONTENTS

Illustrations

ILLUSTRATIONS

ILLUSTRATIONS

xviii

Introduction

There have been art dealers as long as there have been art collectors, which is to say as long as there have been works of art, and art dealing has been big business at some period in the life of every great capital. The social status of the dealer, like that of the collector, has ranged from peddler to prince; some have been ignorant of all values except the monetary, others have been cultivated amateurs; some have been themselves practicing artists, others have subsidized, occasionally victimized, the practicing artist; some have been the proprietors of great galleries, others have sold works of art as a side line. It is safe to say that works of art in public museums throughout the world today have passed through the hands of about an equal number of dealers and collectors, with an equal proportion of love and understanding. In the United States, particularly, the total of works of art in public collections which came there, directly or indirectly, through the efforts of a dozen leading firms is impressive.

In view of this, it is curious how few dealers' names are recorded in the histories of art. Libraries abound with histories of collecting, but no one has undertaken a serious study of the development of the art trade. The late Francis Henry Taylor touched lightly on this phase of the art world as a corollary in his book on collecting, *The Taste of Angels*. Frits Lugt, in connection with his exhaustive compilation of collectors' marks, has done much valuable research, particularly for the art trade of Holland. But the definitive history is still to be written.

Until the 17th century, the art dealer was more agent than shopkeeper, working on salary or commission for wealthy or noble clients. Often he was an artist who advised his patron in the filling of his cabinet, or he was an importer who handled *objets d'art et de curiosité* along with his regular line of silks and spices. Being largely a middle-man, he had little need for storage space, and his noble clientele preferred to be waited upon in their own palaces. It was the rise of the rich burgher class in Holland, themselves merchants and businessmen, that brought about the change; they had no prejudices about shopping for works of art to adorn their homes. Thus the sensible Dutch, who since the 15th century had strictly regulated the trade in works of art through the Guild of Saint Luc, established themselves in shops where they could display their wares and receive their bourgeois clients. Though the agent-artist-adviser formula continued throughout the 18th century—and, indeed, exists in our day—the pattern for the modern merchant of works of art had been outlined. It remained for the 19th and 20th century firms, however, to develop art dealing into a career and a profession.

The art dealer of today is more often than not a man who has prepared himself by years of study in colleges, universities, or such special schools as the École du Louvre of Paris or the Institute of Fine Arts in New York. Some, like the *amateur marchand* of yesterday, choose to deal in works of art because it affords an opportunity to live and work with beautiful objects in a possessive way; others because it is more exciting, and incidentally more lucrative, than a scholarly career; still others, like myself, have grown up in a tradition and a business inherited from their fathers. Almost all are collectors in their private lives.

If I cannot in the space of these pages undertake a history of all our worthy predecessors, I can record the activities of one of the greatest of them, Jacques Seligmann, and some of my own adventures with the heritage he left to me—a vocation and an avocation.

All the works of art reproduced in this book have at some time been in the hands of the firm which Jacques Seligmann founded, first, in Paris and, later, in New York or the firms which stemmed from it, De Hauke & Co., New York, and G. Seligmann et Cie., Paris.

Inevitably, there will be differences of opinion about the interest or merit of some which have been included in comparison with others which have been omitted. The destruction of the files of the

Paris firm made it impossible to trace certain objects which it might have been desirable to reproduce; others have been left out in deference to the wishes of certain collectors, particularly among the older generation in Europe. Furthermore, the technicalities of reproduction quite often dictate a decision to omit an object rather than give a false impression of its beauty and importance. Even so, my original selection ran to more than four hundred objects and the choice of a reasonable number was not easy, for one is naturally attached to every item which has passed through one's hands.

The final choice was thus made with two purposes: first, to point out the variety of fields with which the firm is and has been identified; second, a natural sequence, to demonstrate the evolution of collecting during eighty years. If the selection seems heavy in certain fields, this is due to these very trends in collecting.

To emphasize these two aims, the date of purchase or its approximation has been given for each object, along with the name of the original purchaser and that of the present owner, if they are not the same.

MERCHANTS OF ART

CHAPTER I

Jacques Seligmann
and the Rue des Mathurins

Jacques Seligmann began his career in the art world at the age of sixteen as a humble assistant in the firm of Maître Paul Chevallier, the leading Parisian auctioneer of those days. The auction rooms of Paris, in the Hôtel Drouot, became his university. Nothing comparable to the *hôtel des ventes* of Paris exists in the United States, so an explanation should perhaps be made of its importance as a training ground for the eye and the mind of the art dealer and the collector.

A French auction is an official function and in Paris there are only a limited number of auctioneers. Each is duly licensed by the government, and the office is a highly respected, almost hereditary one. It is, in a manner of speaking, a fiduciary office, for by French law the estate of a deceased must, under certain conditions (usually when minor children are involved), be liquidated at auction. The possessions of rich and poor alike are subject to this law.

Thus day after day at the dusty, dirty old Hôtel Drouot in one of the busiest sections of Paris, twenty-odd rooms are filled with every conceivable kind of human possession, from the trash of metal bedsteads and dilapidated kitchenware to the most treasured items of a great art collection. These come from all corners of France, for while every city has its *hôtel des ventes*, Paris is the most active market. Particularly in past days, collections from all over Europe might be added to the mélange. The natural human instinct for collecting things, the traditional thrift of the French which makes them reluctant to dispose of anything, and their equally traditional respect for

1

works of art as capital investment combine to give variety and fascination to the flood of objects which passes daily through the auction room doors.

Sales often take place without benefit of catalogue. There is little time for preliminary exhibition and none for attractive display. It takes flair, instinct, and knowledge to detect quickly the item of value which may be hidden among the tons of rubbish. Then the finder must make up his mind at once, not only because time is limited, but also because a too long examination may draw the attention of another prospector and the risk of loss or competition in the bidding.

That mistakes are made here is obvious, but what ideal training it is for the eye and the senses! It is in this experimental manner that the surest knowledge is acquired and in the making of mistakes that unforgettable lessons are learned. My father used to call it a "tuition fee" and would add that only a conceited fool claims he never makes mistakes.

It is easy for me to reconstruct that phase of my father's training, for as soon as I was old enough to benefit by it, my father took or sent me to the Hôtel Drouot as often as possible, to go carefully through every room and report my findings. Thanks to his friendship with the officials, I was sometimes allowed to sit at the table next to the expert (in a French auction it is the expert, not the auctioneer, who describes the object for the bidders) and listen to his remarks about each object. While the bidding was going on, there was often time for me to examine the next object and ask if the leg of a chair was not a later addition or the nose on a statue a restoration. It was not necessary for every object to be a fine one—one learns to discriminate only by seeing all kinds. It was my father's conviction that flair, the instinct that makes a man react immediately to quality, was indispensable but was not sufficient by itself; it must be backed by experience. If flair allows one to ferret out the unusual and the beautiful, it is only experience which teaches the responsive eye to detect restorations or out-and-out forgeries.

That Jacques Seligmann had flair there is no doubt, and it must have manifested itself early, for he soon left Chevallier to work with Charles Mannheim, the foremost expert in medieval art and an advisor to the great collecting family of Rothschild. As experience began to give him confidence, he bought and sold an occasional item for his

2

own account, gradually accumulating enough capital to launch his own venture into the art business.

About 1880, when my father would have been twenty-two, he opened what must have been a very humble shop on the rue des Mathurins. I am not at all sure that it was really a shop, perhaps only a room under the family apartment, for Baron Edmond de Rothschild, in describing it to me years later, referred to the activity going on in the courtyard when he called there to see some works of art newly arrived from England. This must have been at the very beginning, for the Baron mentioned that it was shortly after his own marriage in 1878 when he was augmenting the furnishings of his home. "Works of art of all periods were piled one upon another," he said, "but when your father sent word of a new shipment, we always came at once, for should too many hours go by, we would be too late."

The man in his early twenties who could bring a Rothschild hurrying to the unfashionable rue des Mathurins was born in Frankfurt on the Main on September 18, 1858, second son of a moderately successful flour merchant. He talked little of his early life, and I am under the impression that his childhood was not entirely happy. His father died when the children were quite young, and my grandmother, whom I never knew, was apparently a capable and dynamic woman, who successfully managed both the business and the raising of four children. She evidently accomplished the latter with a heavy, and sometimes hasty, hand. My father was devoted to her as long as she lived, but there seemed to be little real understanding between them. Nevertheless, it was doubtless from her that he inherited his energy, his ambition, and his strong belief in discipline for himself and others.

Perhaps it was from her, too, that he acquired his hatred of Prussian militarism. An early recollection of which my father often spoke was the sound of the marching feet of the Prussian army as it paraded through the streets of Frankfort after the victory of Sadowa in 1866 and the vehement indignation of his mother as she banged the shutters to close out the hated sound. Frankfort had always been a free city whose citizens bitterly resented what they felt was enslavement to Prussia. This resentment was a strong factor in Jacques Seligmann's decision to leave Germany at the age of sixteen. Apparently he had learned French, which he spoke fluently, in the excellent German public schools, and it was natural that he should seek his fortune in

3

the land that had always represented, in his own words, liberty and freedom. As soon as he was of legal age he became a French citizen, and he preferred not to remember that he had ever been anything but French.

The France to which he migrated was making an amazing recovery from the Franco-Prussian war and, in concert with the rest of Europe, was embarking upon a great epoch of economic development. The end of the 19th and the beginning of the 20th centuries were to see the growth in number and power of the haute bourgeoisie, who would devote a generous share of their energy and wealth to acquiring works of art. It was an auspicious moment for Jacques Seligmann's venture.

Unfortunately, I know very little about these first years. My father was not given to reminiscences, being completely occupied with the present and future. The memoirs which he started in his later years were destroyed along with the firm's Paris records during the hectic and terrifying days of 1940. My knowledge of the struggling early years has thus had to come from conversations with those who knew him and from press accounts.

At the time of my father's death in 1923, William Roberts wrote in *The Times,* London, "He began in a small way, buying at small prices and selling at small profits. He frequently visited London, traveling third class during the night because it was the cheapest way. When he started on his own account his sole capital was twenty pounds. Part of this he invested in an English purchase which he almost immediately sold to a Paris collector for three hundred pounds."

It was one of the first London purchases which brought him to the attention of Ascher and Charles Wertheimer, proprietors of the great Bond Street gallery. It was to be a long and mutually profitable association. My father, after some debate with himself, took his courage in hand late one afternoon and determined to pay a call at this finest, and most expensive, of London galleries. His English was not then very accomplished, and upon asking somewhat haltingly if he might see Mr. Charles Wertheimer, he was informed by the lordly clerk who greeted him that the gentleman was engaged.

"Engaged?" thought the young caller, "Engaged? Qu'est-ce que c'est que ça?" He quickly ran over in his mind the vocabulary listed under the E's in the little French-English dictionary he had been assiduously studying. "Engaged? Ah, fiancé, bon!"

4

Jacques Seligmann and the Rue des Mathurins

With a triumphant smile he asked the clerk to extend his congratulations to Mr. Wertheimer, excused himself for having come at what was perhaps an inopportune moment, but might he make an appointment? When it was gently explained to him that this was the tea hour, and the Messrs. Wertheimer were simply engaged in that sacred English rite, Jacques Seligmann was so shocked by the idea that afternoon tea might be allowed to interrupt business that he immediately forgot his timidity and interpreted this as only an excuse to be rid of a youth of not-too-prosperous appearance. With dignity but firmness he so insisted that after a few moments one of the two brothers came into the hallway to inquire into this most unconventional behavior.

My father was impressed by the manner of the great dealer, but he was determined not to be defeated now that he had come this far. He explained that he had money to spend, probably not enough to buy the more expensive works of art they handled, but perhaps sufficient for some lesser, neglected items which might have accumulated over the years. Wertheimer was evidently so intrigued by this unusually frank approach that, after making it clear how contrary this was to custom at the tea hour, he personally escorted his visitor about the galleries. He was apparently impressed, too, by the discrimination and enthusiasm of the stranger and made an appointment for the following morning to close the transaction for several objects.

That evening, in his modest hotel room, Jacques Seligmann added up the sums which he had committed and was dismayed to find that his eagerness had carried him considerably beyond his means. There was nothing to do but explain his plight to Wertheimer the next morning. He would not ask for credit, but would they be willing to let him take a part now and set the rest aside for a prescribed length of time? Again his frankness won; Wertheimer was not only willing; he went further and offered to consign the balance rather than reserve it.

The story of the deal I heard from my father himself, but I did not know of the amusing language confusion until a few years ago, though I understand he told it freely. I doubt if it seemed funny to him at the time though, and his embarrassment may have reinforced his later determination to see that his children were not similarly handicapped. As soon as he could afford it, there was an English governess in the house and we grew up speaking English as easily as we did French. Later, we were all required to study German, and it was a rule of the house that we converse in a different language each day at mealtime. In addition, as the eldest son, I was sent several times to England and to Germany, where I lived weeks at a time in private homes, mainly to learn the language. I was also given a short course in the Russian language and learned enough of it to get along years later on the two occasions that I visited Russia.

With the exception of a few big firms of old and honorable tradition, the art business in the 19th century had been a hand-to-mouth affair, a great deal of it done through the offices of an *amateur marchand* or perhaps an artist who acted as advisor and intermediary for a patron. There was much pettiness and considerable misrepresentation, more often through ignorance than through dishonesty, but there was sufficient of the latter for many such stories to appear in the art press of that day.

The average small dealer occasionally acquired an exceptional work of art for little money, a find, and sold it at a large profit, but for the most part he simply bought the poor along with the good and let it go if the percentage of profit was large enough or the need for cash was pressing. Inventories were small and so were profits.

Jacques Seligmann had broader conceptions; he believed that an art dealer could be both connoisseur and businessman. He had a tremendous love for his profession and expressed his faith concretely by a willingness to invest and reinvest his profits in works of art. As soon as a measure of success allowed him to do so, he bought and he kept buying. If an immediate sale for an item did not transpire, he kept it—and bought more. He had little faith or interest in any other type of investment. The stock market held no lure for him even in the days of his greatest prosperity, a position possibly reinforced by the disasters many of his contemporaries had suffered in the crash of the Union Generale of 1882 and the Panama Canal venture of 1892. "How can a man of sound mind who knows his own business have greater faith in the judgment of another for the investment of his money," he used to say, flourishing the cane which he always carried, largely for the purpose of punctuating his words. He had little patience with dealers who put their profits into other activities and none with the art broker, who never invested his own money but bought and sold for the account of another. He reasoned—how can a seller convince a would-be client of the worth of an object, if he has insufficient faith to buy it himself?

Buying was the one phase of the business that Jacques Seligmann al-

6

Plate 1
Jean-Antoine Houdon (1741–1826). "Madame de Jaucourt," 1777, marble, height 26½". Acquired by D. David-Weill, Paris, 1912. Present collection: The Louvre. Gift of D. David-Weill, Paris.

Plate 2a
Antoine Coysevox (1640–1720). "Bust of Robert de Cotte," bronze, height 21″. Acquired by D. David-Weill, Paris, 1910. Present collection: The Frick Collection, New York.

Plate 2b
Leone Leoni (1509–1590). "Bust of Alfonso d'Avalos, Marchese del Vasto," bronze, life-size. From the collection of the Marchese del Vasto e Pescara, Naples. Acquired by J. Pierpont Morgan, 1908. Present collection: The Pierpont Morgan Library, New York.

Plate 3
Jean-Honoré Fragonard (1732–1806). "Garçon aux Cerises," 16⅞″ x 12½″.
From the Prault, Leroy de Senneville and Charras Collections. Acquired by
D. David-Weill, Paris, 1909. Present collection: Private collection, New York.

Plate 4
Franco-Flemish (Arras or Tournai), c. 1435–1440. "Courtiers with Roses," 9′ 7″ x 10′ 11¾
One of a set of three tapestries, presumably made for King Charles VII of France. From t
Sigismond Bardac Collection, Paris. Acquired by the Metropolitan Museum of Art, Rogers Fund, 19(

Plate 5
J. Pierpont Morgan (1837–1913), New York. Portrait by
Frank Holl, 1888, in the Pierpont Morgan Library, New York.

Plate 6
Vienna or Augsburg, 16th century. Book cover, with the arms of Philip II of Spain, gold, enamel and jewels, 18″ x 13″. From the collections of Baron Adolphe and Baron Maurice de Rothschild, Paris. Acquired by J. Pierpont Morgan, 1909. Present collection: The Pierpont Morgan Library, New York.

Plate 7
Etruscan 4th century B.C. Cist, with cover, bronze, height 14⅛″ x diameter 8⅝″. From the Spitzer Collection. Acquired by J. Pierpont Morgan, 1907. Present collection: The Pierpont Morgan Library, New York.

Plate 8a–d
Byzantine, 11th century. Cloisonné enamels, part of a group from the monastery of
Djumati, Georgia, diameter 3¼″ each. From the Swenigorodskoi Collection, St. Peters-
burg. Acquired by J. Pierpont Morgan, 1910. Present collection: The Metropolitan
Museum of Art. Gift of J. Pierpont Morgan, 1917.

Plate 9a
Austrian (Vienna), early 14th century. Hexagonal ciborium, copper-gilt with enamel, 13½″ x 3¾″. From the Abbey of Klosterneuburg and the collection of Baron Albert von Oppenheim, Cologne. Acquired by J. Pierpont Morgan, 1906. Present collection: The Pierpont Morgan Library, New York.

Plate 9b
German, 17th century. Chalice, bearing the date, 1609, and the Wolff-Metternich arms, gold, enamel and jewels, height 9″ x diameter 6″. From the collection of Baron Mayer Karl von Rothschild, Frankfurt am Main. Acquired by J. Pierpont Morgan, 1911. Present collection: The Metropolitan Museum of Art. Gift of J. Pierpont Morgan, 1917.

Plate 10a
Rhenish, early 14th century. Portable altar, surmounted by a reliquary cross, silver-gilt with translucent enamels and jewels, height 10″. From the collections of the Bishop of Lisieux and Wolff-Metternich. Acquired by J. Pierpont Morgan, 1911. Present collection: The Pierpont Morgan Library, New York.

Plate 10b
German (School of Speyer), early 14th century. Altar-tabernacle or casket, translucent enamel on silver, 6⅛″ x 7⅜″ x 5¾″. For the Convent of Lichtenthal, Baden. From the collection of Count Arco-Zinneberg, Munich. Acquired by J. Pierpont Morgan, 1908. Present collection: The Pierpont Morgan Library, New York.

Plate 12a, b
French, 14th century. "A King of France (possibly Jean le Bon or Charles V) and His Consort," marble, height 15½". From the Gaston Le Breton Collection, Rouen. Acquired by J. Pierpont Morgan, 1910. Present collection: The Metropolitan Museum of Art. Gift of J. Pierpont Morgan, 1917.

Plate 13

French (School of Michel Colombe), c. 1510–1512. "Pietà" from the Château de Biron, with donors Pons and Armand de Gontaut, polychromed limestone, height 3′ 6″. Acquired by J. Pierpont Morgan, 1907. Present collection: The Metropolitan Museum of Art. Gift of J. Pierpont Morgan, 1916.

Plate 14
Desiderio da Settignano (1428–1464). "Bust of Marietta Strozzi," marble, height 21⅜". From the Strozzi family. Acquired by J. Pierpont Morgan, 1908. Present collection: The Pierpont Morgan Library, New York.

Plate 15
Jehan Barbet de Lyon (active
1475–1514). "Angelot du Lude,"
1475, bronze, height 45½". From
the Georges Hoentschel Collection, Paris. Acquired by J. Pierpont Morgan, 1906. Present collection: The Frick Collection,
New York.

Plate 16
Antoine Coysevox (1640–1720). "Louis of France, the Grand Dauphin," marble,
height 31 1/16″. From the Wallace-Bagatelle Collection, Paris. Acquired by the
Samuel H. Kress Foundation, 1951. Present collection: National Gallery of Art,
Washington, D.C., Samuel H. Kress Collection, loan.

Plate 17a
Part of the Wallace-Bagatelle Collection at Rue Laffitte.
(Photograph courtesy of the Wallace Collection, London.)

Plate 17b
The garden façade of the Palais de Sagan

Plate 18a, b

French, 18th century. Pair of Louis XVI "Mustapha" consoles, 34″ x 34½″ x 9⅝″. From the Wallace-Bagatelle Collection, Paris. Acquired by Henry Clay Frick, New York, 1914. Present collection: The Frick Collection, New York.

Plate 19
French, c. 1785–1790. Desk of King Louis XVI, 52″ x 62⅛″ x 29″. From the Wallace-Bagatelle Collection, Paris. Present collection: The Metropolitan Museum of Art. Gift of Jacques Seligmann, 1919: "In memory of Mr. J. P. Morgan and as a souvenir of the help which the Americans have given in France during the war."

Plate 20
Edme Bouchardon (1698–1762). "L'Amour taillant son arc," 1744, marble, height 29".
From the Wallace-Bagatelle Collection, Paris. Acquired by Lord Wimborne, London,
1914, by Mortimer L. Schiff, New York, 1923, and by the Samuel H. Kress Foundation,
1950. Present collection: National Gallery of Art, Washington, D.C., Samuel H. Kress
Collection.

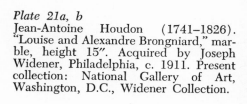

Plate 21a, b
Jean-Antoine Houdon (1741–1826).
"Louise and Alexandre Brongniard," marble, height 15″. Acquired by Joseph Widener, Philadelphia, c. 1911. Present collection: National Gallery of Art, Washington, D.C., Widener Collection.

Plate 22a
Nicolas Lancret (1690–1743). "The End of the Hunt," 23⅝" x 53". One of four over-
doors from the château of Marly-le-Roi. From the Wallace-Bagatelle Collection, Paris.
Acquired by M. Knoedler and Co., New York, 1914. Present collection: The M. H.
de Young Memorial Museum, San Francisco.

Plate 22b
François Boucher (1703–1770). "Cupid and the Graces," 1738, 55½" x 71¼". From
the Wallace-Bagatelle Collection, Paris. Acquired by M. Knoedler and Co., New York,
1914. Present collection: National Gallery of Art, Washington, D.C., Gulbenkian Collection, loan.

Plate 23a
Jean-Baptiste Pater (1695-1736).
"Le Concert Champêtre," 26" x
32¼". From the William Tilden
Blodgett Collection, New York.
Acquired by private collection,
Paris, 1926.

Plate 23b
François Boucher (1703-1770). "The Birth and Triumph of Venus,"
6' 8⅜" x 6' 6". From the Wallace-Bagatelle Collection, Paris. Acquired
by Baron Eugène de Rothschild, Vienna, 1914; repurchased jointly with
Paul Cailleux, Paris. Present collection: The Metropolitan Museum of Art.
Munsey Bequest and Gift of Henry Walters and Germain Seligman, 1928.

Plate 24
Jean-Antoine Houdon (1741–1826). "Sophie Arnould as Iphigénie," 1775, marble, height 26"
From the Wallace-Bagatelle Collection, Paris. Acquired by Edgar Stern, Paris, 1914. Present col-
lection: The Louvre. Bequest of Edgar Stern.

Plate 25
French, c. 1500. "Episode in Feudal Life," tapestry, 10' 4½" x 13' 4". Acquired by Miss Kate S. Buckingham, Chicago, 1922. Present collection: The Art Institute of Chicago, Lucy Maud Buckingham Collection.

Plate 26
Master of the Virgin among Virgins (active 1460/70–1495). "The Adoration of the Magi," 24¾" x 18⅞". Present collection: The Kaiser Friedrich Museum, Berlin. Gift of Jacques Seligmann, 1910.

Plate 27
Jacopo della Quercia (c. 1374–1438). "Madonna of Humility," marble, 23″ x 19¼″.
Acquired by Henry Goldman, New York, 1920. Present collection: National Gallery of
Art, Washington, D.C., Samuel H. Kress Collection.

Plate 28
French, 16th century. "Saint Barbara," marble, height 47½". Acquired by A. J. Kobler, New York, 1924. Present collection: National Gallery of Art, Washington, D.C., Samuel H. Kress Collection.

Plate 29

French (Beauvais), 17th century. "Amphitrite," one of four tapestries after cartoons by Berain, 13′ 10″ x 9′ 10″. Commissioned for the Comte de Toulouse, son of Louis XIV. From the collection of Baron de Hirsch, Paris. Acquired by François Coty, Paris, c. 1921. Present collection: Banque de France, Paris.

Plate 30a
Master of the Saint Barbara Legend (active late 15th century). "Scene from the Life of Saint Barbara," center panel of the triptych, c. 1475, 28½" x 49". Acquired by Musées Royaux, Brussels, 1939.

Plate 30b
Cima da Conegliano (c. 1459–1517/18). "Madonna and Child with Saint Jerome and Saint John the Baptist," 41⅜" x 57⅝". Acquired by Lord d'Abernon, 1922. Present collection: National Gallery of Art, Washington, D.C., Mellon Collection.

Plate 31
Rembrandt van Rijn (1606–1669). "Portrait of Joris de Caullery," 1632, 40½″ x 33″.
Acquired by George Rasmussen, Chicago, 1924. Present collection: M. H. de Young
Memorial Museum (Oakes Collection), San Francisco.

Plate 32
Hubert Robert (1733–1808). "Imaginary View of Rome," 63″ x 41½″. From the collection of Princess Paley, St. Petersburg. Acquired by private collection, New York, 1931.

ways kept in his own hands, even after the firm became too large to be a one-man business, as it quickly did. Within a few years he sent for his older brother, Simon, and his younger brother, Arnold. Simon looked after the books and the accounting, while Arnold's charm and affability made him an excellent salesman. Even when I came into the business as a partner years later, although my father had seen to it that I had every bit of training and experience he could command, he was likely to look upon my buying efforts with a somewhat jaundiced eye.

Jacques Seligmann had a prodigious capacity for work and a vast zest for life; the years at the rue des Mathurins must have taxed him to the full. He was an early riser by nature and upbringing; he was up at six or six-thirty, and so were his children. Even in his later years his work day averaged fifteen or sixteen hours. Somehow, in his youth he found time not only to build a business but to taste the delights of bohemian Paris. The Montmartre of Toulouse-Lautrec was at its zenith, and he spent gay evenings at the Moulin de la Galette and the Moulin Rouge. His tall, slim figure, the small Van Dyke beard (later replaced by a mustache), and a monocle, which he affected at this period, must have blended well with the atmosphere. I do not know whether he actually knew Toulouse-Lautrec, but he talked knowingly of the music-hall characters the artist immortalized.

To recreate the personality and history of my father is difficult. Often, in my imagination I have sought to retrace Jacques Seligmann's steps toward the fabulous career which made him a titan among the international art dealers who helped a whole generation amass great art collections. I believe his character portended his success. He was a dynamic man, radiating power, assurance, and optimism, without arrogance or pomposity. He was swift to make decisions and reach conclusions, not haphazardly, but because his lively intelligence allowed him to gauge soundly after brief consideration. Direct, straight and quick, he had little patience with the devious. He was always particular about his appearance; his hair was kept short, and his rigorously simple clothes were carefully pressed. He never wore a jewel, not even a ring; his watch was strictly utilitarian, its thin chain hardly visible. There was a certain austerity in his inner nature, and these small details of dress were its outward manifestation. He held himself erect and unstooped in his last years, just as he had in his youth.

7

Adventurous as he was in business enterprise, he was steady and conservative in his private life, although a true bon vivant in his enjoyment of a fine meal, vintage wine, good company, and laughter. Few matters irritated him as much as loose living, disorder, or lackadaisical manners. His life was governed by definite rules, and he was a disciplinarian as demanding of himself as of others. Respect and duty toward one's parents and responsibility for the education of one's children were paramount among his precepts. He was genuinely generous, often anonymously. Sure of himself and his conscience, he approached the world without fear. The socially and financially important never awed him. "They have to take me as I am with all my defects," he often said.

By 1900 Jacques Seligmann's family as well as his business had outgrown the rue des Mathurins. That year the family—there were now five children—moved to a more spacious and fashionably located apartment on the avenue Kléber, between the Place de l'Etoile and the Place du Trocadéro, and the business was moved to the Place Vendôme.

The distance by foot from the rue des Mathurins to the Place Vendôme is not great; it can be walked in about fifteen minutes. The distance in prestige is enormous. The rue des Mathurins was, and still is, a street of small shops; the Place Vendôme is the epitome of elegance. The rue des Mathurins is mediocrity; the Place Vendôme is success. I shall never know the story of the twenty years it took my father to travel these few blocks; the balance sheets and inventories destroyed during World War II might have indicated some of the hardships and successes of a growing business. That he could move his family to avenue Kléber, provide us with an ever-ascending standard of living, and at the same time accumulate sufficient capital and a large enough clientele to justify the business address of the Place Vendôme has to speak for itself.

Though I was seven years old at the time of the move, I have no recollection of that first small, obscure shop on the rue des Mathurins nor of the apartment above it where I was born. In fact, it was only when I was almost grown, and for some reason needed a birth certificate, that I discovered that my birthplace was in the 8th arrondissement, not in the more fashionable 16th of the apartment on the avenue Kléber. That my father was the proprietor of a great art gallery

8

on the Place Vendôme, arbiter of all within it, seemed only right and natural to me at that age; in my short remembrance it had always been that way. That it had not always been so for Jacques Seligmann never occurred to me.

As a child, I used to go to the galleries occasionally after school or on a free day to wait for my father. It amused me more to gaze down from the tall shuttered windows upon the busy traffic or to admire Napoleon on his tall bronze column than it did to examine the contents of the great velvet hung rooms. They were dim and a little awesome when there were no clients about to justify the lighting of the big crystal chandeliers. The furniture, delicate with marquetry and ormolu or heavy with carving, was the sort little boys were not allowed to sit upon, and the tempting small bright enamels and jewels were safely out of the reach of small fingers. The sculpture rooms beyond were a little eerie with their solemn company of stone saints and marble kings.

Nevertheless, it was a great treat to be allowed to go to "Papa's Galerie." If Monsieur Jacques were not busy with clients, I would be sent wherever he might be, in the courtyard supervising the unpacking of a new shipment or on one of the four floors directing the arrangement of a display case. I cannot remember today which sculpture my father turned to catch the light just so, or which Sèvres bowl he stroked with his long slender fingers to feel its quality. Still, I am puzzled occasionally by the strange familiarity of objects which to my knowledge I have never seen before. When I first visited the Metropolitan Museum in 1914 and saw four tiny and altogether delightful white enamel and gold angels in the Morgan Collection, I sensed at once that I knew them. My father claimed I could not possibly have remembered, as I was much too young when he had sold them. Perhaps they were in one of those cases; they are exactly the sort of exquisite toylike bibelot which a child would covet.

My most precise memory of those early visits to the Seligmann galleries is of a more mundane nature. My father and my Uncle Arnold were both connoisseurs of food and wine, and the luncheons they gave at Place Vendôme for friends and clients were celebrated, as were the abilities of the Austro-Hungarian cook who prepared them. She had a marvelous hand for pastries, and I can still savor the choice bits which she always reserved for my four o'clock *goûter*.

9

CHAPTER II

A Collector's Paradise: Paris Before 1914

The year 1900 was auspicious for expansion. There were still comparatively few art firms with large financial resources and a growing inventory of exceptional works of art. The number of collectors was increasing, and they came from all over Europe, for Paris in those days was truly a paradise for collectors.

If London competed for control of the art market, it was nevertheless in Paris that the greatest activity was to be found, and to the student, the scholar, and the collector France was supreme. The collections of the Louvre were unrivaled, and there were the lesser museums to draw the specialists—Cluny for the medievalist, the Guimet for the Orientalist, Carnavalet for the historian—and Paris itself for everybody. Versailles spread her splendor at the city gates; Fountainebleau, where the Renaissance and the 18th century were so happily blended, Compiègne, St. Germain, and Chantilly beckoned then, as they do now.

The Grand Dukes of Russia paused in Paris on their annual flight to the Riviera, trailed by the whole noble order: the Stroganoffs, Prince Galitzine, the Paleys, the Cheremeteffs, the Yousupoffs, and Count Pourtales, the German Ambassador to St. Petersburg. From Vienna came the Bendas, the Auspitzes, the Liechtensteins, and the Reitzes. The Bulgarian czar made an occasional visit; nonetheless welcome because he was more interested in selling than in buying, for he had inherited some exceptional 18th century objects.

Among the Berliners were the Mendelssohns, Mrs. Hermine Feist, already famed for her porcelain collection, James and Edouard

10

Simon, Walter von Pannwitz, Oscar Huldschinski, and the Prince von Reuss. England contributed such discriminating collectors as Lord d'Abernon, Walter Burns, Sir Philip Sassoon, and Lord Wimborne. From Brussels came the Adolphe Stoclets, who were just beginning the collection that was to make them world known. These were only a few of the willing and eager collectors, all discriminating amateurs in works of art, which Paris was doing her best to supply.

The move to the Place Vendôme was a logical one for a business with an international clientele. Here were the best hotels, the finest jewelers, the smartest couturiers. In the spacious, high-ceilinged rooms of the new quarters clients could be received in the manner to which they were, or would like to be, accustomed, and the works of art could be displayed to their best advantage. It was a convenient location, too, for the equally important and more permanent Parisian clients, who could easily drop in en route to their homes from the financial district or between a fitting and tea at the Ritz.

Those were the days when international exchange, particularly in works of art, encountered few obstacles. The gold standard prevailed almost everywhere. The solidity of the Banque de France and the Bank of England was soundly based on a universal demand for the louis d'or and the gold sovereign, then worth respectively twenty francs and twenty shillings or five dollars. Fluctuations of one or two points were events of magnitude which automatically created a reverse flow of gold to re-establish the balance. It was quite simple to buy in Germany and, via Paris, sell in England, or vice versa. There were few restrictions on the movement of works of art; Italy and Spain were the only countries which taxed, or sometimes forbade, their export; the United States was the only country which levied duty on their import. It was customary to make transactions in gold or in bank notes, not for fiscal reasons, as there were no income or transaction taxes to tempt the evader, but because it was simpler than writing a check, still a comparatively new procedure in Europe and somewhat suspect. Cash payments were so customary that certain contracts, leases for instance, provided that payment should be made *en espèces sonnantes et trébuchantes,* that is, money which had weight and which jingled.

In retrospect, it seems hardly credible that barely fifty years ago there was such faith in the louis d'or and the English gold pound, and such lack of it in the United States dollar, that European businessmen often hesitated to accept American currency. When Mrs. George Widener bought a set of magnificent 18th century tapestries after cartoons by Boucher from the Wallace-Bagatelle Collection, such a large sum was involved that arrangements were made for staggered payments. Mrs. Widener, of course, was thinking in terms of United States dollars. My father insisted upon payment in gold francs, and I believe he prevailed. This faith in his country's currency was shared by most businessmen, who could not know the reversal of positions which World War I was so shortly to bring about.

Many of the earlier Paris clients of my father I never knew; some I knew briefly in their declining years; others I felt I knew because of objects which passed through the firm's hands and because my father talked of them. Edouard André, for instance, who founded that most interesting and too little known Paris museum, the Jacquemart-André, died in 1894. He and his charming wife, Nélie Jacquemart, the painter, traveled about Europe assembling a collection of wide diversity and eclecticism. Upon the death of Madame André in 1912, the house which they built on the boulevard Haussmann, with its collections, as well as the Château de Chaalis near Ermenonville, were willed to the Institut de France. The installation of the Jacquemart-André, for which Madame André is said to have been responsible, is the first instance of the so-called modern conception of using furniture and decorative objects to create a period background for paintings and sculpture.

Well before my time also were the strange and retiring bachelor brothers Dutuit, Eugene and Auguste, of Rouen. Heirs of a considerable fortune—Auguste is said to have inherited seventeen million francs when his brother Eugene died in 1886—they lived a frugal and cloistered life, animated only by their passion for collecting. Upon Eugene's death in 1902, the entire collection was inherited by the Museum of the City of Paris, the Petit Palais. Its size and quality were astonishing: superb drawings; more than twelve thousand prints, including an almost perfect series of four hundred Rembrandt etchings; a library full of rare books and manuscripts; Dutch little master paintings; and rare classical, medieval, and Renaissance objets d'art.

Chalendon and Aynard of Lyon, Baron Sellière, Victor Gay, Piot of Paris, all were collectors whose names are familiar to art historians, and the catalogues of their collections are important in any good art library. All of them my father knew.

What were the works of art all of them were seeking? Obviously they did not all share the same tastes, but I believe I am right in stating that fine sculpture was in that day among the most sought after and the most valuable. Stone sculptures of the Romanesque and Gothic periods, when they could be found, or marbles of the Italian Renaissance and the French 18th century entranced the discriminating collector—Gustave Dreyfus, for instance, whose collection is now scattered among museums of the world; Oscar Huldschinski, who owned one of Tullio Lombardi's most exquisite profile portraits, now in a private collection in New York; Baron Jerome Pichon, whose collection included the two lovely marble busts of the Brongniard children by Houdon, now among the most beloved exhibits of the National Gallery in Washington. These charming Houdon children were family heirlooms from Baron Pichon's mother, née Brongniard, daughter of the famous architect, and herself subject of a famous portrait by Madame Vigée-Lebrun. Sometime before 1897 the two busts passed into the hands of Sigismond Bardac and it was from him that my father acquired them and subsequently sold them to Joseph Widener.

Baron Pichon was before my time, but I do remember Sigismond Bardac quite well. Of Russian origin, he was one of three well-known banker and collector brothers, Sigismond, Noel, and Joseph. Sigismond was the most active collector of the three and remarkably well-posted about activities in the art world. To be in the know is of considerable importance if one is to be on hand when a collector is in a mood to buy—more especially when he is in a mood to sell. There was always news to be gleaned from Bardac, and sometimes there was the possibility of acquiring some coveted treasure from him. He was never satiated in his hunt for new possessions and occasionally had to part with one in order to acquire another.

It was from Bardac that my father acquired a series of remarkably fine tapestries, known as *La Baillée des Roses,* which were to constitute his first big sale to the Metropolitan Museum in New York. Tapestries at this period were probably next to sculpture in desirability and rarity. Most sought were the already scarce 15th century weavings, the rich gold and silver woven tapestries of the 16th century, usually from the Lowland ateliers, and the very special Beauvais and Gobelins of the 18th century, delicate in texture and color, and designed by Boucher, Fragonard, Casanova, and other leading artists of the day. One hundred thousand dollars was not an unusual price for any of these.

Other collectors were captivated by works of the Middle Ages and the Renaissance—ivories of the 14th century; champlevé enamels of the 12th and 13th, painted ones of the 16th; small Italian bronzes by Riccio, Sant'agata, Giovanni da Bologna; superb majolicas, the deep blacks and yellows of Urbino, the rich lusters of Deruta and Gubbio, the glowing colors of Siena. In the early 1900's these brought prices which now are reserved for Cézannes and Picassos. It is strange today, when these precious small objects seem to have been relegated to the archaeological realm of museums, to remember how they were sought forty or fifty years ago. When the Frederic Spitzer Collection was dispersed in 1893, after the death of that perhaps greatest of 19th century collectors, it numbered four thousand items, from the antique to the 18th century, with scarcely a painting among them. Spitzer had been an art dealer, an Austrian, who came to Paris about 1852 and there made a fortune which enabled him to achieve the dream of all dealers who love their metier—retirement to collecting for his own pleasure. At the time of his death his house on the rue Villejust was popularly known as the Musée Spitzer. The sale, under the direction of Mannheim and Maître Chevallier, still ranks among the outstanding of the century. My father was one of the major buyers, later channeling a number of Spitzer's treasures into other collections.

Highly prized also in those years were exceptional pieces of French 18th century furniture—suites of chairs tapestried with flowers or personages, again Gobelins or Beauvais, for a great distinction was made between these and the weavings of Aubusson, for instance; small precious tables with or without Sevres plaques; large princely commodes or console tables inlaid with exotic woods, adorned with gilt bronzes, or carved, gilded and topped with rare marbles. The commodes and consoles were especially sought in pairs, and certain collectors would patiently wait years to find just the right pair to complete the balance of a room.

Count Moïse de Camondo, of the well-known banking family, was a collector who had a particular passion for objects in pairs. The only period which really interested him was the Louis XVI, and he was not only a connoisseur but a purist and perfectionist. The house which he built on the rue de Monceau, modeled after the Petit Trianon of Versailles, is one of the few perfect houses I have ever seen, a criterion of the Louis XVI style. Architectural symmetry was the ideal and the house as well as its furnishings must reflect it, thus the particular interest in furniture, porcelains, and sculptures in pairs. They lent emphasis to the axes of the halls or the salons and pointed up the perfection of the building itself. Camondo never allowed his desire for a coveted pair to blind him to quality or to proportion; he would wait rather than accept second best. The house is now the Musée Nissim de Camondo, in memory of his only son killed in World War I, and is a part of the Musée des Arts Decoratifs.

If Camondo was somewhat dogmatic as a connoisseur, he was nevertheless delightful as a person. He had a lively sense of humor and a quick wit, which he liked to pit against my father, himself seldom at a loss for repartee. I remember an encounter they had on the occasion of the great fete given at the Château de Versailles shortly after World War I to celebrate its reconditioning, made possible by the generosity of John D. Rockefeller, Jr. The galleries of the Château were open and lighted, the flower gardens were a glory under the illumination, and the fountains sparkled and splashed in spotlights. Hundreds of Parisians and foreigners in gay evening attire had come to witness the splendor. Spying my father and me in the crowd, the Count, a striking figure in evening dress and the black monocle he always wore to disguise a sightless eye, walked quickly toward us. Without preliminary greeting, he put out his hand, and said, "Congratulations, Jacques, I understand you have just bought Versailles!"

Without an instant's hesitation, my father replied, "Thank you, thank you, mon cher ami, but you know, you've heard only half the story. What you haven't heard is that I've already sold it!"

If Jacques Seligmann could not sell Versailles, his clients could find at Place Vendôme furniture to grace a palace; some of it actually had. They could find here also the Savonnerie rugs, sometimes even the rare "black-backgrounds" of the end of the 17th century, upon which to rest such precious pieces; the delightful small terra cottas or marbles by Falconet or Clodion to place on delicate tables; and clocks of marble or bronze and candelabra by Caffieri, Messionier, or Gouthière to decorate carved mantels. These were especially suitable for the larger reception rooms of a collector's house. The smaller, more

15

intimate rooms displayed objects which particularly expressed the personality of the owner. Here were the drawings, more in demand then than paintings (sketches by Fragonard, for instance, brought two or three times their prices of today), and an avid collector might have enough sepias, gouaches, or crayons to line up in two or three rows. Here also were the precious tiny things, gold snuffboxes and *necessaires,* onyx and crystal coupes, each chosen for its quality and the joy of its sight and feel. The more fragile bits, such as the rare yellow and rose Sevres, were usually in small vitrines to protect them from harm.

Like his clients, Jacques Seligmann loved, understood, and reacted with as much enthusiasm to a fine boxwood Virgin of the 14th century as to a drawing of the 18th century, and thus he did his best to supply collectors with what they coveted. There were exceptions. Painting was one field into which he only occasionally ventured, because paintings interested collectors less then than they do today. Classical antiquities was another. He had a particular distrust of the terra-cotta Tanagra figurines for which there was such a vogue, knowing how easily fooled one might be. Also, he refused to have anything to do with the Orient, claiming that he had all he could do to understand and appreciate the art of the Western world, whose heritage was his own, without trying to become an expert in works of an alien culture.

Seeking and acquiring works of art to tempt his clients soon became the most important phase of Jacques Seligmann's business. His problem was increasingly not to sell but to buy. The buying policy of an art firm is the keystone of its reputation; to purchase wisely requires not only knowledge and discrimination but also courage. The art dealer must pay in cash when the opportunity presents itself, and the decision rests entirely on his own quick judgment. The circumstances may involve a multitude of factors quite outside the basic one of aesthetic merit. A change in international politics may have an immediate impact upon the art market; boom, crisis, or slight recession affect it, and, more subtle and harder to foresee, so does shifting public taste. The experienced dealer must evaluate his commitments in these terms, irrespective of his own enthusiasm for an object.

Rivalry in purchasing is in every way comparable to that in selling. There are many stories about the lengths to which dealers of that ruggedly individualistic time went to circumvent a competitor and

16

beat him to a collector who had indicated a willingness to sell. One of my favorites is about my father and Leon Helft, a friend and business rival of long and honorable standing. Both found themselves one evening about to board the same train at a Paris railroad station. Being good friends, they shared a compartment and whiled away the time at a game of cards. As etiquette demanded, neither asked the other where he was going, but each was a little suspicious. When the train arrived at a small city a few hours out of Paris, each reached for his hat and coat and, since there was only one hotel in the town, they shared a hack and with amiable good nights went to their respective rooms. Now, each was certain that the other was after the same goal, but since it lay in a chateau some distance from the town and the hour was late, neither was concerned that evening. Early the next morning, Helft looked out of his door to reconnoiter and saw my father's shoes still in the corridor where they had been placed for polishing. Concluding that Jacques Seligmann was still in his room, Helft confidently finished his dressing and leisurely departed for the chateau. He was greeted there by Jacques Seligmann, his deal completed. On his feet were a pair of rough country shoes which he had slipped out to purchase the night before. Helft's son, Jacques, who recalled this story in his own book of reminiscences, *Vive la chine!,* adds that my father then offered Helft participation in his purchases. This was a part of the tale that my father always omitted in telling it himself.

Not all of Jacques Seligmann's journeys were as short and as easy. To Vienna, Rome, Madrid, London, St. Petersburg, and Berlin, again and again he was on the train, buying, selling, calling on clients and dealers, visiting museums, attending auctions.

CHAPTER III

A Dealer's Paradise: New York Before 1914

As Paris in 1900 was a paradise for collectors, New York was about to become a paradise for dealers. To the art merchants of London or Paris, the American market before the turn of the century had not been impressive, representing only a few clients who could be counted upon to come to Europe year after year. While many of them were lavish in their buying, the total they spent was still small compared to the European business, and with few exceptions, American buying was indiscriminate. Nor were American museums the formidable buying force they are today, most of them being still in their infancy, their vast endowments far in the future. Indifference to the American dollar, erratic and unstable in comparison with the louis d'or and the gold pound, also played a role. Thus, to my father at least, the American market had hardly seemed to warrant the expenditure of time necessary for the long ocean voyage; the results would not have compensated him for the loss of opportunities at home.

But this was changing rapidly. By 1900 a handful of European dealers had already established a bridgehead. Michel Knoedler was one of the first, having come to the United States from France in 1846 as a representative of the engraving firm of Goupil. He had sometime since expanded to original works of art and reversed the usual procedure by then opening a Paris house. Durand-Ruel opened its New York gallery in 1886 and, like Knoedler, handled paintings almost exclusively. Duveen Brothers, then largely concerned with the decorative arts, had started in Boston, but in 1884, they, too, moved to

A Dealer's Paradise: New York Before 1914

New York. Wildenstein, then Gimpel & Wildenstein, arrived in 1901 and established a gallery at 28th Street and Fifth Avenue, the vicinity then favored by the art trade.

Jacques Seligmann had had his share of American business in Paris. He had made substantial contributions to the collection of Benjamin Altman, particularly in the field of early enamels and Renaissance gold and silver work, and had acted for Altman in the purchase of a splendid series of Renaissance crystals in the Spitzer sale of 1893.

There had been at least two sales to J. Pierpont Morgan, in 1901 and 1902, made through Emile Rey, an associate of my father, who had made several trips to the United States and who maintained a small office for my father in New York. There is correspondence in the archives of the Metropolitan Museum dating also from 1902. In that same year Henry Walters purchased a sizable collection of enamels and porcelains, and no doubt the old Paris files would have revealed other sales to American clients. Even so, compared to the business he was doing in Europe, Jacques Seligmann's American affairs were not very important. In twenty-five years of business he had never been to New York, not even to visit his office.

His sudden decision, in 1905, to make the trip, according to a story which he hugely enjoyed telling, was precipitated by his first face-to-face encounter with J. Pierpont Morgan. One afternoon an English collector of porcelains, J. H. Fitzhenry, appeared at Place Vendôme accompanied by a large, forbidding-looking American whom he introduced as Mr. Morgan. Porcelains of all varieties were in great vogue at that time, with collectors avidly buying Dresden, Chelsea, and Sevres at prices which seem great even by today's standards, and it was porcelains that Mr. Morgan sought. After looking about for a while and consulting with Fitzhenry, Mr. Morgan decided to purchase an exceptional 18th century German piece. Made in Hoechst and modeled by Melchior, it was called *Sylvie* and represented a reclining nymph about to be surprised by a shepherd boy approaching from behind a tree.

The porcelain was to be delivered to Morgan's suite at the Hotel Bristol, then a rival of the Ritz on the Place Vendôme. Since Morgan was about to leave Paris, he also suggested that the check be called for at the hotel, and my father, curious about this American who was so well-known in financial circles, decided to go himself. Upon his

19

arrival in the foyer of the suite, he was considerably amazed to see a large number of his competitors, big and little, some with packages, seated or standing about the room. After a rather long wait, which irked my father a bit as he was not used to either calling for a check or being kept waiting, he was shown in. He faced a man quite different in mood from the one he had seen earlier in the day.

Morgan announced brusquely that, after examining the porcelain anew, he had decided it was not what he had supposed it to be and he no longer wanted it. Already irritated by his reception, Jacques Seligmann now had his pride hurt further. He felt his reputation to be at stake, although financially the transaction was of no particular moment. He replied rather stiffly that, of course, he would gladly take the porcelain group back, but before acceding to this, he must know whether it was just Mr. Morgan's change of interest or whether the authenticity of the piece had been challenged.

Now Morgan was irritated. My father recalled that he was completely red-faced as he pounded the table and roared. Morgan, who never liked to admit the presence of a third party in his buying, told my father that the reason for the refusal of the piece was none of his business. But Jacques Seligmann was also a determined man and he persisted. He explained calmly, but forcibly, that if Morgan intended to collect fine objects, he would never succeed if he consulted half a dozen persons about each purchase. Such a course, he said, would only result in dealers working together and arranging commissions with each other.

Such plain talk evidently impressed Morgan, but he would not change his mind, and the purchase was canceled. However, my father's parting words were, "Mr. Morgan, I will see you shortly in New York and prove to you that you have been misled, but not by me."

Then, realizing how much might be at stake, my father, with his characteristic energy and determination, tucked *Sylvie* under his arm and set out for Germany. He showed it to every porcelain specialist of any renown and obtained, in writing, confirmation from each that the piece was not only authentic, but of exceptional merit and a rare subject. He then set out for New York where he presented the porcelain to the Metropolitan Museum of which J. Pierpont Morgan had just been elected president. The charming *Sylvie* was accepted with delight by the museum officials, and this being accomplished, my father called upon J. Pierpont Morgan and told him what he had

20

done. Thus it was that Jacques Seligmann won his most important American client and became the advisor upon whom Morgan most relied in his later years.

As my father's relationship with Morgan grew, so, naturally, did his interest in the Metropolitan Museum, upon which Morgan was bringing to bear the same energy and dynamism that he displayed in his own business and collecting activities. It was doubtless at the behest of Morgan that Edward Robinson, assistant director of the museum and later its first American director, wrote my father in 1906, asking if on his next trip to New York he would be willing to give expert opinion about certain works of art offered the museum as gifts or loans. This recognition by the infant New World museum pleased my father tremendously and, a few months later, he presented to it several works of art, including a 15th century tapestry, a rare Spanish Alcora plate, and a Gothic window. Since he realized the ever present need for funds as well as objects, he added a check for five thousand dollars.

In February of 1907, Jacques Seligmann was elected a Fellow for Life of the Metropolitan Museum, an honor which he greatly cherished and which he often mentioned with pride.

He had acquired an early appreciation of the educational importance of public museums. It was this subject he stressed in interviews with the American press. Only with an active museum could one expect to interest the citizens of a new community in works of art, he said, and encourage them to become collectors, collectors who in turn would aid in the development of the museum, the one acting reciprocally upon the other. He insisted that such an interest should not be limited to the past centuries of Western art but should also encourage contemporary artists. He was one of the rare Europeans to back up this idea with the purchase of paintings by living American artists. He owned several examples of Mary Cassatt and bought canvases by Frieseke, Dana, and Henry Golden Dearth. Whether he would have made some of these choices in later years is moot, but it was a concrete expression of his interest.

Through Pierpont Morgan my father made the acquaintance of William M. Laffan, publisher of the New York *Sun*, who in 1905 became a member of the Board of Trustees of the Metropolitan Museum. Laffan, who traveled extensively in Europe, seems to have been a sort of roving ambassador for the great financier, and ties of

friendship were quickly established between him and Jacques Seligmann. The friendship, however, must have had its tumultuous aspects, for if they generally agreed on the merit of works of art of the
Western world, they were constantly at odds on the subject of Chinese porcelains. My father claimed that few westerners knew
whether they were buying good ones or bad ones, particularly when
it came to monochromes. Since Laffan was considered an expert in
this field—it was he who made the Morgan porcelain catalogue—
their differing points of view frequently led to heated discussion. In
spite of this, however, their strong and direct personalities apparently
held a mutual appeal. Laffan was in some degree responsible, also,
for the firm bonds which existed between my father and Henry
Walters, the great Baltimore collector, for whom Laffan also acted
in an advisory capacity.

It was on the recommendation of Laffan that the Metropolitan
Museum, in 1909, made its first truly important purchase from my
father—the three exquisite Gothic tapestries from the Sigismond
Bardac collection. Popularly known as *La Baillée des Roses*, and extremely rare in type, they are among the most peacefully romantic
tapestries of that charming period when the austerity of the early
Gothic was giving way to storybook chivalry. In them, graceful courtiers wander across a background of three wide bands of green, white,
and red, over which trail blooming roses. It is believed that the set
was ordered, in Arras or Tournai, by Charles VII of France (1422–
1461) and that one of the figures represents the virtuous Agnes Sorel,
La Dame de Beauté, who exercised such a good influence upon this
weak and vacillating king.

The sale of these tapestries unfortunately created a certain friction
between the French museum authorities and my father, which indirectly involved J. P. Morgan as Metropolitan president. The Louvre
had been anxious to acquire these historic tapestries, and for once
had the funds to pay for them. However, they refused to meet Morgan's offer, and my father had no choice except to let them go to
America. According to a press report, just a week later the Louvre
made an offer to Morgan for one of three. Morgan refused to sell.

The period from the turn of the century to 1914 was the golden age
of the American industrial and financial titan. Even if the roster of
great wealth does not necessarily constitute a roster of great collec-

tors, it is nevertheless true that a period of great wealth is usually also a period of great collecting. Upper Fifth Avenue was already strung with Renaissance palaces and Gothic castles, some complete with moat, noble edifices attesting to the fortunes of their owners. Every one of these houses contained works of art and every one of the owners was a collector—if "collector" be defined as a buyer of rare and costly non-utilitarian objects for the adornment of his living quarters. In those years, said Frederick Lewis Allen in *The Big Change,* "A pattern was forming; the American millionaire wanted to live like a prince; and since princes were foreign and princely culture was likewise foreign, he must show his princeliness by living among foreign furnishings and foreign works of art in as great a variety and profusion as could be managed."

After all the appropriate and available spaces were filled with paintings, tapestries, and objets d'art, a few of the wealthy found themselves inextricably involved in the fascination of collecting and were gripped by an overpowering desire to own more treasures. There is no doubt that pride and ego played a role, and for many there was the satisfaction that such a collection would constitute a memorial. There is equally no doubt that many had a basic love of the beautiful. Works of art of great merit have a radiating spirit to which the beholder reacts in terms of his individual sensitivity: "As though the objects themselves," said William Constable in *Collectors and Collecting*, "cast a spell over their owner, to win his disinterested affection. "Thus were created the great American collections, their diversity explained by the personalities of the men who chose them.

There is a great difference between the approaches of collectors today and those of half a century ago. Now there are a greater number of individual purchasers of works of art. The average collector is better educated aesthetically; he has a greater knowledge and understanding, and consequently a greater faith in his own purpose. Obviously, there are few today who can afford to be as careless of cost as were some pre-World War I millionaires, or devote as great a proportion of their fortunes to amass collections as important in size and aesthetic value. There is also a difference in the manner of purchasing. The greater self-confidence of today's collector frequently leads him to avoid the established dealer, in the belief, often mistaken, that he can secure an object at a better price privately or at auction. The collector of the first quarter of the century was inclined to be oblivious of price if convinced that a work had intrinsic merit and that it would add to the prestige of his collection. He preferred to deal with a leading firm, one whose name would add to the value and importance of an object in the same way that a title added luster to its pedigree. Because he himself dealt in large sums and made large profits, he conceded the dealer the same privilege. Moreover, he had powerful competition from fellow collectors, and quick decisions were prompted by the danger of losing a coveted piece should he waver or bargain too long.

Such was the climate, at once simple and complex, surrounding the American collector when Jacques Seligmann decided to enter the New York field. It was typical that he should have gauged it swiftly and accurately on this first visit and, before his departure, already determined to leave the small office at 303 Fifth Avenue in favor of more impressive quarters. It is doubtful that Jacques Seligmann could have achieved the success he did had he remained in his early Paris quarters on the rue des Mathurins or kept only an office in New York. Men of wealth and power preferred to deal with a man whose importance in his own field was comparable to theirs. An understanding of this American psychology, one still foreign to the European mind in those early years of the century, led my father to acquire an appropriately large and handsome house at 7 West 36th Street, then about as far uptown as business dared go. I never saw this place, but I understand that, as at Place Vendôme, the setting was worthy of the works of art and of the clientele which came there.

From 1905 on, Jacques Seligmann spent several weeks each year in New York. In preparation for his periodic visits he would make a selection from the Paris inventory—frequently including objects about which he had already written to a prospective buyer—crate them, and ship them off ahead. Upon his arrival in New York, heralded in the press as some star of stage or screen might be today, he would write more letters, make half a dozen phone calls, and sit back to await developments.

Protocol was a major problem; visits were arranged to avoid conflicts, for certain clients could not be allowed to meet. My father had to prevent, if possible, any suspicion that he had first shown a work of art to someone else and that the present client was seeing the leftovers. Thomas Fortune Ryan and Mrs. Collis P. Huntington were both interested in Italian bronzes, for instance; J. P. Morgan and

A Dealer's Paradise: New York Before 1914

Mortimer Schiff were equally avid for fine Gubbio plates, and Schiff also shared Henry Walters' love for 18th century French objects. Another tapestry fancier might be upset if he found that Otto H. Kahn had acquired a magnificent gold-woven tapestry before he, himself, had had a chance to see it.

When these problems had been solved satisfactorily, and the objects gathered from the four corners of Europe had been dispersed across America, Jacques Seligmann would sail back to Paris to start a fresh search for more. I was twelve at the time of the first New York trip, and I remember with what excitement we all awaited my father's return. Naturally he came loaded with gifts for all of us. The most fascinating to our French eyes were the tins of fruits and other delicacies, still a definitely suspect innovation in France.

We must often have been on Jacques Seligmann's mind during his frequent absences. My lovely young mother had died in 1902, and our care was largely in the hands of governesses and housekeepers. Our education was extremely important to him, especially mine as the eldest son, and my apprenticeship in the art world was seriously begun at about that time. From the age of twelve on I never knew a school holiday or summer vacation in the carefree sense of the word, for I was regularly sent on trips to study languages and acquaint myself with the museums and artistic monuments of Europe. In England I was usually in the charge of Salomon Herz, my father's English partner. Trips to Italy and Germany were supervised by tutors. When I was about fifteen I made a trip to Spain in the company of A. S. Drey, the well-known art dealer, and his younger son, Francis, who was about my age. My most vivid memory of that trip did not reflect my father's program for my study of the history of art.

One day the three of us were traveling by train, probably in a third-class carriage, as I remember the wooden seats. Just as we were pulling out of some small village, a tough-looking man, dressed in a sheepskin coat, jumped into the carriage, brandished a large knife at us and dived into hiding under a seat. There he stayed while we and our fellow travelers, all Spaniards, sat in quaking silence, until the train reached the next village. There two mustachioed police boarded, asked whether anyone had seen the fugitive and made a perfunctory search. We pretended ignorance of the language, the Spanish passengers covered for him, and the officers got off without further ado. As soon as the train had left the village, our stowaway left by the other side of the car, as silently as he had come. By the time we got home, of course, this episode had grown into a really dangerous brush with a Spanish bandit.

Jacques Seligmann was self-trained and it was his belief that no amount of theory could ever replace the training of the eye. He declared with firmness, particularly when irked, that no book-teaching could ever convince him of something that he could not see. Later in his career, when published records were produced to persuade him of the importance of an item, perhaps "just the type that Mr. Morgan would like," his answer was always the same. "Show it to me," he said. "If I am interested I may look at the book, if I'm not, a hundred books won't convince me." Then he might add with a smile, "Paper has great patience and will take anything."

This did not prevent him from seeing that I, and later my brother André, had all the formal teaching in the arts that he could cram into us. While I was still at school, he engaged tutors, specialists in one field or another, for extracurricular classes, beginning with Egyptian and classical antiquities. When I left school, after my first baccalaureate, it was in order to devote my studies entirely to history, chiefly the history of art. Some of this work was with private tutors, especially when I went to stay in another country, but in Paris a great deal of it was at the Ecole du Louvre, the professional school on a university level for the training of art historians and museum curators. The professors were well-known specialists in their fields, often curators at the Louvre or one of the provincial museums, and our work included visits to the collections, accompanied by a member of the museum staff.

We had the benefit of the knowledge of such men as Carle Dreyfus, Curator of Decorative Arts and an authority on the French 18th century, and Marquet de Vasselot, head of the medieval section at both the Louvre and Cluny.

I came to know Carle Dreyfus in a more personal way than as an occasional teacher through his nephew, Robert Aboucaya, who was killed leading his platoon in the first weeeks of World War I and was a companion of my military service. We were privates together, often assigned to the same not-always-pleasant duties, went through officer training school together, and received our second lieutenancies at the same time. We usually tried to arrange our Paris leaves together, and on one of these occasions Robert took me to call on his grandfather, Gustave Dreyfus, owner of some of the most magnificent Renaissance sculptures in the annals of collecting. Gustave Dreyfus showed us around, correcting some of my assumptions, adding his own comments, full of patience for a beginner already entranced with the beauty of marble sculpture, an enchantment which has never left me. Many years later one of my greatest frustrations was my inability to acquire the Dreyfus collection when it was sold.

One of the advantages that acquaintance with the curatorial staff of the Louvre afforded was the rare privilege of occasionally being allowed to handle the objects themselves. Some works of art speak even more eloquently through the tactile sense. I remember with delight the personally conducted tour Carle Dreyfus gave me of the Isaac de Camondo collection of 18th century objets d'art while it was still being installed after its bequest to the Louvre in 1911. Even more exciting was a visit to the Medieval Department, where Marquet de Vasselot put into my hands some of the precious enamels in which the Louvre is so rich—the cloisonnés, the champlevés, the translucents, all veritable jewels of the enameler's art. Enamels, like sculptures, have always held an especial attraction for me.

Through Marquet de Vasselot I was also admitted to one of the great private collections of Paris, that of his father-in-law, Martin LeRoy. I have always suspected that Marquet de Vasselot was the inspiration for his wealthy father-in-law's collecting, as it closely followed his own tastes and interests—rare early Gothic tapestries, primitive paintings, early enamels, and exquisite ivories.

I particularly remember a class in Italian painting at the Louvre, where the professor had been stressing the brilliance of the Venetian palette. As he stood before the monumental *The Marriage at Cana* by Paolo Veronese, he called our attention to the clear yellows, the warm reds, the wonderful greens, and the deep blues. As I stood and gazed at the painting, I began to wonder if there was something seriously wrong with my sense of color. With the best will in the world, I could see nothing but varying shades of dull yellow and duller reds and blues. My puzzlement grew as we went from painting to painting, but I hesitated to question my professor in front of my fellow students. After class, he assured me that the color was really there; I would just have to take it on faith, as it was obscured by the many layers of dirty varnish which had accumulated over the years.

I have had to take it on faith until only a few years ago, when at last cleaning revealed this great masterpiece in all its glory of riotous color. Nor did I ever really see the superb late Titian *Ecce Homo* of the Louvre until it was restored to its original beauty for the great Titian exhibition at the Venice Biennale of 1935. In my student days, the cleaning and restoring of paintings was not the precise science it is today. Most museum authorities viewed it with distrust, and "museum brown" was still the order of the day.

In addition to my formal studies I now had to attend all the important auctions and exhibitions, duly reporting on them to my father if he could not go with me. Sunday afternoon was usually devoted to this pastime, as the Hôtel Drouot was open on Sunday then, and if my father was along, we played a sort of eye-training game. This consisted in standing in the doorway or the middle of the exhibition room and attempting to pick out at once the objects whose quality sang out, those which brought an immediate reaction and stood out from the multitude. This was, of course, without benefit of catalogue or label; attributions change, but quality does not. This kind of first analysis is particularly valuable to a dealer. In appraising a collection to be bought or sold, the value of the best items must approximate the expected total value of the entire collection; otherwise, the proposition is not sound. A dependable estimate is not reached by adding up a hundred small items. Years of training in these quick studies make it relatively easy to sift the masterpieces from the lesser items which even a great collection contains.

As I grew older, my father liked, when it was possible, to take me with him on business trips. In order to make me more useful as a traveling companion, he conceived the notion of having me study shorthand, which would have eliminated the secretary who usually accompanied him. I must admit that this was a skill in which I never became proficient, and he soon gave that up. The international character of the business meant an appalling amount of correspondence, which my father, an inveterate letter writer, enjoyed. No one who interested him was allowed to forget him. He kept three secretaries busy, often dictating in his automobile, cabling to San Francisco for someone's birthday, writing to Edinburgh with congratulations on a wedding or to Vienna simply to see how a friend fared. In French, English, German, Italian, the mail poured in and out. One of my duties was to read the letters and ask questions about things which puzzled me. Another was a weekly visit with the firm's bookkeeper or its attorney, gradually to acquaint myself with the firm's general business procedure.

The rugged schedule my father arranged for me instilled a discipline which has aided me through many difficult periods of my life. Fortunately, I was studious by nature and was particularly fond of history, so research was never a bore to me, though the office routine was sometimes tedious to a boy of sixteen.

My father was a stern disciplinarian who believed that children should be educated to meet any vicissitudes that life might bring, but he was also generous, even indulgent. I had my own horse and could ride every morning, provided I was willing to get up early enough so that it did not interfere with more serious pursuits, for at eight-thirty I had to be at the office. I was given a Renault for my personal use as soon as I was of age to drive it, something quite rare for a youngster in those days. My father had acquired an electric car for himself at a time when other people were still looking askance at automobiles. He simply wanted to move about Paris faster. He never traded his cars until they were past use, no matter how old-fashioned they became. It was characteristic, too, that though he was willing to give me a car, he would send me off to Germany in a third-class carriage lest I be spoiled by too much luxury.

Thursday is the French school holiday, and when there was no important auction for me to attend, I went with my sisters to the Comédie Française where we heard the classic plays of Molière, Racine, or Corneille. My father kept a box at the opera and attended as regularly as he could, for he was fond of music. I suspect, however, that he preferred the lighter variety, such as Offenbach's *Belle Hélène*, of which he knew not only the melodies but the entire libretto. We might catch him dozing in the far corner of the box during the heavier Wagner operas.

CHAPTER IV

The Palais de Sagan

As the first decade of the century drew to its close, Americans had become, as a group, the most important of my father's clients. The same reasoning which had prompted him to enlarge and embellish his New York quarters led him to a new and grandiose gesture in Paris. In 1909, almost overnight and quite unknown to his family or partners, my father bought the *hôtel particulier* of the Prince de Sagan. I was then sixteen, and the Palais de Sagan was to be the scene of my own real entry into the business of being an art dealer.

The Palais de Sagan is one of the most sumptuous old houses in Paris. Ideally located on the rue St. Dominique just off the esplanade des Invalides, near the Chambre des Députés and the Quai d'Orsay, it is an easy walk to the heart of the city. From the rue St. Dominique one sees only the monumental gateway and the tree-lined avenue which leads between the flanking houses. Once inside, the avenue opens into a great cour-d'honneur formed by the classically simple two-story façade of the house and its two lower wings. The terrace in the rear faces upon a garden à la française which once extended for several blocks but now reaches only to the next street, the rue de Talleyrand. The rooms are vast and high-ceilinged, and the magnificent marble stairway is one of the most impressively beautiful in all Paris.

The house was originally built for the Princesse de Monaco in 1784 by Alexandre-Théodore Brongniard, the builder of the Paris Bourse. When the princess fled the Revolution, Sagan with all its furnishings was confiscated and became for a time the Ottoman Embassy. Later, Napoleon presented it to the Count de Siéyès, who sold it to the

Maréchal Davout, Prince of Eckmühl. In 1838 Davout's widow in turn sold the propery to William Hope, a Dutch banker, and from him it passed to Baron Seillière, friend and banker of Napoleon III. In 1873 it was inherited by the Princesse de Sagan, the Baron's daughter. During the latter two ownerships, the Palais de Sagan was the brilliant setting for parties and dinners attended by Europe's highest society, including the royalty of many nations. In its heyday the house was adorned with beautiful paintings and fine works of art. But after the Princess died, the Prince de Sagan, in failing health and a recluse, occupied only two of the smallest rooms of the huge palace.

The gossips of the time said that the Prince and Princess had a rather acrimonious relationship during the last years of her life, and that he always spoke of her as *la vache*. One day, according to a story, when it was necessary for both of them to be present at a reception, she tethered several cows on the lawn and placed him, already somewhat incapacitated, in a chair overlooking the terrace so that he would appear to be commenting upon the scene rather than upon her. However, the old gentleman was not quite so hazy as supposed. As she passed near him, he was heard to mutter quite distinctly, "Chameau," which has an earthier meaning in French argot than its literal translation of "camel."

However that may be, the house was dismal and oppressive when I first saw it, a few days after my father bought it. Some of the ceilings had been redecorated and overgilded during the tenancy of William Hope, whose taste was notoriously bad; a contemporary diary of the Maréchal de Castellane describes an earlier house of Hope's as being hung with silk and "enough gold lace to furnish all the generals of the army." My father's lively imagination had correctly visualized Sagan's possibilities, however, and within a few months the floors had been covered with blue and gold Savonnerie rugs, the crystal chandeliers had been hung, and the overloaded ceilings and walls had been partly hidden by neutral draperies. The open field where the Princess was said to have tethered her cows was now a garden with close-clipped grass, pebbled paths, and a fountain; Sagan was again smiling and welcoming, restored to something of its former grandeur. Even though Sagan offered many times the floor space of the galleries in the Place Vendôme, my father added, for special exhibitions, another building, in the same classical 18th century style, at the side of the garden with an entrance on the rue de Talleyrand.

31

None of us ever lived at Sagan. At the time of its purchase my father also acquired an adjoining property on the rue de Constantine, over-looking the esplanade des Invalides, which then became the family home. The family had continued to grow. My father had remarried a few years earlier, and the children now numbered six.

How, then, was the firm to function with a great establishment of four floors at Place Vendôme (there was no thought of abandoning that strategic location) and an even greater one at the Palais de Sagan? The bulk of the works of art remained at Place Vendôme, pre-sided over by my Uncle Arnold, and here the average clients and the passers-by were received. The important clients, the particular ones, those whose fancy could only be captured by the exceptional, and thus the most expensive, were taken to Sagan. Here they were shown through perhaps seven or eight great rooms to see seven or eight great masterpieces—a painting, a sculpture, a tapestry, or a precious small objet d'art. If none attracted a client's fancy, he was then invited to seat himself comfortably in yet another room and a new group of items was brought to him, again one at a time. So rich was Sagan's display that a contemporary American newspaper correspondent de-scribed it glowingly as "rivaling some of the world's museums."

My father's headquarters, naturally, were at Sagan and it was here that I began my real initiation into the art business. Heretofore it had been largely study and theory. Now I was to learn how the art busi-ness really worked and, particularly, I was to learn something of people.

One of my father's training devices was to have me audit the visit of an important client, my role being to take the place of one of his regular office boys, hand him whatever items he wanted, and make myself unobtrusively useful. It was on such an occasion that I had one of my few opportunities to see J. Pierpont Morgan in action as art collector.

It was in the spring of 1911 in a large room on the west end of the ground floor of Sagan; tall windows opened onto the terrace. The room had been kept simple, with no decoration or works of art; beige velvet hung from ceiling to floor, a height of eighteen to twenty feet. In one corner, hidden by the velvet, was a huge safe. Around a center table, covered with the same material, were a few deep brown leather chairs. On the table my father had placed a stack of large reference

32

books, which were hardly ever consulted, a few pads of white paper, and some pencils.

Morgan had already been shown into the room when I arrived, and from that moment until his leave-taking, I felt dwarfed. The physical proportion between him and me seemed to be three to one; it was not only his actual height and bulk, but his piercing, flashing eyes, his strong, set face, and, above all, his tremendous, radiating vitality.

To me he was awe-inspiring. My father, who, of course, knew Morgan well by this time, showed no timidity or undue awareness of the importance of his client. This was Jacques Seligmann's field; not only was he perfectly at ease, but in the course of the visit he generated his own brand of dynamism—arguing, retorting, and lecturing the great financier, who seemed not only not to mind but rather to expect it. Thinking it over in later years, I came to the conclusion that Morgan probably would have considered it a weakness and lack of certainty about the quality of the treasures offered had my father not taken such a firm and definite stand.

The first items shown, I gathered, were objects which had already been purchased for Morgan's account on a predetermined percentage of commissions or on a definite retainer. For a collector of Morgan's magnitude, the retainer arrangement had the great advantage of eliminating the profit motive on individual purchases: whatever the total figure, the amount received by the art dealer remained the same, much as an attorney, for instance, may handle a firm's legal affairs on a fixed fee basis, irrespective of the work or the sums involved.

Even though these purchases had been decided upon, and Morgan had a keen memory, he had to be convinced again. Possibly he wanted to hear once more the reasons my father had given originally in suggesting the acquisition. It is also possible that, having so little time at his disposal for the study of art, Morgan took advantage of these discussions—my father loved to talk about his "children" and Morgan knew it—to inform himself further about the aesthetic merits and the histories of the treasures he was accumulating.

During this warming-up period my father was gradually taking from the corner safe a second group of treasures. These were purchases he had made for his own account, but had reserved for Morgan to see first. At the beginning Morgan remained seated while my father got up from time to time to go to the safe. But after a little, as the

33

discussion grew livelier, both were on their feet, walking up and down the huge room which suddenly had shrunk to minuscule proportions.

It soon became obvious to me that Morgan was thoroughly enjoying himself. There was no doubt that his purpose was to draw out my father, to be convinced once more, by tone of voice and determination in making a point, of the knowledge and sincerity of his trusted advisor. Had Morgan not been convinced previously of this, of course, he would not have come or, once there, not have troubled to sit down; but it was probably inherent in this man that great transactions must be accomplished with lightning and thunder—otherwise where is the fun? Morgan liked to be faced with a strong personality, one ready to talk back, sure of his ground, and this he got in Jacques Seligmann.

From time to time Morgan would take a scratch pad and make notes, then my father would do the same, and I quickly learned that this meant the collector had added another beautiful object to his mounting aggregate, although no specific words might have been spoken.

So impressed was I, and breathless, watching these two giants, so confused by the size of the figures involved that I lost track of reality when the total amount was reached. Today, knowing the kinds of objects Morgan collected and their prices, I can say that a half million dollars might easily have been involved in such a session.

When it was all over, like ocean waves after a stormy wind have dropped, the tones of the voices lowered, smiles appeared, and Morgan took time to stroke his new possessions, happy, proud, and content. This was Morgan, the private collector.

Not all of the clients who came to Sagan were Rothschilds and Morgans. Some bought one coveted item at a time, paying for it as they could. The first sale I made was to such a collector, a modestly, almost shabbily, dressed man, who appeared one day at Sagan and asked to see Italian majolicas. Since my father was busy, I was delegated to show him around and I soon realized that here was a man of real knowledge. He was particularly fascinated by a dated Urbino plate of great quality, rich in blacks, and bearing the marking of Fra Xanto, to which he kept returning with longing eyes. Finally, with great hesitancy, he asked if he might come in again, just to look at it, as it was far too expensive for him.

Of course I told him he was welcome at any time, and a week or so later he did come back, to gaze once more at the plate and regret his inability to buy it. He told me he was a professor of chemistry at one of the Paris technical schools and already had a small collection of majolicas, so I asked if he would allow me to see them. He seemed delighted at the idea, and when I arrived at his one-room apartment, I found an entire wall occupied by a glass-covered case full of exquisite Italian faience. Realizing the man's genuine interest and obviously limited means, I suggested to him tactfully that if he really wanted the plate there was no reason, as far as we were concerned, why he should not pay for it in installments. He was enchanted, saying he would never have dared to make the suggestion himself, since he felt that ten thousand francs was not enough money to cause us to make special arrangements. If I remember correctly, it took him about a year and a half to settle the account. I am sure he deprived himself of some basic comforts; his was the attitude of the true collector, rich or poor.

Some came to Sagan to sell rather than to buy, and some came to "make a deal." Besides the art dealer who maintains a gallery and owns an inventory of works of art, the art world supports a number of men and women who orbit about it. First, there is what is known in the trade as a private dealer, or amateur marchand, who is usually as much collector as dealer and often sells only because he must in order to form a new collection or to buy at all. Others are frankly intermediaries and make no secret of the fact that they earn a commission by acting as a contact between a dealer and a collector who wishes to buy or sell. Still others are advisors who actually play the role of middle-man but do not wish to appear to be doing so.

Such middle-men have their role in relation to the art dealer, but it is not always a positive one; by that I mean that an intermediary may as easily work against a dealer as for him. It is characteristic of our business that it is easier to dissuade a collector than it is to persuade him. Whether this negative tendency prevails to the same extent in other selling areas, I do not know, but I can well imagine, for example, a man who has a quiet interest in an automobile agency advising a friend who is considering a rival make, "Don't commit yourself today; why not look around a bit more. There are so many models with new improvements." For the moment he is not selling the car for his own interest, but he is preventing a sale by a competitor. The very fact that he is trying, outwardly at least, to keep the eventual client from spending his money is ingratiating, and this strengthens his position for further advice.

The function of the intermediary is a perfectly legitimate one, in no way reprehensible, and an accepted practice in any number of businesses. However, in the huge spending days of the first thirty years of this century, in the art world it sometimes took an oblique character. The intermediary of that day, and even sometimes today, usually did not want it known that he was accepting commissions; many of them were titled members of the aristocracy or otherwise socially prominent. They felt, quite correctly in the society of that day, that acknowledging the source of their incomes would lessen their prestige and their influence. Thus the wealthy collector, usually American, but often European, who had been lavishly entertained by such a man must not be allowed to suspect his host's impartiality. It was up to the dealer, to whom he would lead his new friend, to help him protect his secret. In turn, the intermediary could set his own terms, which were usually high, as were the stakes; this sharing of profits was often worthwhile.

Initiation into the secrets of this practice was one of the great surprises I received when I first began going to my father's office. I shall always remember my amazement, even shock, when I saw the name of a member of the highest nobility signed to a receipt for a very large commission. It was a blow to my youthful faith in humanity, an affront to the "vertue" of nobility, the old spirit of chivalry I had been taught to revere as above petty mercantilism. I had no peace of mind until I had an opportunity to discuss this matter with my father. He burst into laughter at the vehemence of my feelings and teased me unmercifully about the rarefied atmosphere of the imaginary world in which I was living. He went on to tell me that this same nobleman had, in fact, telephoned only a few hours earlier to ask for a large advance to arrange a party at one of the most exclusive clubs, solely for the purpose of impressing a new collector. Sure enough, the social columns of Paris newspapers a few days later ecstatically described the event as one of the most brilliant of many a season.

One of this noble company of intermediaries, who was by the time I knew him perfectly open about his need for the means to live in grandeur, was the Marquis de Castellane. When I first met him he was

36

still Count Boni, and I was a very young man, much impressed by this alluring embodiment of the *grand seigneur,* haloed by the glamor of his past marriage to Anna Gould, one of the wealthiest American women of the day. My father had known him when he was still enjoying this affluence and was building the famous Palais Rose at the corner of the avenue du Bois and the avenue Malakoff. (To my mind, this much admired house never acquired the grace one would have expected time to lend it, perhaps because the insufficient grounds never allowed one to see it in its proper perspective; it needed the park and vistas of its inspiration, the Grand Trianon of Versailles.) There Castellane lived for a while, and since the interior was to be decorated in the grand manner, it was as a client that my father met him. Castellane had great faith in Jacques Seligmann's judgment, and an even greater one in his own. In his book, *How I Discovered America,* he says of his collection, "As my wonders accumulated and as my inborn flair for judging and purchasing developed, I became obsessed with the idea of forming a kind of art trust before prices became as high as I knew must inevitably be the case in a few years. If my scheme had materialized, I should have been one of the richest men in the world. But my brothers-in-law, who neither knew nor cared anything about art, were actively hostile towards any trust which did not touch metals or railways."

A spendthrift in his youth, Castellane remained one to the end. Few men, even in those days of comparatively easy money, spent as much as he did on lavish living and entertaining. But where such extravagances might have seemed ostentatious in another, somehow they never did with Boni. He was to the manner born; a reincarnation of his noble ancestors who had played their roles at the court of France. A paragraph in his book in which he described his "dream castle" reveals something of this side of him, as well as his wit:

In imagining what Paradise for me would be like, I saw a chateau perpetually in progress . . . salons where I could walk and reflect, constantly being decorated by numerous workmen who never finished —painters, artisans, sculptors working without cease at the new works which I would inspire.

From the windows, I would see a vast park, a prolongment in nature of the architecture of my habitation. Its lines would correspond to those of the building and become its frame, thus giving it an aspect of solidity

37

and logic. Columns, statues, monuments would be there on trial, to be adopted only if they realized perfect proportions, each object completing the ensemble.

Then, I would live near a town peopled by antiquarians, among whom I would find again, Seligmann, Kraemer, Davis, Duveen, those in whose establishments I had found the greatest satisfactions of my terrestrial life. Some persons would perhaps rather not find these men there in Paradise, but I myself have never begrudged them the fortunes which they made at my expense and I am grateful to them for the joys which they brought me.

Traits which in another might have been considered arrogant, in Castellane were tempered by a disarming smile and a charming manner which explained and excused them. It is not difficult to understand the influence he could exert on both men and women, for he had an incredible feeling for the magnificent. Those who aspired to live like kings could not ask a better teacher of the art than Boni de Castellane.

He admits freely in his memoirs his activities as advisor, and his judgments upon some of the American collectors he knew are interesting, for their insight as well as their bite. Pierpont Morgan, whom he called a sort of nabob, was "infinitely more of a real art lover than any of his compatriots and possessed a soul above dollars! He, nevertheless, grasped with the avidity of a furniture mover the beautiful things which were suggested to him—I sometimes thought him more of a passionate collector than a true artist." Daniel Guggenheim, Otto Kahn, Joseph Feder, and George Blumenthal he names as "superior to the generality of (American) connoisseurs."

I am sure that many who received Castellane's invitations gladly allowed themselves to be taken, for, after all, it is often not the amount involved so much as the manner in which it is asked. If in addition, one was invited to enjoy a social function where the distinction of the guest list was surpassed only by that of the food and wine, how could one—why should one—be resentful of so small a price for so much offered?

The Marquis de Biron was not an intermediary, but an *amateur marchand*. He belonged to the oldest French nobility and thus was related to some of the most celebrated families of Europe, a fact which gave him entrée to collections otherwise inaccessible to the average collector or dealer. Biron was a realist; long before I actually

38

met him, I had heard of him as the man who had not hesitated to sell the tomb of his ancestors. If this was not quite true, it was near enough; the two magnificent 15th century stone groups which he sold to J. P. Morgan through my father had stood in the Chapel of the Chateau de Biron, and two of the kneeling figures in the *Pietà* do represent his ancestors, Armand de Gontaut and Pons de Gontaut, Bishop of Sarlat.

In all but gentleness of birth and love of fine objects, Biron was the antithesis of Castellane. My earliest recollection of the short, stocky marquis is one of astonishment at his dress, for he habitually wore at least three topcoats and a heavy muffler wound about his neck, the whole topped by a bowler hat. This would lead one to believe him unusually sensitive to cold, and perhaps he was. If so, discomfort did not induce him to heat his apartment, which was always frigid.

I had known him for several years and seen him often at Sagan before my father took me to call upon him at his apartment on the rue d'Aguessau. It was more like a warehouse than a home, with works of art of all types scattered helter-skelter about the place. I particularly recall the empty 18th century picture frames which hung on the walls or were stacked in odd corners. I was too young then, and not sufficiently attuned to the more subtle nuances of the art world, to understand the intrinsic quality of these delicately hand-carved and gilded wood bibelots. It was only later that I realized with what exceptional taste he had chosen them, and I sigh with envy today when I recall them. What is more, they would be worth their weight in gold.

My own conviction about Biron is that he was essentially a collector, one truly infected by the bug, that he simply could not resist the temptation of a bibelot of quality or of a fine drawing, and that he had to sell in order to buy. In contrast with Castellane, he lavished no money on himself or on entertainment: he was a bachelor and his manner of living was frugal, almost Spartan. There did appear to be one exception to this, however, an exception which fits well with his connoisseurship—he had the palate of a gourmet. Many years later, when we met by chance at one of Bordeaux's famous restaurants, he asked me to join him at the meal he had chosen, complete with the choicest wines, and it was a real masterpiece. I believe that he himself owned some fine vineyards in the Bordeaux country where the Biron family seat is located.

Biron was the type par excellence of the *amateur marchand,* who buys and sells works of art. He had no shop or gallery, with all the paraphernalia of trade, but could be approached about some fine thing he had acquired, asked to show it and to name a price. Sometimes Biron would answer that it was not for sale, often because he genuinely wanted to enjoy it for a while, more often because he felt that time would enhance its worth. And he was frequently correct. He liked to build up a collection of drawings by a particular artist, sometimes taking years to do it, and then to sell them as a group, as he did with his superb Tiepolos and Guardis, for instance.

Being in touch with a great many private collectors, Biron sometimes sold to them directly, but he worked chiefly with a few leading firms, selling outright or occasionally buying in joint account with them, putting up half the cost price and sharing equally in the profits. He realized that these firms, with their American clientele, could obtain better prices than he, and it was on this basis that he operated with my father.

Such connections, however, did not prevent him from selling at auction, as he did in 1914—a speculative venture in which the title "Marquis de Biron Collection" played a prominent role. This does not imply any misrepresentation of the quality of the items, for they were all chosen with great taste by a connoisseur of the first rank in his somewhat restricted field of interest, the 18th century.

After World War I, Biron moved to Switzerland, and I never failed to call upon him in his Geneva apartment whenever I visited that lovely city. It was here, on one of my last calls before his death, that he reiterated to me an oft-repeated axiom: "Germain, have but two worldly possessions—great works of art and gold." The first I have, the second is less easy to come by and less heart-warming to own.

Alphonse Kann was a different type. He had the elegance and sybaritic taste of Castellane, but not his arrogance. He was as knowing in certain fields as Biron, and as sensitive, but lacked his misanthropic nature. His background was that of the Parisian haute-bourgeoisie—I believe he was related to the collector, Edouard Kann. When I first met him he was guiding and advising some of the leading Paris collectors. I assume that he continued to do so up to his last years, but apparently he realized fairly early that his endowments and his access to collections could more profitably be used in buying

40

and selling, directly or otherwise. As an amateur marchand he could have the pleasure of collecting and the profit of selling.

Thus he gradually invested in works of art until he built up collections known the world over. This was achieved in most skillfully worked out successive steps, the like of which I have never seen elsewhere. He first concentrated on 18th century French furniture, bibelots, pastels, and drawings; while this first collection was decorative and tasteful, it was comparatively banal. He sold it at the top of the market. It was after this that his remarkable flair and understanding began to show itself as he turned to the Romanesque and Gothic. The sculptures of wood or stone, the early enamels and ivories, the illuminated manuscripts, the drawings, that he ferreted out from unknown hiding places were of top quality. A number of the treasures in American collections came originally from him, finding their way across the Atlantic largely through the offices of the leading art firms. The auction of this phase of his collecting, again at the top of the market, in New York in 1927, gave only a faint idea of the quality of the works he had owned. Though some very attractive items were included, it was actually the liquidation of a glorious past. Kann was already interested in new fields, the Near East, African sculpture, and, above all, modern paintings.

Within a few years he went through a complete new evolution, as he progressed from the more conservative Manet and Renoir, to Bonnard, and finally to the abstract artists. When I last saw him, shortly before World War II, it was at his exquisite home, a *thebaide* at St. Germain, just outside Paris. Here a large room was devoted to his important library and the walls were covered with modern paintings. Facing me across the luncheon table was his latest acquisition, a superb abstract Picasso of the great 1910–1912 period. When I asked him whether he would consider selling it, his answer was, No, he paid a high price for it, but was certain it would some day be worth much more. How right the man was.

It took courage to invest his original small capital and then reinvest it in this fashion, but it also took an astute knowledge of present and probable trends of the market. Alphonse Kann seemed to have a sixth sense for gauging the market, and when he concluded that it was time to switch fields, he did so with an understanding and a feeling for quality which shunned the mediocre and the so-called bargains.

Honest and knowing intermediaries can often be of great service to both the dealer and the collector, particularly to the novice collector, who might easily be led to purchase dubious works of art or outright fakes. He can also be of considerable help with the type of collector who has an exalted opinion of his own knowledge and believes himself capable of discovering masterpieces outside the usual channels of trade. How often have I heard a man boast of some fantastic purchase he has made through the good offices of a friend—a masterpiece hidden away in the home of a family who did not wish to sell through a dealer, only directly to a collector. It would seem that the very unlikelihood of such a situation would make a collector shy away from it, if for no other reason than the astounding coincidence of his appearance on the scene at the exact moment when the family had decided to sell. It would have been so much simpler for the owner to make arrangements with any one of a half dozen international firms, always ready and willing to entertain such a proposition. Granting that one such exceptional case is credible, it is just not possible to take seriously the claims of certain collectors that all their works of art have been accumulated this way. I believe that I can truthfully say that I, personally, have yet to encounter an unknown masterpiece in such a collector's house.

It is with this type of conceit that an intermediary may be useful, not only to the dealer, but equally to the misguided collector about to squander his money. One day at Sagan I received a visit from an Italian art historian, a highly cultivated and congenial man who was happy to supplement a meager income by the usual commission upon sales he arranged. He asked whether I knew Mr. X, who wanted to purchase important paintings. I knew Mr. X, but considered him a hopeless case, since he was the type who refused to do business with dealers. However, should my friend succeed in bringing Mr. X to Sagan, I would be delighted, and I proceeded to show the art historian paintings of a kind which I understood his client fancied. Next day this charming man returned, somewhat crestfallen, to tell me that I was right; Mr. X flatly refused to go to any dealer, wishing to purchase only directly from private parties—what could I suggest?

I had no suggestions to make and, after weighing the situation for a few minutes, my friend asked, "Would it make sense, do you think, to show him one of your paintings, the beautiful Tiepolo, for instance, in his hotel room or at my apartment? That is, if you are willing?"

42

This is a type of operation which I loathe and under ordinary circumstances would not entertain. But I was fond of my Italian friend, and the challenge amused me, so I acquiesced, adding, "Make up a good story. It will be that as much as the painting that your client will buy!"

Exactly twenty-four hours later, my friend returned, without the painting, and answered my questioning look by pulling a roll of bank notes out of his pocket. "I made up an excellent tale," he said, "I told him, too, that the owner was in immediate need of cash, that it was a matter of hours, as the painting was on the verge of being sold to a dealer. That got him!"

Several years later I chanced to be in the home of Mr. X, and he related to me with almost malicious glee the story of his extraordinary luck in acquiring this marvelous Tiepolo, which was practically sold to a dealer when Mr. X appeared just in time to snatch it away. I did not disillusion him.

This type of know-it-all, suspicious-of-dealers collector is also largely responsible for the well-known racket of "planting." As the term implies, this is the practice of placing a given item, even a whole collection, in appropriate surroundings which purport to be the original setting. Entire castles have been furnished in this manner. The practice need not involve fraud as far as the works of art themselves are concerned, for they may be of the highest quality. Nevertheless, it is a spurious enhancing of value by means of a false background, and it must be confessed that even prominent dealers have themselves been taken in by such maneuvers, especially in countries not their own.

In 1912, three years after the purchase of Sagan, a most unfortunate family quarrel brought to an end the unique and ideal cooperation which had existed for more than twenty-five years between Jacques Seligmann and his brother, Arnold. Simon, the third brother, had retired some years before. There is no quarrel so bitter as a family one and, as a sudden tropical storm swiftly uproots trees and smashes buildings, so was the house of Seligmann shaken to its foundations. When the lawsuits were over and the droves of arguing attorneys had departed, there was no longer one firm, but two. Arnold remained at 23 Place Vendôme under the firm name of Arnold Seligmann & Cie., while Jacques consolidated his activities at Sagan as Jacques Seligmann & Cie., later to become Jacques Seligmann et Fils.

Thus there came to an end the powerfully single-minded firm, and there is no doubt that it was to the detriment of both brothers. The sum total of such a combination is considerably greater than any of its component parts. The partnership of Jacques and Arnold, whatever the deficiencies of one or the other, represented a higher potential of efficiency than either of them could attain as rivals.

It seems strange, I know, to write that I do not really know the cause of the quarrel, but this is partly explained by my own life at that time. I had turned eighteen and had decided to volunteer for military service rather than wait to be drafted at twenty. It was a move which my father favored, as once finished with my two years I would be of an age to take my place in the business and could continue my career without interruption. I was determined to be an officer and to this end had enrolled in physical training classes especially designed to fit one to pass the rigid requirements of a candidate. Thanks to the marks I received there and in my previous schooling, I was accepted with a rating sufficiently high to permit me to choose the garrison where I would serve. Thus, although I was variously stationed in Paris itself or at comparatively nearby Le Havre and Rheims and could spend my leaves at home, I was still not there enough, nor close enough to the situation to know all the details of the differences which had arisen between my father and my uncle. Naturally, too, the subject was avoided at home as much as possible, for my father, who could talk with vehemence about any subject which interested him even mildly, would go into a rage of towering proportions about Arnold and those whom he believed had influenced him.

To whom would such a separation be most profitable? It must be obvious to anyone with a knowledge of the art world—or, for that matter, the general business world—that so dynamic a firm in a highly competitive field could not have developed without arousing jealousy, envy, even fear or hatred. The stakes involved were high; one does not juggle with millions without fomenting intrigues and coalitions directed toward upsetting the balance of success. Together the two brothers were an indestructible force, working for the greater name of Seligmann; separated they could perhaps be outdone by competitors.

It would be foolish to pretend that my father was an easy man to work with or for; few brilliant and dynamic men are. Uncle Arnold was often irked by his dictatorial methods. I know that he had been resentful for some time of my father's keeping the buying so firmly in his own hands. I suspect that it was the acquisition of Sagan, and the consequent drawing away from Place Vendôme of many of the finest objects and many of the most important clients which precipitated matters. Since my father spent most of his time at Sagan, Arnold had, perforce, had a freer hand and this taste of independence, doubtless encouraged by outside interests, emboldened Arnold to make demands to which my father was not willing to concede.

Whatever the cause, from then on the two brothers fought their competitive battles separately, and with visors down.

Family ties were strong in Jacques Seligmann; aside from any business consideration, the separation was a sadder blow to him emotionally than he would ever have admitted. Fortunately, the work he loved was the panacea to cure both hurts, and he submerged himself in the challenge to show the world, and particularly his brother Arnold, how much he could again achieve alone, as he had in the beginning.

Certainly the internal difficulties of the firm do not appear to have hampered either Jacques Seligmann's buying or his selling. A random coverage of the art press for the years 1912 and 1913 finds his name repeatedly conspicuous among the buyers at important auctions with only the publicly recorded purchases totaling hundreds of thousands of dollars—the Buisseret sale in Brussels, the Lanna and Lippmann sales in Berlin, the Jean Dollfus and Jacques Doucet sales in Paris, the Rita Lydig sale in New York, the Charles Wertheimer sale in London. This last must have had a special, even sentimental, quality for my father, for Charles Wertheimer, who died in 1912, was one of the brothers whose tea Jacques Seligmann had so naively interrupted twenty-five years earlier. When my father presented his check for the sum of the day's purchases—more than twenty-seven thousand pounds or about a hundred and thirty-five thousand dollars—I like to think he remembered that earlier occasion when even a hundred pounds would have made so much difference to him.

One of the problems presented by the division was the loss to my father of the Place Vendôme address, where for many years clients had been accustomed to find him. To get around this difficulty, space was taken on the ground floor of 17 Place Vendôme, between the old firm and the Hotel Ritz. The move brought about another law suit with my Uncle Arnold, which was settled in my father's favor. This address was soon abandoned in favor of quarters in a business building which my father purchased at 9 rue de la Paix, a location which the firm of Jacques Seligmann & Cie. maintained until it was closed by the Nazis in 1940.

Headquarters, however, were at the Palais de Sagan, and some means had to be devised to fix its importance more firmly in the public eye. My father had never been particularly addicted to exhibitions, even though he had added the auxiliary building at Sagan for that purpose. But now well-advertised public showings, particularly those for the benefit of some worthy cause, seemed a logical method of bringing the art-minded public, as well as the choice collectors, to Sagan. An ideal opportunity was offered in the spring of 1912, when J. P. Morgan agreed to allow the exhibition of the marvelous group of ivories from the Hoentschel collection before they were shipped off to America. Later, in the early summer of that year, the height of the Parisian social season, Sagan was turned over to a committee, headed by the Comtesse Greffuhle, which had organized a huge exhibition of contemporary painting and decorative arts. Both, naturally, brought tremendous crowds of the art-minded, the merely curious, and the fashionable to Sagan.

To open the fall season, the great rooms of Sagan were hung with a fabulous display of some of the finest tapestries ever gathered together by a private collector, again J. Pierpont Morgan. This exhibition, too, had a distinguished sponsoring committee, as it was a benefit for Les Amis du Louvre—a gesture not without its ironical aspects, as my father and J. Pierpont Morgan had more than once incurred the displeasure of the Louvre over some work of art which had left France. Whether by design or accident, however, the display tactfully included only one example which had come from a French collection. Nor was it a French work, but one of the two sumptuous Crucifixion tapestries of Bernard van Orly, woven in Flanders for the ancient collection of the Dukes of Berwick and Alba. My father had acquired it for Morgan from the Jean Dollfus sale, and in the dispersal of some of the Morgan properties in 1917, it went to Joseph Widener who left it to the National Gallery at Washington. Another famous example, and an extremely rare subject, was a great Credo of the 15th century, the only complete example known. It had come originally from Spain, from the Sambolo family.

All the rest, twenty-nine in all, carried the provenance of Knole House, the venerable and justly celebrated family seat of the Sack-

46

villes at Sevenoaks, Kent, England. Morgan had purchased them through my father when death duties forced Lord Sackville to raise immediate cash. All of them dated from the 16th or the early 17th century, and two, a *Legend of Saint Veronica* and the *Miracle of the Two Children,* were superb examples of the rich gold and silver woven technique. (The *Saint Veronica* is now in the Robert Lehman Collection). A handsome catalogue was compiled by Seymour de Ricci to commemorate the occasion, and a leading American art journal extolled the exhibition under a headline reading, "Rare Gothic Tapestries Exhibited at Sagan . . . in the newly re-decorated premises of the premier French professional collector."

The most beautiful and most thrilling of this prewar series of exhibitions at Sagan was undoubtedly the Loan Exhibition of Medieval and Renaissance Art, held in May of 1913, for the benefit of the French Red Cross. The organizing committee was headed by the Marquise de Ganay, herself a collector of knowledge and great taste. The reception was graced by His Majesty, King Alfonso XIII of Spain, the social lion of the season. Again, a beautiful catalogue was published, with a special deluxe folio edition in which all of the three hundred and forty-five examples of the choicest Medieval and Renaissance objets d'art were illustrated. Not one of them came from a museum and not one of them was for sale; they were the prized possessions of private collectors. As I look through the catalogue today, I am struck anew by the beauty and quality of the objects it contains.

It is fascinating to consider the exhibition, too, from the standpoint of the history of collecting, for it was the debut of the American collector as lender to Parisian exhibitions. For the first time, objects from American collections re-crossed the Atlantic at the invitation of the sponsors of a great exhibition. If anyone had the desire and the will to duplicate the exhibition today—and what a revelation it would be to a generation who believe that only painting is great art and that painting begins with Manet—it would be possible to do so almost in its entirety. The roster of American lenders would be much longer and those lenders would be largely American museums, thanks to the generosity of such collectors as George Blumenthal, Senator William A. Clark, Jules Bache, Philip Lehmann, Mortimer Schiff, and, of course, John Pierpont Morgan.

CHAPTER V

The Fabulous Barons de Rothschild

The patronage of the various members of the great international banking and collecting family of Rothschild had a considerable influence on the early success of Jacques Seligmann. When such discriminating and experienced collectors display faith in the taste and ability of a young antiquarian, others are sure to follow their lead. If any Rothschild was aware of his importance to my father there was never any evidence of it in word or deed. In the early days of my father's career when he must often have been pressed for ready cash and anxious to make a sale, there was never any suggestion of awareness of the possibilities this offered. On the contrary, their attitude toward him seems always to have been one of generosity and a special kindness. It was natural, then, that Jacques Seligmann felt a devotion to the Rothschilds beyond the natural respect of a businessman for a valued client. It is greatly to be regretted that he himself never recorded his memories of these associations, for my own experience with the older generations of the family was limited.

What a magnitude of artistic treasure might be assembled were it possible to draw up a great catalogue under the global heading of the Collections of the Barons de Rothschild! Generation after generation —in Paris, in London, in Frankfurt, in Vienna or Berlin or Naples— every Rothschild has been a collector. Some have been so largely in the sense of guarding and enjoying the great works of art which they inherited. But each Rothschild I have known, to the present generation, was and is an *amateur* in the truest sense, which implies both knowledge and taste. Few catalogues exist to give even a vague idea of what such an aggregation once represented or represents today.

48

The Fabulous Barons de Rothschild

If in recent years certain works of art from Rothschild collections have changed hands, some of the smaller collections dispersed, or others donated to the nation, for generations nothing of importance left the hands of the family. It was a generally accepted tradition that works of art were never sold upon the death of their owner, but were bequeathed to the male descendants. Probably no private collection outside a royal one has ever existed which could rival such an assemblage. Even the Wallace Collection, also assembled over generations, would be small by comparison with the aggregate of the Rothschild collections in the last generation.

It is curious, then, considering the volumes which have been written about the financial and political activities of the Rothschilds, how little exists about the role they have played in the world of art. Such a lacuna in the literature of collecting can perhaps best be explained by the determination with which they have always avoided publicity. Outside the inevitable financial news, the only press they have tolerated has been in the field of sport; after all, if the Baron Edouard's horse won at Longchamps, it was a little difficult to disguise the fact of ownership. But on the subject of art acquisitions, nothing ever appeared. A remark which the Baron Edmond once made to me is typical (and almost identical to one made much later by another great gentleman and collector, Henry Walters): any publicity about his purchases would end his patronage. My father, naturally, respected this reticence.

From the few words my father occasionally allowed himself on the Rothschilds, I assume that he had been closest to Baron Alphonse and his younger brother, Edmond, both sons of the famous Baron James, founder of the Paris branch. He was well acquainted, too, with the third son, Baron Gustave, and his cousin Baron Adolphe, who came to Paris after the closing of the Naples house. He seems to have known Baron Salomon less well. The collections of the Viennese Rothschilds —Barons Alphonse, Eugene, and Louis—as well as those of the Frankfurt Goldschmidt-Rothchilds, also owed many of their treasures to Jacques Seligmann's efforts. However, this chapter is concerned with those living in Paris.

The oldest member of the family whom I ever met was Baron Alphonse, a prodigious figure who was then head of the firm. I was a boy when the Baron died in 1905, but he must have impressed me, for I remember his appearance quite clearly—his tall, spare figure and his white mutton-chop whiskers. Some years later I met his widow in an encounter which also made a deep impression on me. I happened one day to be standing on the steps at the doorway of Sagan when I saw walking toward me from the entrance to the court-yard, a small white-haired woman clothed in black. The nearer she came, the less impressed I was with her appearance. The woolen suit she wore was of the style of the nineties, fastened to the neck with small, round cloth-covered buttons and ornamented only by a white collar of the Gibson girl type. Her brisk pace revealed high button shoes under the long skirt. On top of her head perched a small black hat, difficult to describe except that it looked old-fashioned and cer-tainly not elegant. Young, and quick to jump to conclusions, I was sure that here was someone with a hard luck story and I thought to spare my father by disposing of the matter at once, so I awaited her where I was.

As she approached the foot of the steps, she stated in an assured voice that she wished to speak with Mr. Jacques Seligmann. I replied, rather haughtily, I am afraid, that my father was too busy to receive anyone at the moment. Having by this time reached my level at the top of the short flight of steps, she looked me up and down with an icy glance, drew herself up to her small height, and said, "Just tell him anyway that the Baroness Alphonse de Rothschild wishes to see him."

Lightning could not have struck me more effectively. By then I saw the coupé of the Baroness, complete with coachman and foot-man, drawn by two superb, spirited horses, negotiating the narrow entrance. Had she remained in her coach until it had entered the courtyard, what a personal service she would have rendered me. When the Baroness saw my father, she was good enough to ignore my foolishness and allowed him to present me, though I am sure that I detected a small twinkle in her eyes as she smilingly gave me her hand to kiss. To this day, whenever I find myself about to assess a new acquaintance or a new client on the basis of dress, her image is apt to appear before my mind's eye.

Baron Alphonse's father, Baron James, had built the large house on the rue Laffitte, which is now the headquarters of the bank, and the fabulous Château de Ferrières, a few miles east of Paris, which has now become a historic landmark. An intimate of Louis-Philippe, Baron James was a frequent visitor at the French court, and in turn was favored with the King's presence at receptions or the celebrated hunting parties at Ferrières, noted for its game preserves. Later, Napoleon III was also a guest at the château, though it is said that Baron James neither liked nor trusted him.

Ferrières was built in 1857 by the English architect, Sir Joseph Paxton, and decorated in the 19th century conception of Renaissance style—thus more 19th century than Renaissance, but nevertheless imposing. Eugène Lami, the charming and witty artist who recorded the colorful life of the courts of both Louis-Philippe and Queen Victoria, is reputed to have been in charge of interior decorations; the walls of a small salon are frescoed with Venetian scenes signed by him. Like all the Rothschild houses, it was filled with works of art of the past—paintings, furniture, superb tapestries and a ceiling by Tiepolo. At the close of the war of 1870, Ferrières was commandeered by the Prussians for the use of William I and Bismarck during the peace negotiations. In World War II it was again occupied by German invaders.

Baron Alphonse inherited the Château de Ferrières, along with the leadership of the Paris firm, upon the death of Baron James in 1868. In Paris he occupied the Hôtel de la Vrillière, just off the Place de la Concorde at the corner of the rue de Rivoli and the rue St. Florentine. More familiarly known as the Hôtel de Talleyrand, the house had once been owned and occupied by the Duc de Talleyrand, Prince de Bénévent, the "weathervane" statesman, who had begun his career as a priest and given his allegiance first to the church and then successively to each new form of revolution and government. It was there, after the final defeat of Napoleon, to whom Talleyrand owed his huge fortune and his titles, that he lavishly entertained France's enemies of the day before—the Russians, the Prussians, and the English. Baron Alphonse's son, Edouard, lived in the Hôtel de Talleyrand until the beginning of World War II. In his lifetime it was a veritable treasure house, where quite literally every room contained great works of art. After World War II the Hôtel de Talleyrand became the headquarters of the Marshall Plan, the American aid program in Europe. It has since been used by agencies of the U.S. government.

The member of the Rothschild family whose memory I particularly cherish is Baron Edmond, youngest of the three sons of Baron James, not only for the great kindness he always showed me and the time he was willing to spend with me, but especially because in my relationship with him, the memory of my father was alive. Baron Edmond was already seventy-eight years of age when my father died in 1923. My father was the link between us, and I feel sure that the real reason for the interest the Baron evinced in my visits to him or his to me was the opportunity it gave him to reminisce. He found me a ready listener, as I was always eager to know more of my father's early career and the collectors of his time.

The first clear memory I have of this tall, slender man, truly aristocratic in character as well as in appearance and manner, was at Sagan shortly after World War I. I may still have been in uniform. He had come for the purpose of visiting the "treasure trove," as he called the steel and concrete vault which my father had built in the basement for the safekeeping of the most precious small items. Among the objects stored there on this occasion was an exceptionally fine group of gold-enameled snuffboxes recently acquired from a well-known collector. Picking them up one by one and delicately turning them about in his long tapering fingers, Baron Edmond admired them knowingly as the two men argued their relative merits. Then holding out a particularly lovely one, he turned to my father and asked, "What valuation do you put on this one?"

"Oh, roughly 200,000 francs," answered my father.

After a few more minutes of examination the Baron said, "Well, I think I'll indulge myself—I'll take it."

"And what will you give me for it," said my father solemnly. "You asked for my valuation, not my selling price. That would have to be considerably higher."

Of course, Baron Edmond bought the box—and for the price mentioned. This little skirmish, of a type which can only happen between the best of friends, is indicative of the mutual trust and common understanding which had grown between them.

To give an adequate idea of the extent of the collection of Baron Edmond would be a formidable task. His interest had no boundaries. I believe he knew as much of pre-Christian art as he did of Medieval or Renaissance; and though the representation of French 18th century art in his collection was considerable, I would not venture to say that it was unsurpassed by other fields.

A heavy doorway at Number 41, Faubourg Saint Honoré, was all that the passer-by could see of Baron Edmund's town house set amidst gardens which led through to the avenue Gabriel. Once inside the walls, it seemed remote indeed from that busy thoroughfare. A monumental stairway led up to the formal reception rooms on the first floor, and on the second was the big family living room where I was always received. Basically Louis XVI in style, but with something of the 19th century in its comfortable informality, its contents alone would have constituted a lifetime achievement for many an ambitious collector. On the walls, hanging in two or three rows, were some of the world's great paintings, Goya, Rembrandt, Fragonard, and 16th century portraits.

One day, while awaiting the Baron who was still occupied with a previous caller, I was shown into a small room which I had never seen before. There, in vitrines and on the walls, was displayed a dazzling array of Romanesque and Medieval works of art, none of which were known to me. My pleasure at this unexpected aesthetic treat should have been enough for one day, but, such is the perversity of human nature, my appetite was only whetted, and my curiosity aroused to see what was behind other closed doors. When in a little while I was shown into the sitting room and found my elderly host in a mellow mood, I ventured to ask the privilege of seeing more of the collection. Knowing that the Baron was easily fatigued—he was then past eighty —I suggested that perhaps the keeper of the collection, his secretary, or even the butler might be delegated to escort me. Not at all, he would do it himself.

Passing through a dark corridor opening from the opposite end of the room, he led me into two lovely rooms furnished with some of the most exquisite examples of Louis XV furniture it has ever been my pleasure to see. Ornamented with delicately chiseled ormolu and dainty Sèvres plaques, they were fit to grace the apartments of a queen or a royal mistress which, if I remember correctly, was their origin, though I have forgotten whether at the Château de Bellevue of the Marquise de Pompadour or Louveciennes of Madame du Barry. The Baron noted in passing that my father knew the pieces well, from which I gathered that he had had some responsibility for their acquisition.

Returning through the same corridor, now lighted from the open doors, I could see that the walls were lined with a series of small gouaches which I stopped to examine. To my delight they were by Lavreince, Baudouin, and other rare French 18th century artists who are the joy of the truly discriminating amateur of that refined and

53

sprightly period. When I voiced a mild protest at such charming works being hidden in this obscure passageway, his reply was that of a man who not only cares much for works of art, but who also feels the responsibility of their ownership. They were so placed to protect them from the daylight which in time would spoil them, a sad truth too often disregarded.

Baron Edmond owned another exquisite house on the very out-skirts of Paris, in Boulogne just off the Bois, where he frequently went in the spring, and a château at Armainvilliers just east of Paris near Gretz. I once had occasion to drive there with him. It was late autumn or early winter, and the partly closed house was dreary and cold, yet fascinating because of the works of art throughout.

Though it is naturally difficult to tempt a man of eighty who has been collecting all his life and who has houses full of art treasures, Baron Edmond's visits to me were never dull, for his comments on anything shown him were lively and interesting. He was extremely fastidious in his tastes and had very set ideas about the ideal condition of a work of art. Arriving one day at Sagan, he prefaced his visit with the usual statement that he was not interested in buying anything, and anyway, with his failing sight, he could no longer enjoy art ob-jects. Nevertheless, he did enjoy the few items I considered worthy of his attention, chosen from a wide range to suit his eclectic taste. I had purchased, only a few days earlier, a delightful small painting by Fragonard, a version of *Dites, donc, s'il vous plaît*. One of the witty family scenes carried out in a broad, brilliant technique, it was a canvas in every way suitable for the Baron's collection. I asked an assistant to bring in this little gem, not telling Baron Edmond what he was to see. The man had hardly entered the room, holding the tiny canvas's back to us until he could place a small easel on the table, when Baron Edmond exclaimed, "No, I do not wish to see it!"

My face evidently showed my astonishment, for he added in an accusing tone, "You've had it cleaned!"

"You're perfectly right, Baron," I replied, "but how on earth did you know without even seeing the face of the canvas?"

"Because I smell it!"

The answer was so unexpected that I had to laugh. It was true, of course. The painting had been returned only that morning from the restorer and the odor of fresh varnish was quite noticeable.

Put in front of him he greatly admired it, nevertheless, but said with a sigh, "If only you hadn't cleaned it, I certainly would have bought it."

Of no avail to explain that the old yellow varnish had completely hidden the radiant color and subtle shading; useless to tell him that had he seen it in the condition in which it was, he certainly would not have wanted it. He just answered, "Never mind. To me the painting has lost something, reeking of varnish as it does. What a pity, for it is indeed an exquisite thing, and I congratulate you upon owning it."

Baron Robert, son of Gustave and thus a grandson of James, occupied a lovely house in the avenue de Marigny just opposite the Palais de l'Elysée and, in the country, the equally charming Château de la Versine. To my knowledge, he was the only Rothschild, at least of the older generations, who deviated from the more conservative fields of collecting into the modern. He had allowed himself to be tempted by Renoir and I particularly recall, in the avenue de Marigny house, a truly superb canvas by that artist, *Rosiers à Wargemont,* probably painted around 1875–1880. Its quality was in keeping with the other masterpieces he owned.

All the Rothschilds were, and probably still are, collectors, amateurs of the beautiful; but people who live continuously among masterpieces attain standards of discrimination which make them difficult to tempt. Yet no member of the family that I ever knew appeared satiated or bored by their own or other people's works of art. Baron Edouard, for instance, whose collection left little to be desired in either quality or quantity, could not resist when something particularly alluring came his way. When he and the Baroness appeared at Sagan on the opening of the exhibition of the Philippe Wiener collection, I greeted them as guests at a social function rather than as amateurs looking for further treasures. Before they left, however, two or three small but delicately beautiful items had acquired a new home.

Still another example of this continuously living interest in art was Baron Henri, who, though son of Baron James of the London Rothschilds, made his home in Paris. His professional field was medicine rather than the traditional finance, and he was an active participant in the various scientific and charitable institutions founded by members of the family. One of these was the hospital for tubercular children at Berck, near Le Touquet, and another the *Laiterie* in Paris, a milk station for indigent children. It was he who founded the famous

Institut du Cancer where Madame Curie worked, and his son, Baron Philippe, still carries on his father's interest in and patronage of this institution.

Though most of the Rothschilds are tall and slender, Baron Henri was of medium height and somewhat rotund, with an air of bonhomie and easy good nature. He had a passion for the theater and wrote a series of plays under the nom de plume of André Pascal, a number of which were produced and attained some popular success. He served as a Captain in the French Medical Corps in World War I and his elder son, Baron James, was a pilot in the famous Guynemer Squadron. The latter and the younger son, Philippe, also distinguished themselves in World War II, holding the rank of Major in their respective branches of Air Corps and Army. Captured during the fall of France, Philippe de Rothschild was sent to a prison camp in Morocco, from which he escaped at the end of 1942 to join General de Gaulle in London.

Baron Henri, as one might expect from his literary bent, was much interested in books and manuscripts; his collection is now in the Bibliothèque Nationale. But he also had a taste for fine paintings, whether by a great name or by a charming minor master such as Boilly, of whom he was particularly fond. His collection was renowned, too, for an exceptional group of Guardis and Chardins; he was author, under the name of Pascal, of a book on the latter artist. Many of his paintings were inherited, but he continued to add to the collection until it ranged through period and country, including Goya, Frans Hals, Nattier, Drouais. It was he who acquired the superb La Tour, *Portrait of Duval de l'Epinoy,* when it reached one of the highest prices paid in the fabulous Doucet sale of 1912. It is now in the Gulbenkian Collection.

He also owned an exquisite group of gold-enameled snuffboxes, which had belonged to the Baroness Salomon de Rothschild, as well as other objets d'art. These, his library, and his paintings were divided between his lovely home on the grounds of the former Folie de la Muette near the Bois de Boulogne and his country place, the celebrated Abbaye des Vaux-de-Cernay near the forest of Rambouillet. An amusing, if perhaps apocryphal, news note appeared shortly after the Doucet sale to the effect that Baron Henri was building the home in the Bois to protect his art treasures because he found the vibrations of the buses on the Faubourg St. Honoré disturbing to the pastel of the La Tour. Greater love hath no man for a work of art; if true, it was entirely compatible with the feeling of the Rothschilds.

If the cause of, even the necessity for, the reticence of the Rothschild family is understandable, the art historian can only mourn it, for no one has ever known or will know the extent in quality and quantity of the works of art owned through the generations by these fabulous collectors. Particularly impressive would be its universality of taste, for there was no period of Western art in which some one of these noblemen was not interested. If it is natural enough that some of the German and Austrian collections were overweighted with German silver of the later Renaissance, the Parisian collections, on the other hand, were handsomely provided with the greatest works of the French 18th century. The collection of early woodcuts, engravings, and etchings which Baron Edmond made (and bequeathed to the French nation) is close to perfection.

The roster of great painters would be complete: from Van Eyck to Vermeer to Ingres; Rembrandt, Rubens, Van Dyck, Franz Hals, Boucher, Fragonard, Goya, Gainsborough, Reynolds. All are represented, some by canvases not even recorded in the *catalogues raisonnés*.

Their appreciation of certain rare types of craftsmanship was exceptional, and until a few years ago it was only in the Rothschild collections that one could truly study the exquisitely delicate faience known as St. Porchaire d'Oiron, created for the personal use of Henri II and Diane de Poitiers. The same could be said of the precious 16th century enamels of Limoges, the sumptuous portraits by Leonard Limousin, the highly decorative plates and ewers, a group rivaled only in the Louvre; or of the delicate, creamy so-called Medici porcelain and the Deruta and Gubbio plates iridescent with chamois and ruby luster.

Although the Rothschilds did not concentrate on any one period or any one type of object, my personal experience has been that a certain caliber of man reacts to a kindred quality in periods of art. Historical cycles of unusual dynamism, effervescent with new activities, new discoveries, and vital personalities, generate works of art which express the aspirations and ambitions of the patrons who commanded them, as well as the artists who created them. Thus the works of the Renaissance in both Italy and France subconsciously appeal to psychological or even metaphysical affinities in later generations.

57

It may be argued that the attraction is more historic than aesthetic, but I disagree. Certainly in the case of the Rothschilds, the historical side was academic, immersed as they were in making history themselves. No, it is because these precious creations, made for such dynamic personalities as the Medicis, the Sforzas, François I, reflect the temperament of the men who made them, the men who ordered them, and the men who later collected them. Similarly, great examples of French 18th century art offered the refinement, measure, and beauty essential to a high degree of culture. That this kinship between the personality of the collector and the art which attracts him has been neglected by scholars is somewhat surprising in our days of introspection and psychoanalysis.

Despite the wall of reserve which the Rothschilds have built about themselves and their art treasures, they are far from reluctant to share their good fortune with the public. Though catalogues of public exhibitions almost never list a Rothschild name, if one could assemble all the works of art which they have lent anonymously, both the total number and the quality would be impressive. In addition, they have made munificent gifts to the museums of Paris.

Great works of art have a quality of immortality which is often more enduring than the personalities of the men who made them, the men who commissioned them, or the collectors who may be the instruments of their preservation. To the true art lover who is at the same time a philanthropist (and the terms are by no means synonymous), the preservation and public enjoyment of the work of art is sufficient reward. But it is only just that from time to time their names be rescued from the relative obscurity of museum labels and commemorative tablets.

Many visitors to the Louvre know the Boscoreale treasure—that stunning group of 1st century Roman silver which was such a sensation when it was recovered from the ashes of Vesuvius in 1895—but how many recall that it was the generosity of Baron Edmond de Rothschild which placed it there. Later his heirs also gave to the French nation his great collection of xylographs, engravings, and etchings, one of the most complete and discriminating ever made by a private collector.

Baron Adolphe was donor of a superb group of Gothic and Renaissance objects and a long list was added by the Baroness Nathaniel. More recently, Baron Guy de Rothschild and his two sisters presented

58

to the Louvre a magnificent portrait of the Countess Doria by Van Dyck in memory of their father, Baron Edouard. The already fabulous stacks of the Bibliothèque Nationale were further enriched by the books and autographs of Baron Henri, who also contributed generously to the collections of Cluny. The enumeration could go on endlessly.

In recognition of the encouragement they gave to the arts and sciences—their personal interests included many intellectual and aesthetic fields—both Baron Alphonse and Baron Edmond were elected *Membres de l'Institut,* the greatest honor that France can grant in the fields of higher learning. It is surprising, however, that no greater place was made for them on the boards of those very museums in which the Rothschilds were, and certainly still are, so keenly interested. Is this perhaps again because their reserve and modesty kept them from accepting such posts, assuming that they were offered?

CHAPTER VI

St. Petersburg, 1910

In the late fall of 1910, my father assigned me to my first important mission. Carrying it out involved me in an Arabian-nights journey to St. Petersburg, capital of all the Russias and principal seat of the Czar. As I look back upon it, I wonder at my father's temerity; I was not quite eighteen.

Going to Russia in those days was no small undertaking, not that it has ever been exactly easy. Where travel to Austria or Italy, for instance, involved nothing more complicated than buying a ticket and reserving a sleeper on the international wagons-lits, a journey to Russia involved a good many more problems. First, one needed a passport and a visa, for until World War I, Russia and the United States were the only nations of the Western world requiring these documents. Then, looming large among the obstacles, were the severe cold for which one had to prepare and, most formidable of all, the language. As soon as one crossed the eastern borders of Germany into the Slav-speaking countries, knowledge of French, English, or German was of little avail. Fortunately, I did have a smattering of Russian, but had I known none, it would not have marred to any great extent my youthful excitement at the prospect ahead. Anyway, if one could manage to overcome the language barriers of the journey, not the least of which was bargaining with the droschky driver, one's troubles were over, for St. Petersburg society at home spoke either French or German, if not both, and Russian was reserved strictly for addressing servants and peasants.

The Russia of those days was still in the feudal period. True, there were no suits of armor, and the gowns of the beautiful women were of the latest Parisian mode, but the manner of living was nearer that of the 15th century. Life was centered about a few thousand persons who, one felt, had the right of life or death over the rest of the populace. This *vulgum pecus*, toiling for the few, was occasionally granted certain privileges and enjoyments according to the good grace of the overlord, but, as in all tyrannical oligarchies, nothing in the life of the lower strata had permanent character, dependent as it was upon the mood of the all-powerful master.

This impression of the nothingness of the individual began at the border, where all passengers were required to descend and traverse heaps of snow to board the wider gauge Russian train. Falling in line between beautifully uniformed Cossacks, whose long knouts were an indispensable part of their accoutrement, a tedious inspection of our passports ensued. Some travelers were openly favored with repeated salutes and clicking of heels, rushed out with their baggage, and given their liberty at once. Others, not so fortunate as to belong to the nobility or to be directly employed by them, were thrown back into the herd and told, menacingly, to wait. Officers of the army or navy had privileges, too, of course, but few of the untitled ever reached this rank. The bags of the commoners were opened and searched, not so much for dutiable goods as for dangerous literature which might fall into the wrong hands and give the worker unfortunate ideas of another world where liberty and equality had meaning. One Czarist tradition which has not been liquidated!

When one is almost eighteen and fate has granted such an adventure, with a maximum of comfort and no immediate worry except the obvious one of getting through these tiresome formalities and on to St. Petersburg, such observations touch one lightly. It is only later that comparisons and impressions crystallize into understanding. Once out of the toils of the threatening Cossacks and back on the train, steaming slowly across the everlasting vastness of the Russian plains, white and silent under their thick mantle of snow, or through the dense forests of pines and silver birches, life in Russia seemed only stirring in its novelty and strangeness. As day after day the same roadless landscape unfolded, snow and more snow, dotted here and there with a miserable hamlet, even a casual young student of history might be led to wonder how there could have been a man so daring as to imagine that he could nourish a conquering army in this wilderness. Had Napoleon made this journey before undertaking his campaign, would he have ventured it?

I thought, too, of my father, as a young man, making this same trip by third-class carriage. He had been among the first of the Parisian art dealers to undertake the long trip to Russia, which, with limited means and no friends, could have involved real risks. After several visits, and considerable persistence, Jacques Seligmann had finally gained access, via the front door, to fabulous palaces into which, in earlier years, he could hardly have penetrated by the tradesmen's entrance. Behind these palace walls were untold numbers of works of art of all periods, but particularly those of the French 18th century, accumulated through years of princely collecting. Due to the indifference of some owners and the cupidity of others, usually heirs rather than actual collectors, my father was able to carry back to Paris treasures which eventually found their way into the cabinets of his clients. Conversely, he had also acquired important Russian clients, including no less a personage than His Majesty, Nicholas II the Czar of all the Russias. According to a New York newspaper, my father had enjoyed "one of the rare distinctions of the world in being admitted alone to the presence of the Czar."

It was the Grand Duke, H. I. H. Nicholas Mikhailovitch, who had presented my father to his uncle the Czar, and, naturally, the Grand Duke was one of the first persons upon whom I called. A grand seigneur in the fullest sense, with all the prerogatives and functions, military and civil, pertaining to a direct blood relative of the ruler, he was also a great scholar. *Membre correspondent* of the French Institute, his St. Petersburg palace, one of many throughout Russia, was a center where savants, scientists, and collectors met. As a great admirer of Napoleon, the Grand Duke was much interested in documents relating to the life of the French Emperor as well as in works of art of that period. He collected miniatures by the leading Directoire and Empire artists and was collaborating with the French collector, David-Weill, in compiling a corpus of late 18th century miniature painting. What happened to the manuscript after the events of 1917 ended the life of this exceptional character, I do not know.

A few days after my courtesy call, His Imperial Highness invited me to join one of his intimate luncheons. It was served in one of the smaller rooms, by half a dozen footmen in imperial livery, to a dozen intellectuals and scholars, plus as many dignitaries of His Highness' household. The afternoon was well along when we arose from the table and the Grand Duke excused himself, saying he had been called unexpectedly to the Czar's palace. Most charmingly he inquired whether I would like to be driven anywhere; if so, a sleigh was at my disposition. Feeling the need of exercise after abundant food and wine, I declined with thanks, explaining that I was just going back to the Hotel de l'Europe and would enjoy the walk.

Winter daylight lasts only a few hours in St. Petersburg and it was already dusk when I started down the avenue, looking extraordinarily broad with its snow-covered sidewalks. As I strolled along, fascinated by the strange sights, I suddenly heard behind me, muffled by the crisp, heavy snow, the wild sound of galloping horses and shouting men. I looked back, and instinctively threw myself against the wall of the nearest house, for coming at full speed was a troika, preceded by a detachment of Cossacks flaying their knouts to right and left to whip pedestrians out of their path. My first thought was that the erect man in uniform must be the Czar, for only he would dare such a display of omnipotence and such complete disregard for the lives of his subjects. To my utter amazement, the demigod of the troika, I could see as it passed me, was none other than my recent host, the *membre correspondent* of the *Institut,* the fine *causeur,* the dilettante collector, the Grand Duke Nicholas Mikhailovitch, wrapped in his furs, oblivious to the scene before him.

Fortunately time has a faculty of glossing over the unpleasant, and one generally remembers the sunnier moments. These few weeks, of which I still retain certain vivid images, seem now like a dream given a measure of reality only by the strength of the emotions the memories revive. In spite of the brilliance and sophistication of prewar life in Paris, London, Berlin, or Vienna which deservedly captured the imagination of many a traveler, their atmosphere was truly pale and shadowy in comparison to that of St. Petersburg.

Partly European, yet still oriental in its sumptuous luxury, in its depravity, and in its indifference to western morals, the standards were completely different. Work was apparently unknown among the few thousand privileged. Money was made by those one employed for that purpose, and the privileged who received it had the greatest disdain and disregard for it. It was considered small, petty, even in bad taste, to talk of money. The high nobility ignored even the meaning of the word and carried none on their persons, the touch of so low a commodity being left to the secretaries and the butlers. True, one might carry a bound purse to be tossed to a mendicant with a gesture which seemed, and probably was, disdainful, but was to them only a most natural one. It was simply the remnant of a centuries-old tradition of feudalism, when the only career worthy of a nobleman was the military. He, as overlord, had all the privileges incumbent upon rank, however far he considered these prerogatives should go.

Thrown by circumstances into this whirl of idleness and easy enjoyment, I partook for a few weeks of all the liberties offered by a society the like of which I could not have conceived. The night life was, of course, the most fantastic part of this world; for many it was the only life, since there were few hours of actual daylight. The round of parties ended in the early hours of the morning and, allowing a few for sleep, it was again dark when the social whirl recommenced.

A focal point in St. Petersburg was the Hotel de l'Europe where, around tea time, the smart world, hardly out of bed, began to gather. Here mingled both society and the demi-monde, for the lavish life naturally attracted women from all strata hoping to be noticed and, setting virtue aside, to achieve prominence in the capital. The opera, the ballet, the many theaters furnished opportunities for a would-be protector to claim an opening for a newly discovered "star." The women represented in their beauty all the cosmos that is Russia— tall blondes from the north with milky white skin, dark houris from the south with a perfume of lemon all their own; beauties from the mountains or from the steppes, witty and quick, or languorous and unhurried. Wherever one went in the deadly cold, the same amazing sight struck the eye, men and women alike muffled in precious furs of ermine, chinchilla, sable, or mink. Under them the women wore the latest Paris creations of a sumptuousness rarely seen elsewhere in such profusion—lamés, velvets, brocades, cut with deep decolletage to display the rivers of precious stones and pearls which flowed beneath the lovely heads sparkling with diamonds. Seen in such lavishness, jewels and furs lost all importance as such, and reverted to their true purpose, the enhancement of the beauty of a particular woman. Their monetary value had no meaning, for the fortunes of their donors derived from estates as big as provinces. The majority of the men were in uniform—officers of the imperial guard, cavalrymen, Cossacks whose belts were strung with pistols and cartridges. Those who did wear the conventional black evening dress, added their own notes of color in bright sashes or decorations dazzling with

64

pearls and precious stones. This gay and glittering throng whiled away the early hours of the night at regally set dinner tables laden with suckling pigs and whole sturgeons amidst a hothouse setting of flowers and tropical plants, with vodka and champagne flowing freely.

As the night wore on and the larger parties broke up, there came the most stirring part of the entertainment, at least to the eyes of the young westerner, the drive to The Islands. Over the frozen Neva in sleighs or handsome troikas with the horses trotting their peculiar gait to the silvery tinkle of bells, one drove at full speed to the inns on the small pleasure islands which studded the river. Here the party continued, in the private rooms of some inn, where orchestras of tziganes entertained with exotic music and dances. By that hour the women seemed even more sensuously tantalizing, and the shoulder straps of their gowns did not appear to be as taut as they had a few hours earlier. Outside, the moon, which had silvered the already white landscape, set in its turn, and the twinkling stars smiled down at the singing and dancing groups, oblivous of time.

Interesting as it was to observe and partake momentarily of the life of the great of Russia, to visit private collections or study royal ones in the public museums, the business purpose of the journey could not be forgotten. This was the first important mission ever entrusted to me and I was determined not to fail in it.

My father had delegated to me negotiations preliminary to the purchase of the Swenigorodskoi collection of early Russo-Byzantine enamels, one of the most important of its type in existence. Alexander Swenigorodskoi was a Russian collector of the 19th century who had become interested in medieval art during a trip to Spain in 1864. He had collected so successfully that when, like so many collectors, he developed a new passion, the Stietglitz Museum in St. Petersburg is reported to have bought the first collection for one hundred and thirty-five thousand dollars. The new interest, for Byzantine enamels, had been awakened by another trip, this time to the Caucasus, and by the time the second collection was catalogued in 1892, it was even more celebrated than the first.

Swenigorodskoi was no longer living, and his enamels had passed to another wealthy Russian collector, M. P. Botkine. Botkine's interest ran from Tanagra figurines, of which he had hundreds, to Renaissance decorative arts, and he had amassed a large, but unfortunately not always discriminating, collection. He, too, was keen about Byzantine enamels and if he acquired them with an uneven perception, there was still the nucleus of his collection, the forty-two pieces from the Swenigorodskoi collection, all of superb quality.

The exquisite little plaquettes, made in the 9th, 10th, or 11th centuries in the delicate and fragile technique of cloisonné enamel on gold, originally decorated icons, holy books, and other ecclesiastical objects, as well as secular jewelry. Among the most beautiful, for example, are nine rondels depicting heads of Christ, the Virgin, and various saints which originally adorned a silver-gilt icon in the Monastary of Djumati in Georgia.

The problem was to find out whether the owner was ready to sell and, if so, at what price. Thus stated, it seems simple enough, but in the art world there are always wheels within wheels, and this was particularly so in those days of the free-spending big collectors. In the first place, Mr. Botkine received few people and then only those particularly qualified to appreciate his collection. The name of Seligmann would have been an open sesame; in fact, my father knew Botkine well. But that would create another difficulty; for negotiations begun in the name of Jacques Seligmann ran the very real chance of pushing the price of the enamels beyond any reasonable figure.

It was well known that Jacques Seligmann was J. Pierpont Morgan's chief art advisor, and the name of Seligmann in connection with these small precious objects, which were exactly the sort of thing the great American collector most enjoyed, would immediately have spelled Morgan. Money played no role when Morgan had his heart set on a work of art and, though Europe was rich in those days, there were few things, material or spiritual, which could not be bought if the price was right—the honor of women or men, their titles, their homes, even the tombs of their ancestors. On the other hand, Morgan allowed no one to take advantage of him, and if Jacques Seligmann had succeeded over a period of years in gaining the full confidence of the great financier and becoming one of his leading advisors, it was because he had made Morgan's interests his own. My father's business ethics were extremely strict, and no amount of money could have induced him to budge from a stand which he considered proper. Thus, while the profit on a transaction could be very large, he never hesitated to say so, and Morgan understood such

66

language. He recognized that a business must be profitable and respected this, provided he felt the exchange was clear-cut. These considerations made it imperative, in my father's opinion, that he secure
the best terms possible when buying for Morgan's account.

I was not told at the time whether my father was acting independ-
ently, in the case of the Swenigorodskoi enamels, or for the account
of Morgan. I have learned since that the latter was probably the case.
He had already felt out Botkine on the subject of selling, and now I
was to go to St. Petersburg, confer with a Russian nobleman who was
a great friend of the collector, and see what could be done about
obtaining a firm price. After considerable discussion, I agreed somewhat reluctantly to the Russian's suggestion that he present me as a
friend, a young man of means, interested in collecting, who wished
to remain anonymous for reasons of his own. Europe was full of in-
cognito traveling nobility, and I desperately hoped that I was being
taken for such. Then, as soon as I should have succeeded in obtaining a price, I was to wire to my father, who would come posthaste.
Meanwhile, after first seeming anxious to purchase the exquisite bits,
I was to waver and hesitate, until the arrival of my father.

Since Paris was not just an overnight journey from St. Petersburg,
the days of waiting were torture for me. I worried about whether the
owner would change his mind and decide not to sell or, worse,
whether some other buyer would cut in. I was never more glad to see
my father than the day he arrived in St. Petersburg and I could bow
out of the picture after making one last call with him upon Botkine.
In his role of the eminent expert, my father took advantage of the
occasion to give me a lesson in the connoisseurship of early enamels.
Botkine's collection contained a number of items which purported to
be 9th or 10th century but were actually made much later, and my
father could compare them and show me why one was early and another was not. Now since Jacques Seligmann had a firm price, he
could deal directly with Botkine and consummate the purchase in
his own name.

My anxieties were even then not quite ended, however. My father
was not returning directly to Paris, and it was up to me to carry the
precious load back to France. If it is easy now to tell that the little
gold sheaves arrived safely, my days and nights then were far from
pleasant. Across practically the whole of Europe, through border
after border, the precious box was most of the time hidden inside the

berth where, pretending illness, I remained as constantly as circumstances allowed. This was not for reasons of customs; there were no customs regulations restricting the movement of works of art or of gold, and these were both. Moreover, I carried a note from the French embassy in St. Petersburg testifying to the bona fide ownership of the enamels. It was decided not to declare them for two very good reasons: to avoid, first, the voluminous red tape which a declaration would have entailed at every frontier station and, second, the inevitable gossip over the great value of such small objects and the possibility of this reaching the ears of the light-fingered gentry who frequented the transcontinental railroads. It was with real relief, and some self-satisfaction, that I finally saw them deposited in the safe in Paris and could go back to remembering the delights of my stay in the land of the Czars.

CHAPTER VII

J. Pierpont Morgan

Late in December, 1912, Jacques Seligmann arrived in New York on the French liner *La Provence* and was interviewed at the Ritz-Carlton by a reporter from the New York *Herald*.

"This year has been a busy one for me," he said. "I had to look after the packing of Mr. Morgan's collection. . . . In a fortnight [it] will be in New York. . . . Nobody can imagine the beauty and rarity of Mr. Morgan's collections. I, who have had every article in my hand, cannot find words to express its marvelous beauty and quality. No museum can compete with him. He has gathered a number of unsurpassed translucent enamels."

He might have added, had he been in a reminiscent mood, that almost the first purchase Morgan made from him was an enamel in 1902—an exquisite chalice in silver gilt that he got from the Baron Albert Von Oppenheim collection in Cologne. It was made in the 14th century for the church of San Michele in Siena. Also, there was the lovely copper-gilt ciborium from the Klosterneuberg Convent in Austria, one of the most precious examples of early 14th century champlevé, that he bought in 1906. The same year he added the gold and enamel bookcover from the Imperial collections of the Hapsburgs and the unique tiny altar-tabernacle, another translucent piece made in the 14th century. It originally belonged to the Convent of Lichtenthal in Baden, Germany, and came from the collection of the Count Arco-Zinneberg. To my father's mind, the loveliest and rarest of all was the delicate little portable altar, no bigger than a man's hand, which was already more than a hundred years old when it belonged to its first recorded owner, a 15th century bishop, Thomas Basin of Lisieux. It had come from a German nobleman along with

69

the great jeweled ciborium which bears the arms of the Wolff-Metternich family and the date 1609.

Actually the interview continued in a less personal vein. "When his [Morgan's] collection is seen as a whole, which has not been the case up to now, it will be a revelation to the world and will give the inspiration to his countrymen to follow his example. Europeans must come here to study, and Americans will love all those wonderful genuine things. There will then come a desire to purchase similar treasures, and the people will see what Mr. Morgan has done, because these genuine articles are very rare, and today no one is wealthy enough to make another collection like Mr. Morgan's. . . . Look what he has done for his country. You can be proud to have such a citizen, for they are rare. . . . Can you imagine the treasures stored in the Metropolitan Museum?"

One could not possibly imagine, and to enumerate all of Morgan's fabulous purchases would be an enormous task—even just those which came from my father. Sometimes Morgan bought single items, often he acquired whole collections. The Baron Albert Von Oppenheim collection of objets d'art, for instance, which was purchased in two groups in 1905 and 1906, included several hundred objects of superb quality. One of the choicest was a Carolingian ivory plaque dating from the 9th century. One of the rarest was a delicate Byzantine reliquary of cloisonné enamel on gold which had belonged to the Fieschi family, whose most illustrious member was Pope Innocent IV, said to have owned the reliquary and its enclosing 13th century ivory casket.

Morgan's taste was eclectic in period and type, as long as the quality was outstanding. In 1907, he acquired, with equal enthusiasm, an exceedingly rare Etruscan bronze cist, with its cover, dating from the 4th century B.C. (it had once been in the Spitzer collection); outstanding examples of the rich lustered majolica from Gubbio, which he particularly loved; and two pieces of rare 16th century faience from Saint Porchaire d'Oiron, one a saltcellar bearing the crescent of Diane de Poitiers. All these were comparatively small things which he could keep in his own cabinet, but the monumental 15th century sculptures from the Château de Biron could only go in a museum. They, an *Entombment of Christ* and a *Pietà*, attributed to the school of Michel Colombe, went directly to the Metropolitan Museum upon their arrival in New York and have been there ever

Plate 33
Jean-Honoré Fragonard (1732–1806). "Dîtes, donc, s'il vous plaît," 16¼″ x 19½″. Acquired by Fritz Thyssen, Essen, 1928. Present collection: Folkwang Museum, Essen.

Plate 34b
Henry Walters (1848–1931), Baltimore. Portrait by Frank O. Salisbury, in the Walters Art Gallery, Baltimore.

Plate 34a
Herbert N. Straus (1881–1933), New York

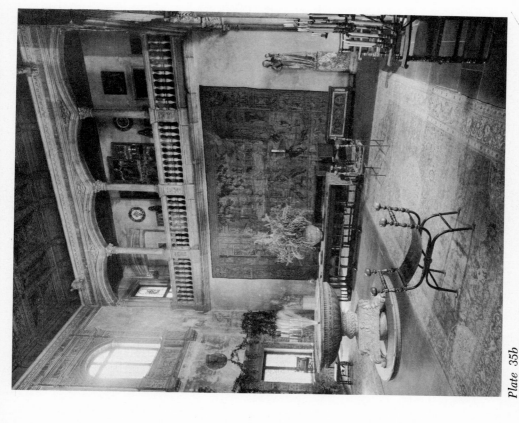

Plate 35b
Marble patio, early 16th century, from the Château of Vélez Blanco, Spain, as installed in the Blumenthal House on Park Avenue. (Photograph courtesy of the Metropolitan Museum of Art, New York.)

Plate 35a
George Blumenthal (1858–1941), New York. Portrait by A. Dechenaud, in Mount Sinai Hospital, New York.

Plate 36

Joos van Gent (active c. 1460–1480). "The Adoration of the Magi," tempera on linen, 43″ x 63″. From the collection of the Dukes of Frias, Convento de Santa Clara, Medina de Pomar. Acquired by George Blumenthal, New York, 1924. Present collection: The Metropolitan Museum of Art. Bequest of George Blumenthal, 1941.

Plate 37
Hugo van der Goes (active 1467–1482). "Portrait of a Donor with Saint John the Baptist," 12¼"x 8¾". From the P. A. Borger Collection, Arnhem. Acquired by Henry Walters, Baltimore, 1920. Present collection: The Walters Art Gallery, Baltimore.

Plate 38
Mosan, 12th century. Gable end of the Chasse of Sainte-Ode (Amay, Belgium), silver and silver-gilt, 23 1/16″ x 14 7/8″. From the Magniac Collection, London. Acquired by Henry Walters, Baltimore, c. 1912. Present collection: The Walters Art Gallery, Baltimore.

Plate 39a
Suzanne de Court (Limoges), 16th century. "The Passage of the Red Sea," enamel plate, 20⅜" x 15⁵⁄₁₆". Acquired by Henry Walters, Baltimore, 1928. Present collection: The Walters Art Gallery, Baltimore.

Plate 39b
South German, 16th century. Knight's gold enameled necklace, length 18". From the Ester-hazy Collection. Acquired by Henry Walters, Baltimore, 1923. Present collection: The Walters Art Gallery, Baltimore.

Plate 40b
Spanish (Valencian), mid-15th century. "Saint George and the Dragon," lustered earthenware, diameter 17⅞". From the Sigismond Bardac Collection, Paris. Acquired by George Blumenthal, New York, c. 1909. Present collection: The Metropolitan Museum of Art. Gift of George Blumenthal, 1941.

Plate 40a
French (Limoges), 12th–early 13th century. "Annunciation," champlevé enamel, 13½" x 12⅛". Acquired by George Blumenthal, New York, c. 1913. Present collection: The Metropolitan Museum of Art. Gift of George Blumenthal, 1941.

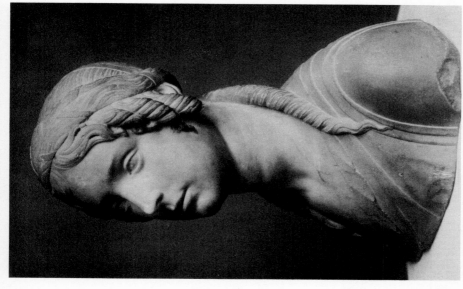

Plate 41a
Tullio Lombardi (c. 1455–1532). "Bust of a Young Woman," marble, height 17½". From the collection of Eduard Simon, Berlin. Acquired by George Blumenthal, New York, 1929. Present collection: The Metropolitan Museum of Art. Bequest of George Blumenthal, 1941.

Plate 41b
Tullio Lombardi (c. 1455–1532). "Bust of a Woman," marble high-relief, 18⅛" x 15¼". From the Oscar Huldschinsky Collection, Berlin. Acquired by Richard Weininger, New York, c. 1926.

Plate 42a
Attributed to Jacopo Sansovino (1486–1570).
"Saint John the Baptist," bronze, height 20⅝".
From the collection of the Empress Frederick of
Germany. Acquired by Henry Walters, Balti-
more, 1926. Present collection: The Walters Art
Gallery, Baltimore.

Plate 42b
Andrea Riccio (1470–1532). Bronze lamp,
height 9". Acquired by Richard Weininger,
New York, c. 1925.

Plate 43

Master of Soriguerola (Catalan), late 13th century. Altar frontal, "Saint Christopher." Acquired by Luis Plandiura, 1925. Present collection: Museum of Art, Barcelona, Luis Plandiura Collection.

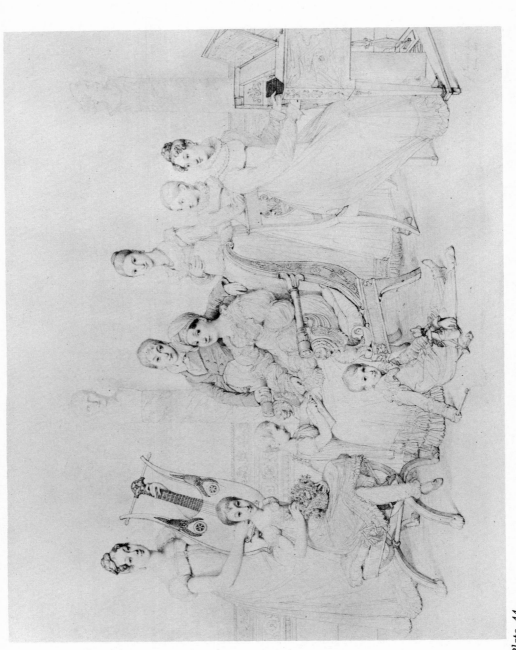

Plate 44
J. A. D. Ingres (1780–1867). "Family of Lucien Bonaparte," drawing, 1815, 15¾" x 20½". Acquired by Grenville L. Winthrop, New York, 1936. Present collection: The Fogg Art Museum, Harvard University. Grenville L. Winthrop Bequest.

Plate 45b
Sir Thomas Lawrence (1769–1830). "Portrait of Mirza Abu Talet Kahn, Ambassador of Persia, 1810, 35½" x 27½". Acquired by William M. Chadbourne, New York, 1927.

Plate 45a
Jacques-Louis David (1748–1825). "Portrait of Napoleon I," 1807, 34½" x 23¾". From the Wallace-Bagatelle Collection, Paris. Acquired by Grenville L. Winthrop, New York, 1925. Present collection: The Fogg Art Museum, Harvard University. Grenville L. Winthrop Bequest.

Plate 46a
Eugène Delacroix (1798–1863). "Musiciens arabes," watercolor, 1836, 16¾" x 23". (Study for the painting in the Musée de Tours.) From the Collections Demidoff, Bouruet-Aubertot, Duval, Faure, Marmontel and Tabourier. Acquired by Emil Bührle, Zurich, 1953.

Plate 46b
Théodore Chassériau (1819–1856). "Combat arabe," 1855, 15½" x 18½". Acquired by Grenville L. Winthrop, New York, 1935. Present collection: The Fogg Art Museum, Harvard University. Grenville L. Winthrop Bequest.

Plate 47
Pierre-Auguste Renoir (1841–1919). "Portrait of Monsieur Choquet," 1874, 18½″ x 14½″. From the collection of the Prince de Wagram, Paris. Acquired by Grenville L. Winthrop, New York, 1930. Present collection: The Fogg Art Museum, Harvard University. Grenville L. Winthrop Bequest.

Plate 48

French, late 15th century. "Quo Vadis," tapestry, 9′ 4″ x 16′ 7″. From the collection of Paul Blanchet de Rives, Grenoble. Acquired by Sir William Burrell, Berwick-on-Tweed, 1933. Present collection: The Burrell Collection, Glasgow Art Gallery and Museum.

Plate 49
French (Beauvais), 18th century. "Motherhood and Infancy," tapestry from the series, "Four Ages of Life," commissioned by King Louis XVI, after cartoons by François Casanova, 1778, 10′ x 6′. Acquired by Herbert N. and Therese K. Straus, New York, 1931. Present collection: Cincinnati Art Museum.

Plate 50b

Peter Gaertner (active 1524–1537). "Ott-Heinrich von der Pfalz," drawing, 16⅜″ x 12¼″. From the collection of the Prince of Anhalt-Dessau. Acquired by Gifford Cochran, Lamoine, Maine, 1932.

Plate 50a

François Quesnel (1543–1619). "Portrait of Monsieur de Canisy," c. 1596, 15″ x 10¾″. One of twelve Quesnel drawings from the Fevret de Fontette Collection (1765) acquired by Herbert N. and Therese K. Straus, New York, 1927.

Plate 51a
Antoine Watteau (1684–1721). "Two Studies of a Woman," drawing *aux trois crayons*, 7½″ x 8¼″. From the Crozat Collection. Acquired by Herbert N. and Therese K. Straus, New York, 1931.

Plate 51b
Jean-Honoré Fragonard (1732–1806). "Les Jets d'Eau," watercolor, 10½″ x 15¼″. From the Collections Varanchon de Saint-Geniès, Marquis de Lucay and Baron Leonino. Acquired by private collection, Paris, 1936. (Present whereabouts unknown; looted during World War II.)

Plate 52
Maurice Quentin de La Tour (1704–1788). "Portrait de M. de Laideguive, Notaire," pastel, 1761, 36″ x 30″. From the William Tilden Blodgett Collection, New York. Acquired by Francisco Cambó, Barcelona, 1927. Present collection: Museum of Art, Barcelona, Francisco Cambó Collection.

Jean-Honoré Fragonard (1732–1806). "Portrait of Monsieur de la Bretèche," 19″ x 16½″. Exhibited: Copenhagen, "L'Art français au XVIIIᵉ Siècle," 1935, #75. San Francisco, "Golden Gate International Exposition," 1939, #114. Bibliography: René Huyghe and Georges Grappe, *L'Amour de l'Art*, July, 1935. Louis Réau, *Fragonard*, 1956, p. 173, Plate 195. S. Rocheblave, *French Painting in the 18th Century*, 1937, Plate 53. Acquired by private collection, New York, 1947.

Plate 54
Hans Holbein, the Younger (1497–1543). "Portrait of Sir Henry Guildford," diameter
4¼". From the Eugene Pelletier Collection, Paris. Acquired by the Detroit Institute of
Arts, 1926.

Plate 55
Benvenuto Cellini (1500–1571). "Venus and Amor,"
bronze, height 6". Acquired by August Lederer, Vienna, c. 1927. (Present whereabouts unknown.)

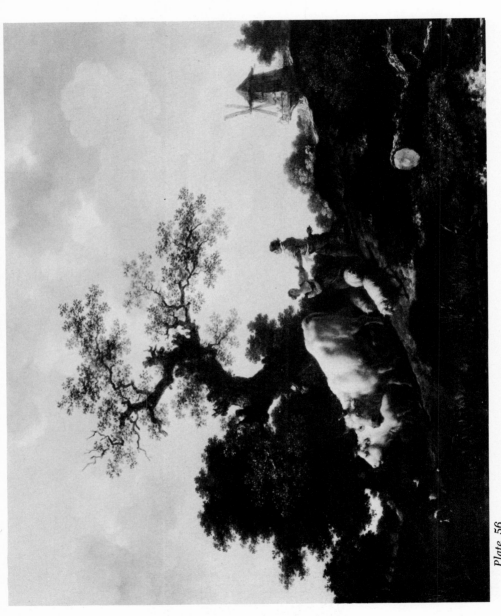

Plate 56

Jean-Honoré Fragonard (1732–1806). "La Rentrée du Troupeau" ("Annette et Lubin"), 25¼" x 31½". From the collection of the Marquis d'Harcourt, Paris. Acquired by Theodore T. Ellis, Worcester, 1929. Present collection: The Worcester Art Museum, Worcester, Massachusetts.

Plate 57
Francesco Guardi (1712–1793). "The Judgment of Paris," 16¾" x 21⅞".
Acquired by private collection, Switzerland, 1934.

Plate 58
French, c. 1480. "Portrait of a Monk in Prayer," 13¼″ x 9½″. Acquired by Ernst Rosenfeld, New York, 1930. Present collection: The Metropolitan Museum of Art, Fletcher Fund, 1937.

Plate 59
Andrea del Verrocchio (1435–1488). "Alexander the Great," marble, 22½″ x 14½″. Acquired by Herbert N. and Therese K. Straus, New York, 1927. Present collection: National Gallery of Art, Washington, D.C. Gift of Therese K. Straus.

Plate 60
French (Burgundian), 15th century. "Virgin and Child," polychromed limestone, 4′ 5″ x 3′ 5½
From the Convent of the Nuns of Sainte-Claire, Poligny. Acquired by the Metropolitan Museum
Art, Rogers Fund, 1933.

Plate 61
Lucas Cranach, the Elder (1472–1553). "Portrait of Freiin von Schenck-Winterstein," 1528, 31¼″ x 21¼″. Acquired by Gifford Cochran, Lamoine, Maine, 1933. Present collection: Sir Thomas Merton, Maidenhead Thicket, England.

Plate 62a
Pierre Bonnard (1867–1947). "La Palme," 1926, 44″ x 57½″. Acquired by the Phillips Collection, Washington, D.C., 1928.

Plate 62b
Edouard Vuillard (1868–1940). "Femme Balayant dans un Intérieur," c. 1892–1893, 18″ x 19″. Acquired by the Phillips Collection, Washington, D.C., 1939.

Plate 63
Henri de Toulouse-Lautrec (1864–1901). "Jane Avril sortant du Moulin-Rouge," 1892, 40″ x 21½″. Acquired by Samuel Courtauld, London, 1929. Present collection: The Courtauld Institute, London. (Reproduced by courtesy of the Home House Trustees.)

Plate 64a
Georges Seurat (1859–1891). "Study for 'La Parade,' " 6¾" x 9⅞".
Acquired by Emil Bührle, Zurich, 1951.

Plate 64b
Georges Seurat (1859–1891). "Le Phare de Honfleur," 1886, 26" x 32".
Acquired by private collection, London, 1933.

since, two of the most remarkable French stone sculptures in America.

Two sculptures bought the next year, 1908, a bronze bust of Alfonso d'Avalos, Marchese del Vasto, by the 16th century Italian, Leone Leoni, and an exquisite marble of Marietta Strozzi by Desiderio da Settignano, or perhaps Mino da Fiesole, remained at Morgan's East 37th Street home. The Morgan house had already been enlarged in 1906 by the addition of the handsome marble library on the 36th Street side, for Morgan had never ceased to add to his library, and the house was overflowing with illuminated manuscripts, autographs, and rare books. It was a source of great satisfaction to my father that he had helped acquire most of the works of art with which Pierpont Morgan had chosen to surround himself in the new den. Even after Morgan's death, when some of his possessions were sold or given to various institutions and the building opened to the public, certain early purchases remained in their places about the shelves of this room, as they do today.

Until a short time ago, when it went to the Frick Collection, there also stood at the entrance to the Morgan Library one of the rarest treasures of the collection, the heavenly *Ange du Lude*. I had always taken it for granted that this unique and delightful bronze, signed by its maker, Jehan Barbet of Lyon, and dated March 28, 1475, had passed through my father's hands. When the Morgan Library staff so graciously undertook to verify the pedigrees of the various items about which I needed confirmation, the scanty records about the *Angelot* seemed to indicate that Morgan had bought it directly from the Château du Lude, near Angers, where it had stood for many years. This seemed odd to me, for it was not Morgan's way to buy direct, but I could only assume that this was an exception. Quite by accident, I found in the preface to the catalogue of the residue of the Georges Hoentschel collection, sold in 1919 after the death of that great collector, a reference by Arsène Alexandre to the acquisition of *l'Angelot adorable du Château du Lude* as one of the great triumphs of Hoentschel's collecting career. Alexandre says it left France, after Hoentschel had had a moulage made and presented to the Musée des Monuments Français at the Trocadero. With this clue, it was possible to discover in the records of Hoentschel purchases made by Morgan, the date of acquisition, April, 1906. Still there was no mention of Jacques Seligmann. Nevertheless, I feel certain that this most beguiling of Gothic angels came to America through my father. For it was through him that Morgan acquired in that same year the 18th century collection of Georges Hoentschel, and through him, again, that the medieval objects were purchased in 1911. Thus it seems logical to believe that it was also through Jacques Seligmann that the sale of the *Ange du Lude* was negotiated.

However that may be, it is fact that in later years my father never failed to comment upon the Angelot when we passed it in the Library on our way to see Belle Greene, the Director. Since it is a lovely and rare object, this in itself is not extraordinary. A fine work of art need not have ever been his for him to admire it, but my own attachment to the lovely bronze angel prompted me to try to re-establish the facts. Whether my claim is fact or fancy, the beauty of this unique reminder of medieval spiritual artistry remains great.

In spite of this impressive list, and it is only a sampling of objects which came from my father in these early years, the most staggering acquisitions of Morgan have not yet been mentioned. In 1910 he purchased an unparalleled collection of Rouen faience, two hundred and two pieces, which had been selected by the former director of the Rouen Museum, Gaston LaBreton. From him, too, came three rare 14th century French marble figures probably representing Charles V, Jeanne de Bourbon, and the Dauphin, later Charles VI. Later in that year, as a result of my trip to St. Petersburg, Morgan acquired the Byzantine enamels of the Swenigorodskoi collection, which Director Edward Robinson described in the Metropolitan Bulletin in June of 1914 as "among the most extraordinary gatherings of Byzantine enamels ever brought together." Originally there were forty-three pieces, but in one of those charming gestures of which Morgan was capable, two of the precious bits were given to the Louvre in Paris; the remainder may be seen at the Metropolitan Museum today.

In 1911, my father secured for Morgan two more spectacular collections—twenty-nine of the finest tapestries of the Renaissance from Knole House in England, and, crowning the whole, the second half of the Georges Hoentschel Collection. Georges Hoentschel was a Parisian, a successful architect and decorator, whose passion for collecting beautiful works of art was almost as great as Morgan's. I remember well how he looked, as fastidious in his dress as he was in his collecting, slender, so erect of carriage that he appeared taller than his medium height—the epitome of what was then called the "cavalry officer type." His architectural activities naturally included an interest in woodwork, *boiseries,* and all the forms of French 18th century decorative art, but with Hoentschel it was more than a professional interest, it was also a hobby. He gradually assembled a unique study collection which today at the Metropolitan Museum serves as an encyclopedia of the technical skill, the ideals of proportion, and the beauty of detail which artisans and artists achieved under the direction of the great 18th century builders. It must always be borne in mind that in 18th century France, architecture was the dictator and that all artists, with the exception of the easel painters, were submitted to the instruction of the architect to whom, as to the conductor of a great orchestra, no detail was too small to be considered with careful measure. Thus, if we find today in the Hoentschel Collection whole *boiseries,* along with them are the decorative painted panels made especially to fit into them, the tapestries, and the thousand and one small or large bits of exquisitely chiseled ormolu especially designed to match as door knobs, hinges, or window catches. In 1906, Hoentschel sold this entire assembly of decorative elements, stone and marble sculptures, furniture and bibelots, to J. P. Morgan, through Jacques Seligmann. Morgan at once presented it to the Metropolitan Museum.

If this collection is a criterion of the quality of Hoentschel's taste and knowledge in one direction, it by no means conveys the full scope of his interest. Following a general trend of his time, he had for several years been withdrawing from this first love in favor of a new mistress, the Medieval. While he had already acquired a few exceptional items, such as the *Ange du Lude,* it was the proceeds of the Morgan sale which enabled him to enlarge his scope, quantitatively and qualitatively. Thus, Pierpont Morgan, called with some justice, a collector of collections which other men had labored to perfect, in this case was accessory both before and after the fact, for he also acquired the second Georges Hoentschel Collection, in two installments, in 1911 and 1912.

This comment upon Morgan is by no means uncomplimentary. The true amateur, which I believe Morgan to have been, despite suggestions to the contrary by some of his biographers, looks first for quality, but to him pedigree is also of importance, if for no other reason than the historical continuity which is so much a part of the aura surrounding works of art. Distinguished provenances, such as those attached to many of the medieval enamels of the Hoentschel collection, for instance, certainly do not add to their aesthetic worth, but they are intensely interesting to the historian of taste. The extremely important 13th century chasse with vermiculate background had once belonged to Lord Zouche; the beautiful 12th century ciborium came from the Braikenridge Collection; others were from Chandon de Briailles, Stanislas Baron, and Sigismond Bardac.

In the final group acquired from Hoentschel in 1912—the ivories, the religious silver, and the sculptures—were objects which had come from the most discriminating collectors of the late 19th and early 20th centuries. Guilhou, Boy, Charles Stein, Spitzer, Molinier, all are names which appear and reappear like leitmotifs in the exhibition catalogues of the time. At the height of the vogue for medieval works of art, any one of these pieces was worth a king's ransom. When it was rumored in the American press in January of 1912 that Jacques Seligmann had bought this last group for Morgan, my father, in confirming the story a few days later, refused to name the price paid. He did say that it was much more than the reported million francs, then about two hundred thousand dollars, and that it was the finest collection of early Limoges enamels and ivories in the world, containing some pieces unequalled in the Louvre, Cluny, or any other museum.

But what was one man to do with as many works of art as Morgan now owned? His New York home and the Library were full. There were objects on loan to the Metropolitan and to the Morgan Memorial of the Wadsworth Atheneum in Hartford. The rest were scattered about the world—the section of the Oppenheim collection purchased in 1906 immediately went on loan to the Victoria and Albert Museum; other loans were made to the National Gallery of London; his own house there, Prince's Gate, was overflowing, as was Dover House in the country; and some objects were still stored with my father.

Rumors and speculation naturally were rife. The *American Art News* of December 25, 1909, in an item headed "Important if True," quoted a cable dispatch to the New York *American* from its Paris correspondent: "Mr. J. P. Morgan means to bequeath to his country a museum not second to the Louvre. Such is the gossip among the antiquaries in Paris, London, and Rome. Napoleon the First plundered Europe for art treasures to make the Louvre. Why should not Morgan do likewise? The Seligmanns of Paris, the Agnews of London, and the Imberts of Rome hold that he can and will."

In 1912 that same publication relayed another European rumor that frequent and lengthy conversations held in Rome between Morgan and one of the Rothschilds were for the purpose of founding an art trust tending to control the prices of objects of art. Again gossip had it that the whole Morgan collection would go to Hartford, as the Metropolitan was too slow in arranging a wing to house it; but this was thought to be only a goad to prod the city fathers into action in appropriating the necessary funds.

The Morgan-Rothschild rumor was absurd on the face of it. The other two, in spite of the somewhat waspish tone of the European commentator, echoed what was more or less general opinion. Morgan had been a generous donor to the Metropolitan since his first gift in 1897, adding new ones each year, and he had been its president for almost a decade; but no one knew for sure what his intentions were.

One thing, however, seemed clear: the import tax which until 1909 was levied on works of art had weighed heavily against the chances of Morgan bringing to the United States the vast bulk of his collection which was still in Europe. For a good many years it had been hoped that the Congress of the United States would alter the existing laws to permit the entry of such items free of duty. My father often mentioned the topic and, with his crusading spirit, called to the attention of influential men the duty's detrimental effect on American art and education. How could museums be developed if collectors were to be penalized by heavy import duties? And they were heavy. I have in my files a copy of a 1906 invoice made out to an American collector, which shows that on a total of some thirty thousand dollars, almost seven thousand was for customs duty.

My father cited particularly the example of Pierpont Morgan. As long as such laws were in force, he said, the Morgan collections would remain in Europe, making it quite clear that they would not be sent home until they could enter duty free. In later years my father used to say that the new legislation finally passed by Congress was due to the personal activities of Morgan and certain of his friends, among them the brilliant Senator Elihu Root.

The Payne Bill was passed in 1909, and early in 1912 shipment of a major part of the Morgan collections was begun from London and Paris. Apparently it was still not definitely decided when and how they would be shown or housed, for Morgan arranged for a customs appraiser from the United States to go to London to inspect the boxes as they were packed, so that they would not have to be opened on arrival but could go directly to the third floor of the Metropolitan Museum to be stored.

Jacques Seligmann was entrusted with the huge task of packing and shipping the three hundred and fifty-one cases which arrived at the Metropolitan Museum between February 15, 1912, and January 29, 1913. The London branch of the Seligmann Galleries under the direction of Salomon Herz had as its chief activity the supervision of the shipment and, more important, the preparations for shipment. This, in view of the number of objects which had to be removed from their various places and the care with which such objects had to be packed, took months. Once begun, shipments went forward at the rate of one or two a week.

The three hundred and fifty-one cases contained purchases from all sources. The great Raphael Madonna, for instance, which occupied an enormous case, did not come from my father; nor did the magnificent Fragonard room which is now in the Frick Collection. There is, in fact, a precise indication in the shipping lists that on August 17, 1912, the fourteen Fragonard panels were shipped in four cases, Numbers 167–170, with the handsome catalogue "arranged for Mr. Morgan by Messrs. Agnew." Jacques Selgimann mentions them in the interview quoted above as "one of the things which cost Mr. Morgan the most . . . (for which) . . . I am sure that he can get two or three times what he paid."

Despite the volume, none of these shipments contained manuscripts or rare books which formed a separate part of this truly fantastic collection. Nor should it be forgotten that even after the removal of these cases, there still remained at Prince's Gate enough paintings and other fine objects to keep it a worthy place to receive its owner and his distinguished guests.

Letters in the archives of the Metropolitan and items in the press indicate the sequence of the shipments: "seven cases containing items from the second part of the Hoentschel Collection"; "four cases containing Sevres porcelain"; "five cases with the balance of the Sevres" and "seven cases of Dresden porcelain"; a "case containing snuffboxes and miniatures"; or "three cases with seven paintings." Shipment No. 5 had been scheduled for the ill-fated SS *Titanic* on April 27, 1912, and missed the sailing only because it was not ready in time. Another case contained thirty-one tapestries, twenty-nine of them from Knole House. It is not just the number which is impressive; it is the realization of what was represented in rarity and quality. The mere listing of cases is dry of romance but it does at least imply the staggering proportions of this collection, assembled within a decade, of the most refined creations made by hands of men over ten centuries.

The last case was shipped on January 29, 1913. On March 31, John Pierpont Morgan died in Rome after a brief illness. He was not to see it all assembled at the museum to which he had given so much time and devotion.

When Morgan's will was made public, it was found that the disposition of the collection had been left in the hands of his son, John Pierpont Morgan, Jr. Its exhibition would be held in abeyance pending the formalities which attend the settlement of so vast an estate. The official valuation of the collection made in 1916 was something over twenty million dollars, but the figure of sixty million estimated by *The Times* in London in 1913 was undoubtedly nearer the mark. The Bulletin of the Metropolitan of June, 1913, announced that the exhibition would be held as soon as it could be prepared, "in order that the public . . . might see and enjoy the most famous collection of works of art that has been brought together in our generation." Edward Robinson, the Director, estimated the aggregation at more than 4,100 objects; of these, some 3,000 were eventually presented to the permanent collection of the Museum by J. P. Morgan, Jr., in memory of his father.

These dry figures and facts do not do justice to John Pierpont Morgan, the collector. His role as banker and financier, his part in the history and the industrial development of his country are well established. But the immensity of his vision, his capabilities for unselfish and altruistic action, and, most of all, his sensitivity toward the aesthetic values of works of art have not been fully appreciated. As Francis Henry Taylor wrote, "Pierpont Morgan was the greatest figure in the art world that America has yet produced, a visionary and a patron such as we never knew before, nor ever shall again."

The devotion of Jacques Seligmann to this gigantic personality is not hard to understand, and, in turn, no greater compliment can be paid him than to have been over these important collecting years the trusted advisor of J. Pierpont Morgan.

CHAPTER VIII

The United States, 1913

In the autumn of 1913, most of Europe felt that war was imminent. The Kaiser, on his way to the Middle East, had reaffirmed his often expressed intention of seeing the Berlin-Baghdad link established by the completion of that railroad. The "peaceful penetration" of Morocco by the brothers Manessmann had already started. The bellicose Agadir incident of 1911 was still strong in memory. Moreover, the might of the German Imperial Navy was offering an increasing challenge to the British. Nevertheless, I do not believe that my father anticipated a real conflict, or if he did, he must have been so sure of French strength that he felt the possibility need not interfere with a project he had planned for some time, an extended journey throughout the eastern half of the United States.

Having just completed my first integration into the French army, I now had my coveted second lieutenant's commission, an achievement which gave me a certain pardonable pride, as the standards of even a reserve officer in the peacetime French army were high. I, personally, did not share my father's equanimity about the future and had already subscribed to a further few weeks of army training for the following spring. There was no compulsion about this, but, convinced as I was of the impending danger of war, I felt the necessity of a better knowledge of the officers under whom I would serve and the men I was to command. This further training was somewhat against my father's wishes, as he was impatient to have me free. Already the firm's attorneys were drawing up the partnership agreement of Jacques Seligmann et Fils. In spite of my father's apparent disregard of the rumors of threatening war, he seemed to be constantly harassed by a sense of little time to pass on to me his knowledge and his experience. Every phase of my instruction and all my experiences with the business world were now on double time. If the American voyage was a holiday, with my stepmother and one of my sisters accompanying us, it was also a part of my training.

I was excited and curious, eagerly anticipating my first views of the new world about which I heard so much. As I wandered alone about the streets of New York, lost in the hum of this fabulous bee-hive, I felt insignificant and lonely amidst an almost menacing, un-leashed power and might. Young as I was, I had an undefined im-pression of boundless possibilities, of extremes reaching to climactic heights of success and dismal depths of failure with few in-betweens. The glory and brilliance of Fifth Avenue against the miserable de-jection of Sixth Avenue under its rattling el; murkiness and poverty next door to scented luxury.

My first impressions were brought back to me vividly some years later when Marczell von Nemes, the well-known Hungarian collector and *amateur marchand,* was on his own first trip to New York. Ad-dressing me in German, he said, "New York is the first city I have ever seen which measures up to my own importance." All newcomers to New York, whether foreign or American, are gripped by the ex-citement and exhilaration of the atmosphere, but surely few have expressed it with such arrogant complacence.

As a consequence of the separation of Jacques and his brother Arnold, a new gallery had been opened in New York that spring for the firm of Jacques Seligmann & Company. A suitable property had been chosen, the former E. H. Harriman house at 705 Fifth Avenue, on the northeast corner of 55th Street, a bold step northward from West 36th Street and a direction which many art firms were later to follow. The manager and a partner of the new American firm was Eugene Glaenzer, a well-known figure in the art world who had been particularly active in the field of Barbizon paintings, then at the height of their popularity. He had suitably inaugurated the new galleries with an exhibition of "Portraits of Fair Women," an appro-priate choice since it was a benefit for the cause of women's suffrage, under the aegis of the Women's Political Union, with Mrs. Philip M. Lydig as chairman.

Shortly after Glaenzer came into the firm, my father unwittingly made him the victim of one of his typically unexpected and forthright statements to the press. Jacques Seligmann, perhaps goaded by some recent occurrence, had stated in a final interview as he left for Paris, that he intended to install a room of fakes in the new 55th Street house for the edification of the public. It was doubtless a spur of the moment idea, but the press seized on it with joy and a headline "Seligmann To Open Fake Picture Museum." When a reporter followed my father to Monte Carlo where he was vacationing, he declared, "I have definitely decided to open such a room in my New York house . . . it may make me enemies, but I hope to save collectors from buying fakes as genuine." He emphasized, however, that it would be objets d'art only, adding, "I am not a picture dealer." Eugene Glaenzer naturally came in for considerable sarcasm from his colleagues about managing a gallery of fakes. My father did make the collection, buying a few pieces to add to his own "mistakes" which he had always kept, but the war intervened before the room was installed. Eventually he presented it to the museum at Cooper Union Institute to be used for study purposes. It remained there until recently when, having served their purpose, the objects were sold and the proceeds used for the purchase of genuine ones which are carried in the museum's records as gifts of Jacques Seligmann.

It was doubtless at the behest of Eugene Glaenzer that the Cooper Union became the recipient of this somewhat peculiar, but extremely useful gift. He was a friend and frequent guest of the Misses Eleanor and Sarah Hewitt, descendants of the great Peter Cooper and trustees of the Cooper Union. It was he who later introduced me to these delightful elderly ladies who, in the years immediately following World War I, maintained one of the few real salons, in the French sense of the term, in New York.

The Misses Hewitt were truly captivating personalities. They still lived in the old family house at 9 Lexington Avenue, next door to their brother, Erskine, and, while thoroughly aware of the social changes about them, chose to ignore them. One had the impression that all clocks had stopped just before the turn of the century. For them, the automobile had not yet been invented and their horse-drawn coupé was possibly the last seen on the streets of New York. They patronized such fashionable dressmakers as Worth or Paquin, but the sumptuous materials of their gowns were still fashioned in the old modes, as were their hats.

But what character it all had! The Hewitt house was one of the last bastions of an older American aristocracy, where culture and manners played a greater role than money, where the strictest standards were maintained and apparently suffered no exceptions. Brought up as I was in the old European manner, accustomed to calling and leaving cards, I felt quite at home in this environment, a Victorian oasis in the hustle and push of New York life. Here one was in the age of top hats, morning coats, and striped trousers, and here certain topics of conversation were taboo unless suitably enshrouded with wit and elegance. Cocktails were unknown, one was offered sherry or port. Excellent wines were served with the meals, and the cuisine was refined but without extravagance. Both ladies spoke flawless French and had an impressive knowledge of French literature past and present, though they were apt to be severe about the newer works if they presented any vulgarity, a cardinal sin they could not condone. When one of the Misses Hewitt said, "He (or it) is vulgar," that was tantamount to dismissal.

Younger people, particularly, were severely measured for their manners, and I was therefore especially careful to abide by their ritual, a call at the beginning of the season, leaving cards if they were not at home. Otherwise, I would not be eligible for a Sunday luncheon invitation, when they entertained small groups of guests from their social set of old New York families, visitors from Newport or Boston, or foreigners of distinction. One season, having failed to call as early as usual, I tried to make up for this dereliction by presenting myself on their at-home day and was greeted with, "You have been detained much longer than usual in Europe this year." It was at once a reprimand and a compliment, for it indicated that my absence had been noted, but they were inclined to overlook and forgive it.

Particularly amusing to me was the complete disdain in which these delightful ladies held newcomers in New York's constantly changing society. The opera was still one of the great social bulwarks; but a box did inevitably change hands from time to time. I commented upon such a change to one of the Misses Hewitt, and mentioned a name which, in my ignorance, I thought was of their social milieu. The answer was, "Mrs. A. . . . . ? And who is she? I have never heard of her." Evidently they were not on calling terms.

The chief outside interest of the Misses Hewitt was the Cooper Union Institute, and when I met them they had only recently acquired in Paris the celebrated Decloux library of rare books, prints, and original drawings, all related to French decoration. This exceptional and precious collection, which they gave to the museum together with the lovely 18th century room in which it is kept, is a mine of information for the student of decorative arts. I spent many delightful hours perusing it, both at their home and at the Institute.

The dissolution of the old firm and the shipping of the Morgan collection had kept my father in Europe for almost the entire year, and he was now seeing the new galleries fully installed for the first time. From his new office he immediately set about making the appointments with friends and clients which were to plunge us into a frenzy of social and business activities.

One of our first calls was upon Belle da Costa Greene in the newly built Morgan Library, still a private institution. Her fascinating personality made a lasting impression upon me, which the years strengthened rather than altered. She was young and slender, quick in her movement, and already well established in the reputation for the mot juste which has made her something of a legend in the art world. One of her most important functions during Morgan's lifetime, in addition to those usual to a librarian and curator, was to protect him from the innumerable schemes designed to gain approach to the all-powerful, the great spender. His eagerness to add great works of art to his collection, regardless of cost, made it worthwhile to stoop to almost any method to gain his ear, and it was Belle Greene's difficult and delicate task to gauge quickly and correctly the quality of a caller before reporting to Morgan.

One had only to see her in action to know with what agility and firmness she met such problems. I am sure she realized that a laissez faire policy would have been much simpler and safer for her own future, as Morgan was impatient, but laissez faire was never Belle Greene's way. Morgan had as absolute faith in her intuition and judgment of men as he had in her remarkable instinct for and knowledge of works of art. First appointed in 1905 as librarian, a specialist in incunabula, manuscripts, and rare books, her province rapidly extended to other territories, until no field of aesthetic endeavor escaped her intellectual grasp. She and my father had established a firm friendship, based on mutual respect and a mutual devotion to the same man. Their first meeting after Morgan's death the preceding spring held sad memories for both of them.

82

Most of the people upon whom we called during my first New York visit were collectors of knowledge and taste with whom my father had long established friendships, based on a common love of works of art, and with whom he wished me to become better acquainted. With collectors of such standing, a home call offered an opportunity for my father to comment, favorably or otherwise, about a new trend in collecting, to give or to ask an opinion. For me, meeting these American clients, some for the first time, seeing their homes and their collections, was a continual education and delight, even though at times these visits could be rather trying. I was in the ambiguous position of partaker and on-looker, endeavoring at once not to say the wrong thing, and yet not to give my father's clients the impression that I had a speech impediment or was stupid. I shall always remember gratefully Mrs. Collis P. Huntington for her quick sensitivity to my predicament and her gracious manner of putting me at ease when we called. Mrs. Huntington was an interested collector of 18th century French objets d'art, and although her conversation was with my father, she somehow managed to convey that I was included in the deference she showed the visiting expert. When we were about to leave, she insisted that I come again, without my father, to take a cup of tea with her and see at leisure the collection in the big 57th Street house.

George Blumenthal, the dynamic American partner of the French banking house of Lazard Frères, was an old school friend of my fathers'; they were born in Frankfort in the same year. He was still living then on West 53rd Street and there is little to say about his collection at that time, except that it contained excellent examples of Barbizon painting, his first collecting love, for he was only beginning the important role he was to play in American art circles.

Of greater moment then were the activities of his attractive, elegant, and cultivated wife, Florence, who was not only endowed with a refined taste, but had a true student's approach to art. She had been much impressed with the house of Mrs. Jack Gardner in Boston and realized the possibilities such a program of construction offered if a greater orthodoxy were observed in the architecture itself and in the decoration of the individual rooms. She had therefore set about assembling the essential elements around which her house, and each of its rooms, would be built. It was a grandiose scheme, the like of which had never before been undertaken in such completeness.

Every capital work of art was to be chosen before the actual building began, if it were to have a fundamental role in the architecture, so that it would fit ideally into the place planned for it both in physical proportion and in relation to the aesthetic scheme. The nucleus about which the house-to-be was planned, had just been purchased from my father—a galleried Spanish Renaissance patio, two stories in height and entirely of marble. It had been originally in the palace of Don Pedro Fajardo, the first Marquis of Vélez, at Vélez Blanco, and dated between 1506 and 1515. Around it would be grouped the reception rooms of the ground and second floors. Naturally, much of the talk on this visit had to do with this absorbing subject.

Henry Walters, to whom my father was particularly devoted, also was on our calling list, but I gained little knowledge of his collection on this trip, since his New York apartment was then only a pied-a-terre in a small 42nd Street hotel. He kept few works of art there, and we did not go to his Baltimore home.

One of the most interesting characters we saw was George Kessler, the champagne king. He was the American representative of a well-known French champagne firm, and from early morning he drank, and offered to his guests, champagne frappé in handsome silver or gold urns. I never learned whether this was really an acquired taste or simply a business routine. He spent much time in Paris, and his wife became a devoted Francophile whose indefatigable activities in war relief won her the gratitude of the French. It was she who founded the Permanent Blind Relief War Fund which supported a hostel for blinded officers and soldiers in the Château de Madrid, and an industrial school for the blind. She personally financed the industrial school throughout the war, and my father, at her solicitation, took over the rent of the hostel.

Thanks to my father's educational efforts, Kessler had embarked on a collecting career, and, at the time of our visit to New York, he was busy embellishing a recently purchased house at Auteuil. That he derived a very real enjoyment from his acquisitions was patent, and he seemed genuinely grateful to my father for having awakened this new interest. One of the dividends which accrue to an art dealer who truly loves his metier is to watch a casual whim grow into a real appreciation.

One day we went to Philadelphia to lunch with Joseph Widener in his home at Elkins Park, by far the most palatial American establishment I had yet seen. Widener was about to purchase from my father four well-known stone groups, *The Seasons,* by Claude Gillet, to be placed in the garden which the French landscape architect, Jacques Greber, was designing, and their placement was discussed. They had been made originally for the Château de Valenton of Madame de Pompadour; now they were to adorn a garden in the new world.

Impressive though the house was, the collection itself had not yet achieved its full splendor, and it still contained certain paintings, among them English portraits, which were later sold or exchanged. The great Donatello statue was already at the far end of the long gallery, but the magnificent *Feast of the* Gods by Bellini and the stupendous Rembrandts were still to come.

I had met Thomas Fortune Ryan in Paris a few months before our 1913 trip to America, when he was sitting for his portrait by Sorolla. My father had given Sorolla the hospitality of Sagan, possibly at the request of another American patron, Archer Huntington, a great admirer of the Spanish painter. Sorolla occupied a studio at Sagan for several months, during which time he also painted the portrait of Jacques Seligmann which appears as frontispiece to this book. The original is still in the rue de Constantine house in Paris, now occupied by my brother. I liked Ryan at once, for under the rather forbidding outward aspect of the tobacco magnate there lay a delightful sense of humor and a deep humanity. He owned a fine collection of Medieval and Renaissance objects, housed in a long gallery on the top floor of his Fifth Avenue home, but on this visit, I was especially anxious to see the Rodin sculptures about which he had talked in Paris. Rodin was much in vogue in those days, but Ryan's collection, like that of Mrs. John W. Simpson, belonged to the late period of the great French sculptor's work, which is today considered less significant to modern art.

Jules Bache in this winter of 1913–1914 had not yet attained the financial peak he was later to achieve. His friends, in future years, talked of Jules Bache, B.C., and Jules Bache, A.C., Before Chrysler and After Chrysler. Whether a great part of his fortune actually came through a transaction in Chrysler Motors is of no great moment here except that it may explain the quickened tempo of his collecting after that date. At any rate, when we called upon him, he was still living on East 67th Street and had not yet moved to the Fifth Avenue mansion where his collection was shown for so many years before it finally went to the Metropolitan. However, he already owned the charming *Billet Doux* of Fragonard, which I had known and loved through reproductions, and I was moved to see the original painting.

Our call was something in the nature of a peace mission, for my father and Jules Bache had been on rather cool terms for a while because of Jacques Seligmann's plain-spoken opinion about what he considered a mistaken purchase by Bache. My father never hesitated to speak his mind if he felt it his duty, even though his frankness might alienate a client. However, he and Jules Bache had known and esteemed one another over a period of many years, so that the rift was healed, and a few days after our call, Bache asked us both to lunch with him downtown.

My acquaintaince with William Randolph Hearst also dates from this trip. Though he and my father had known each other for several years, and Jacques Seligmann had secured for Hearst several of his quality items, here, too, there had arisen a certain coolness, probably for the same reason. My father was in some doubt as to whether Hearst would see him, but evidently all was forgiven, because our whole party was invited to dine at his penthouse on Riverside Drive. I remember well how Hearst looked at that time—very tall, still quite slender, long of arm, and with an impassive face in which only the handsome eyes seemed to move. Though he had not yet reached the fame he was to achieve, if one should judge the success of a man, as some cynic has said, by the number and quality of his enemies, William Randolph Hearst was already well on his way.

My most vivid recollections of that visit are the height of the ceiling in the great apartment, the magnificent early tapestries, and the superb group of Hispano-Moresque earthenware of the 15th and early 16th centuries. This was a field in which my father was a connoisseur, and he was happy to see again, beautifully shown in glass cases, the chamois-and-blue plates and the rare alberelli which had been acquired from him. I dare say Hearst's collection in that field was the most important outside Spain. Next to these works of art, rather austere in their severity of design, was a large collection of German silver of the late 16th and early 17th centuries, over-ornate, and of little interest to my father. These two contrasting groups were the collector's great pride.

In later years I saw Hearst frequently. He went regularly each summer for several years to Bad Neuheim to take the cure, and that was one of the best opportunities to approach him. Even there art dealers from all Europe were constantly in attendance, and it was always a question as to who would get his ear at the right moment.

The buying methods of this dynamic personality were very strange; nobody I have known showed simultaneously such a voracious desire to acquire and so little discrimination in doing it. Hearst often purchased superb examples of real aesthetic merit, but he also acquired hundreds of items of no artistic or historic interest. There was a legend—or was it fact?—that his mother had left him a specific fund, the interest of which had to be spent yearly on works of art. This, if true, might account for some of his otherwise inexplicable eccentricities.

Contrary to the majority of men of business acumen, Hearst loved to dicker, a practice of dubious value in the art world, leading rather to bargaining than to bargains. Thus, through the years I did business with William Randolph Hearst, I never derived from it the true enjoyment I felt with his great contemporaries. An art dealer's pride and satisfaction is not entirely measured by the total amount of money a client spends; it is measured also by the quality and the exceptional character of the works of art chosen. The dealer wishes to feel himself a guide and mentor, and, because he recommends and encourages the purchase of an object he considers fitting, he is willing to assume a special moral responsibility. But when, contrary to the dealer's better judgment, the client purchases less fitting items, the art dealer loses interest in the client. It becomes then, purely a business transaction, devoid of the human ties which connect the true collector and the art dealer who enjoys his profession. Financially our relations with Hearst were satisfactory, but we derived little pride from his acquisitions of a more or less decorative nature. Too often they were the leavings of a collection we had bought up in toto for the sake of a few fine pieces.

Ironically enough, it was through Hearst that I sold one of the most regal marble statues of the French Renaissance that the firm has ever owned. He had introduced me to A. J. Kobler, an editor of one of the Hearst magazines, and it was he who bought the lovely *Saint Barbara*. The Saint, a little under life size, is represented in full length, holding a chalice in her left hand; the rich material of her dress delicately moulds her youthful figure, and her long wavy hair falls over her

87

shoulders and down her back; her bearing has all the elegance and refinement which typifies the Renaissance period in France. In addition, the warm, mellow patina, close to ivory, which the ages have added to the usual coldness of marble, imbues the very material with a sense of life.

Who was the sculptor, the Pygmalion—for one does not fashion such a work of art without falling in love with the model or the achievement—who created it? Unfortunately, as is so often the case with sculptors of the earlier periods, he remains without a name. Opinion leans toward someone from that group of artists who worked at the Church of Brou near Bourg, in France, and who built the tombs of Marguerite d'Autriche and Philibert le Beau in that lovely shrine of elegant figures and marble lace. The only other creation of a like splendor that I know—the one always reminds me of the other—is the Certosa of Pavia. The two, Pavia and Brou, are among the few architectural jewels left to us from a period which created so many.

Our New York stay was a continual round of entertainment. We went to luncheons, teas (the cocktail hour was not yet born), dinners, the theater, the opera. Hospitality was so spontaneous and generous as to be quite strange and altogether delightful to Europeans who, hemmed in by reticences and a certain amount of xenophobia, could not conceive this kind of easy-going, full-hearted gesture to foreign guests.

It must be admitted that we were definitely in need of a few days' breather in Montreal and Quebec when we left New York to begin our tour of the Middle West. Our time in Canada was largely devoted to sightseeing, but we did make one business call, to see Sir William Van Horne whom my father had recently met. Sir William was President and Chairman of the Board of the Canadian Pacific Railroad, and his knighthood was in recognition of the days of his general managership when that great road was pushed to its completion. Now well along in years, he had turned to collecting and had assembled one of Canada's outstanding private galleries.

Thence we made our way through snowbound Canada on to Chicago and the Blackstone, at that time the city's most modern hotel. From our windows we could see the open railroad tracks along the as-yet-unbeautified lake front and the Chicago Art Institute, sitting practically astride the tracks. Coming from New York, with our eyes

88

still dazzled by the brilliance of the Morgan Collection, then being installed for exhibition at the Metropolitan, our first impression of the Art Institute, the museum of the second largest city in the United States, was by comparison a dreary one. But this was 1914; the Hutchinson, Ryerson, Bartlett, Deering, Palmer, Worcester, and Coburn collections which were to make the Institute a mecca for students from all over the country, particularly for French 19th century painting, were not yet at the museum. What a change has been wrought there in forty years.

There were, however, collectors aplenty in Chicago, some with the daring to acquire paintings by the little-considered Impressionists and Post-Impressionists at a time when they sold for what today seems a song. Mrs. Lewis L. Coburn, for instance, was then living at the Blackstone, and we saw upon her walls paintings which now are key pieces in the Institute's collection. The Deerings, whom my father knew well, were, unfortunately for us, wintering in Florida, but we saw Mrs. Blackstone's collection of Chinese porcelains, and we called on the Potter Palmers, the McCormicks, and the Armours, whose homes were mostly still on Prairie Avenue, then the milieu of the wealthy.

Miss Kate Buckingham was one of the last to move from this stronghold of Chicago society, but our acquaintance with her dates from the 1920's when she was beginning the great Gothic Hall in the Art Institute which bears her name. Impressed by the personality and accomplishments of Florence Blumenthal, it was under her guidance that Miss Buckingham started the project, and it was, I believe, due to the untimely death of Mrs. Blumenthal that the scheme did not progress along the lines originally planned. Several objects destined for this hall were acquired from my father, one of the most precious being a rare early French tapestry representing two delightful huntresses, a hawker and other attendants, against a mille fleurs background.

To our French eyes, this sprawling, gusty city of Chicago held a fascination all its own, and aside from our more aesthetic pursuits, we took in such utilitarian projects as Ogden Armour's packing plant and the Sears Roebuck mail-order house, both American industrial phenomena which amazed us.

We made a side trip to Toledo to call upon John N. Willys, the automobile manufacturer, then proceeded to St. Louis, the westernmost point of our journey, and returned to New York by way of Cincinnati and Pittsburgh. Looking back on it today, I realize what an unusual opportunity I was given. Even now, with travel so swift and easy, there are few foreigners who see as much of the country on a first visit.

In Cincinnati, the Charles P. Tafts were still living in the gracious and beautiful early Federal house which is now the Taft Museum, far too little known and appreciated. Mr. Taft had acquired a number of his excellent enamels from my father, and it was a pleasure to us to see them in their new setting and a real delight to take tea with these hospitable people so representative of American tradition and refinement.

Though Jacques Seligmann was excited by the driving power and industry of these midwestern cities and the dynamic men who were building them, he often referred to the trip as a pure waste of time for an art connoisseur. My own impressions and reactions were then too numerous and varied to be crystallized. Today, I consider myself fortunate indeed to have witnessed the first steps of the infant American museum world. In terms of years, it represents half a century, a rather frightening span in a human lifetime, but how infinitesimal a measure for a country and its culture. Particularly does it seem short when one looks at the museums, today filled with distinguished works of art, then often bare of really worthy objects to fill the handsome buildings. It was this condition which provoked my father to ask the reporters who interviewed him in Buffalo if it would not have been better to buy works of art with the money lavished on the building of the Albright Gallery, even if these masterpieces must be housed elsewhere temporarily, rather than to have so fine a shell with nothing in it.

This did not, I am afraid endear Jacques Seligmann to Buffalo, but it did represent the point of view of a European, conditioned to finding great treasures in the humblest surroundings. Squandering money on buildings without objects to fill them, was a neuralgic point with Jacques Seligmann, and many were the arguments he had on the subject, for he was a born campaigner and the more difficult the cause, the more vehement he was. Perhaps he was right fundamentally, but he failed to make the necessary allowance for the youth of the country, the temper of the swiftly growing young cities, and the American "bigger and better" psychology. A magnificent building

90

was a symbol of importance and strength, with the value of the contents judged in terms of the container. Such buildings served their purpose as an incentive to a local collector to bequeath his works of art and his fortune to the native museum.

Andrew Carnegie understood the strategy of the empty building which, as Stewart H. Holbrook relates in his *Age of the Moguls,* he often referred to as bribes to tempt the city fathers to do their duty. Many a collection has been lost in later years because a would-be donor's city was too parsimonious to house his works of art fittingly and safely.

Thomas Fortune Ryan once said to me in the course of a conversation much later in which I had evidently made some unconsidered remark about American mores: "Don't try to reform America, you have to take it as it is, with all its defects; but think of the qualities which make up for them!"

CHAPTER IX

The Wallace-Bagatelle Collection

When it was announced, shortly after our return from the United States in the early spring of 1914, that Jacques Seligmann had purchased a marble bust by Jean-Antoine Houdon, representing the 18th century tragedienne, Sophie Arnould, from the Paris collection of the late Sir Richard Wallace, it created something of a sensation in the art world. Rumors about the fate of the collection had been rife for more than two years; here at last was something definite. An American art journal reported that Mr. Seligmann had confirmed his purchase of the Houdon, but denied that he was taking any steps toward the acquisition of the rest of the collection. Yes, the interview quoted him, it was true that the Wallace Collection was valued at around two million dollars; no, he knew nothing of the rumor that it was to go to Widener. My father must have had a lot of fun with that interview. It was strictly true that he was taking no steps toward the purchase of the rest of the Wallace Collection from the Château of Bagatelle. He already owned it.

The transaction, which he closed before we left for the United States, remains unique in the history of art dealing. It is the only instance I know of a dealer taking the tremendous gamble of paying nearly two million dollars, in cash, for a collection which he had never seen and for which there existed no catalogue, no expertise, nor even an adequate inventory!

Considered in the light of the history of the Wallace-Bagatelle Collection and its founders, this spectacular gamble seems a fitting final episode to a story of strange legend and stranger fact. Involved in it are great names of England and of France, names which made headlines for daily papers and gossip for contemporary tongues. An aura

92

of mystery and strangeness seemed to enshroud the actions of almost everyone connected with the Wallace Collection. The men who made it and the persons who inherited it were pronounced individuals with driving personalities. Jacques Seligmann himself was by no means the least of these, and the circumstances under which the sale was made were strictly within the tradition.

The Château de Bagatelle had its origins in the 18th century. It was charmingly situated near the banks of the Seine in the Bois de Boulogne, once the property of Madame la Maréchale d'Estrées, a grande dame of the court of the Regent, who built a house there in 1720. Just across the river there already existed another small pavilion belonging to the Duc d'Orleans which was called Brimborion, a trifle, and thus it seemed quite natural to call the new house a bagatelle. Located as it was on the road to Versailles and not far from the Château de La Muette where Louis XV was to find considerable charm, Bagatelle became a convenient halt in the restless movement of the court and one reads of the brilliant receptions the Maréchale gave there for the Regent and later for the young and dashing Louis XV.

In 1756 the property passed to the Marquise de Monconseil, and from 1770 to 1775 was owned by the Prince and Princesse de Chimay. All of them entertained lavishly for kings and court with plays, luncheons, and supper parties. One such occasion was a fete honoring the father-in-law of Louis XV, King Stanislas of Poland.

In 1775 the estate took the fancy of the younger brother of Louis XVI, the Comte d'Artois, later to reign briefly as Charles X. He was a profligate young man with no consideration for popular feelings or public funds and, in true princely fashion, decided to do away with the now somewhat shabby old house, and build another more in keeping with his exalted position. François-Joseph Belanger was designated architect, and Thomas Blaikie was called from England especially to landscape the grounds in the new vogue of the so-called English garden, a change involving major rearrangements of natural contours to accommodate the intricate paths, grottos, miniature rivers, and waterfalls. Such small, intimate houses, exquisite in every detail, served as weekend hideaways or hunting lodges for Paris society and were commonly called by the often-not-inappropriate name of *folie*. Bagatelle quickly became known as the Folie d'Artois. Even in the Comte's time, however, the original name was not forgotten.

93

Teased by his sister-in-law, Marie Antoinette, about the slow progress which his new *folie* was making, d'Artois is said to have made a wager with her that the new house would be ready to receive her en fete when the court returned to Versailles from its annual trek to Fontainebleau, just sixty-four days hence. And this master stroke was achieved in a grandiose manner. Contemporary accounts tell us that nine hundred workmen were employed night and day, and that scarce materials were commandeered on the roads without regard for their true destinations.

The wager between the Queen and the Comte, we are told, was for a stake of 100,000 francs, but the first accounting of the cost of the *folie* showed an expense of 600,000 francs, before interior decorations, furniture, and works of art. It is difficult to express 18th century values in modern terms, but there can be little doubt that this represented more than a million dollars. When d'Artois received the congratulations of the Queen, and presumably the hundred thousand francs, he is supposed to have replied, "Ce n'est rien qu'une bagatelle."

In 1789, at the outset of the Revolution, d'Artois was one of the first to emigrate, and twenty-five years were to pass before he again saw Bagatelle. The Revolution of 1830 once more upset the ownership, and it is with the advent of the Orleans branch that we approach the final royal relinquishment of the château. Louis-Philippe, a constitutional king who had to keep his private expenses separate from the nation's budget, and was thus less profligate, decided to sell the *folie*. In September, 1835, it was purchased by an Englishman, Richard Seymour, Lord Yarmouth, later to be the Fourth Marquess of Hertford. Lord Yarmouth, like his father, the Third Marquess of Hertford, was a great collector, a lover of works of art, and an extremely wealthy man. He was also, with other members of his famous family, a Francophile who spent most of his time in Paris, where he already owned a townhouse in the rue Laffitte, then a particularly brilliant residential section.

Yarmouth immediately began to restore Bagatelle to its original beauty and to furnish it in keeping with its style and his own predilection for the French 18th century. Once finished, and its name restored, Bagatelle again became the scene of royal entertainment, for Yarmouth numbered among his close friends the Emperor Napoleon III and his wife, the Empress Eugénie. It was in the *parc* of Bagatelle

94

that the Prince Imperial received his first riding lessons, in a ring especially built for his use.

In 1842, Lord Yarmouth succeeded to the title and fortune of his father. That same year, a young man known to all familiars of the household as "Monsieur Richard," legally changed his name from Richard Jackson to Richard Wallace. Exactly who he was remains uncertain. Some claimed him to be the son of the Third Marchioness, whom he always called "Tante Mie Mie," and thus the half-brother of the new Lord Hertford. Others believed them to be father and son, though Lord Hertford referred to Wallace only as "a dear friend." Later historians say that Wallace was actually the son of the Fourth Marquess and one Agnes Jackson whose family name was Wallace. Whatever the relationship, the two men were strongly alike in taste, manner, and political tendencies, as well as in their love for France and for works of art. Exquisite taste and refinement were exhibited by Richard Wallace in the purchases he made with and for Lord Hertford as they added further sumptuous works of art to the collection. The few existing documents lead one to wonder whether Richard Wallace may not have become a greater collector than his benefactor. It is quite conceivable that the later acquisitions of the Wallace Collection, as it is today at Hertford House in London and as it was at Bagatelle and rue Laffitte, were actually made by Richard Wallace rather than by Lord Hertford, as has been generally believed—perhaps a rather academic question, but puzzling to art historians.

By the end of the 1860's the political fortunes of France were rapidly deteriorating. The weak and sick Emperor, lost in dreams dominated by the memory of his majestic uncle, Napoleon I, ill-advised by court flatterers, and misled by his military chiefs, fell headlong into the trap of Bismarck, the Franco-Prussian War. Lord Hertford, old, ailing, and disheartened by this blow to his beloved France, passed away in August of 1870.

Richard Wallace was revealed as his heir.

Devoted to France as had been his benefactor, Wallace remained there throughout the war, helping with every means in his power to alleviate the sufferings which followed in its wake—the siege of Paris and the bloody Commune during which so many great monuments, spared by the Revolution of 1789, became a prey to fire and looting.

He organized and financed three ambulance corps, founded and endowed the Hertford British Hospital, and spent vast sums to aid the besieged. Later he installed the hundred drinking fountains "for man and beast" still known as "Wallaces" to Parisians.

In recognition of his many benefactions, Richard Wallace was made a Commander of the Legion of Honor in France and knighted by Queen Victoria. Lady Wallace, however, was never received at Her Majesty's court; Sir Richard did not marry her until after the death of Lord Hertford, though she had already borne him a son. She lived quietly at Hertford House, while Sir Richard divided his time between London and Paris.

The situation in France had driven Richard Wallace to ship a large portion of his French collection to England, where many of its objects were included in the great Bethnal Green exhibition of 1872, while the London home, Hertford House, was being readied for it. As might be expected with so celebrated a collection there was much speculation as to the intentions of Sir Richard regarding its final disposition. His English friends believed that he would leave it to England, while his French intimates asserted that he had often expressed his intention of giving it to the city of Paris. He did neither. When Sir Richard died in 1890, his entire estate, with the exception of a few specific legacies, was left to his widow. When Lady Wallace herself died in 1897, it was her will which left the art contents of Hertford House to the British nation. The will also brought another stranger into the Hertford-Wallace story: John Murray Scott, to whom she bequeathed, except for minor bequests, the entire residue of this incredible estate, including the Château de Bagatelle.

If a link of consanguinity existed between Hertford and Wallace there was no such tie to explain the fabulously generous gesture to Scott. John Murray Scott was the son of a Scottish doctor living in Boulogne who had attended Lord Hertford. The charming manners and brilliant qualities of the young man had apparently attracted Hertford and Wallace, who employed him as their secretary. He gradually rose from this post to one of confidence and high trust, becoming finally the indispensable friend and man of affairs. It is said that Lady Wallace, after Sir Richard's death, relied upon Scott for everything and that it was on his insistence that the London portion of the Wallace Collection went to the nation, rather than to Scott himself, as she had wished. The evidence seems to indicate that in this she was also carrying out the wishes of Sir Richard.

The Wallace estate included numerous castles and houses in England, but it was mainly in Paris, at Bagatelle and the rue Laffitte house, that John Murray Scott chose to spend his time. Perhaps no better picture of the man himself, his gigantic physical stature, his general culture, and his mode of living, can be found than the vivid one presented by Miss Vita Sackville-West in her charming book, *Pepita.* However, many of the incidents related occurred during the most impressionable years of the author's childhood and early youth, in truly exceptional surroundings, and the praise lavished upon Scott by her mother may well have qualified Miss West's objectivity. Furthermore, as the only child of Lady Sackville, whom Scott so deeply cherished, her account may also be colored by his role of bachelor uncle who enjoyed spoiling a young girl.

Despite the fact that Sir John (he, too, was knighted by Victoria) became a Trustee of Hertford House and was a man of taste, greatly interested in art, we have no indication that he added anything of importance to the Wallace Collections. Some might ask what he could add to so rich an endowment, but a true collector and amateur ceases to be one only on his deathbed!

As the 20th century opened, the work of embellishing Paris, started by Baron Haussmann under Napoleon III, was again under way. Among the plans were the *aménagements* of the Bois de Boulogne and the western part of the city, then developing fast, so that the very existence of Bagatelle as a private residence was threatened. Did Sir John realize that Bagatelle might be expropriated or was it simply that old age and other cares made it seem wiser to part with the property? In any case, in 1904, he sold this historic chateau to the city of Paris and moved its contents to the rue Laffitte house.

Quite wisely, however, since they would have been considered an inherent part of the property, he first sold at auction the statues which ornamented the gardens and the façade of the house. Many of them were marbles of large size and there would have been no room for them in the house on the rue Laffitte, already bursting with the contents of Bagatelle added to its own sumptuous furnishings. Thus the sculptures outside the house had already been disposed of before Jacques Seligmann came into the picture. It was then that the

Baigneuse of Houdon, now in the Metropolitan Museum, was sold to Benjamin Altman.

Sir John also inherited vast groups of works of art in England, specifically, as listed by Robert Cecil in the Burlington Magazine of June, 1950, "The estates and contents of Sudbourne House . . . Sir Richard's Irish estate . . . such works of art . . . at Hertford House as were not bequeathed to the nation under Lady Wallace's will . . . and it is known that his (Sir John's) own London house was full of works of art inherited from Lady Wallace." Thus, "Wallace Collection" in a provenance does not necessarily mean that the object was formerly at Bagatelle or that it was part of the acquisitions of Jacques Seligmann. His purchase was simply, if simply can be used in this connection, that part of the collection which was in the rue Laffitte house at Sir John's death in 1912.

His death added one more curious chapter to the saga of Bagatelle and created a stir which my generation has not forgotten. Lady Sackville, wife of the Third Baron Sackville of Knole, was willed the sum of 150,000 pounds and the entire contents of the house on rue Laffitte. Although Sir John left the bulk of his estate, amounting to well over a million pounds, to his brother and his two sisters, they nevertheless contested the bequest to Lady Sackville, on the grounds of "undue influence," and the ensuing trial became a cause celèbre. In 1913, after memorable days spent in court fighting the case, Lady Sackville emerged victorious, the sole owner of the Paris portion of the Wallace Collection.

It is impossible to give in a few words a description of this beautiful and high-spirited lady, whose own life was so colorful and romantic, and I leave this to her daughter, Miss Vita Sackville-West, whose book *Pepita* is vivid and charming. I would give a great deal, however, to have been present at the various interviews which took place between Lady Sackville and my father, for it is now that Jacques Seligmann steps into the story. The meetings of two such determined individuals, of pronounced personality, must certainly have had their own special flavor.

Actually, they had met a few years earlier when my father had arranged the sale of the twenty-nine Knole House tapestries to J. Pierpont Morgan. Just when Jacques Seligmann first approached her, or, perhaps, she approached him, about the sale of her French holdings, I am not sure. I do know that it was well before the settlement of the lawsuit. Lady Sackville was not averse to selling. She was extravagant by nature and perhaps the heavy expenses of an earlier legal battle over the succession of her husband to the Sackville title, the death duties, and the upkeep of Knole House, made the prospect of a large sum of ready money a welcome one. Obviously, however, she could take no definite steps until the suit was settled. Furthermore, the house on the rue Laffitte was under legal seal, and the objects it contained could not even be seen. Nevertheless, Jacques Seligmann entered into a legal covenant with Lady Sackville whereby, should she win the suit, he would become the sole and absolute owner of the entire French collection of Sir Richard Wallace at an agreed price. Because of the loss of the firm's Paris records during the recent war, I cannot state the exact amount involved, but my recollection is of a figure slightly under two million dollars. I should like to emphasize that in accordance with my father's invariable practice, this sum was paid in cash, from his own funds, without recourse to loans or to mortgages. Miss Sackville-West states in *Pepita* that her mother received 270,000 pounds, which accords well enough if one takes into consideration deductions necessarily made for attorney's fees, inventory costs and other expenses. *The New York Times* front-page story of the purchase used the figure of $1,400,000.

At this point one must marvel at the courage and instinct of Jacques Seligmann, for *he had never seen the collection*. With its history and all that has been written of the Wallace-Bagatelle Collection, it would be natural to assume that all the world was familiar with the contents of Bagatelle and of the rue Laffitte house, but such an assumption would be erroneous. These were private houses, open only to friends of the families who lived in them. Thus as a basis for making his offer, colossal even for a man used to deals of magnitude, Jacques Seligmann had only three indications.

The first was knowledge of a few objects which Wallace had lent during his lifetime to certain important public exhibitions in Paris, and he may have read two articles on the contents of Scott's rue Laffitte house which had appeared in the English magazine *Connoisseur* in 1910 and 1911. The second was a manuscript list on which there was no description whatsoever, simply the barest indication, often insufficient to identify the items even after we had seen them, and useful only to check them by number and to help in a process of elimination. My father, perusing the list, tried to identify the items he knew, but ran into such laconic lines as "a marble statuette," which he surmised might be the Cupid of Bouchardon, or "marble figure of a woman," which might mean the Lemoyne portrait of Madame de Pompadour, or "portrait of a young woman with head-dress," possibly referring to the Houdon. The third indication available to him, and the most valuable, was what he knew of the quality of the Wallace Collection at Hertford House in London. He reasoned that if items of such exceptional quality and importance as those he could identify were on the manuscript list with such insignificant captions, it was likely that others would prove of equal consequence.

In his autobiography, Bernard Baruch tells of an interview with J. Pierpont Morgan on an investment opportunity in sulphur which the Morgan firm had asked Baruch to investigate. An initial capital investment of half a million dollars was required, and Baruch stated that he was willing to gamble half that out of his own funds. To which Morgan replied, icily, "I never gamble!" I wonder what Morgan's reaction would have been to my father's approach to the Wallace-Bagatelle purchase.

There is no record in any country, as far as I have been able to discover, of any comparable transaction in the whole history of the fine arts. The late Andrew Mellon was twice involved in art purchases of much larger totals, but he knew precisely what he was buying. Among dealers, Lord Duveen made several spectacular and well-publicized purchases of collections which cost several millions, but each had been offered for public sale with well-expertized catalogues. Furthermore, they were often financed by bank loans. Long after the event, I continue to believe that no man but Jacques Seligmann would have had the courage to take such a huge gamble. If the enormity of what he did left my father openly unperturbed, it was still with relief that we viewed the profusion of riches when we were at last allowed to inspect the house at 2 rue Laffitte. I knew, of course, that millions of gold francs had been paid for these accumulated works of art, and I had perused the noncommittal list, but I had not seen even the few objects which my father already knew. To me it was like entering Ali Baba's cave. His simple but daring reasoning had been correct. Almost every item was of the quality of Hertford House—but in what confusion!

All over the floors, piled up in corners, some carefully covered with slips, others wrapped in papers or, more often, with only a heavy coating of dust to protect them from sight, were some of the greatest sculptures of the 18th century and luxurious pieces of furniture made for the royal family. There, rolled in a corner, was the famous set of tapestries after cartoons by Boucher, now in the Philadelphia Museum. Standing on a table was the small marble figure by Lemoyne. Over there, its companion in size and quality, was the first version of the *Cupid Bending His Bow* of Bouchardon. Yonder was the superb Houdon bust of Sophie Arnould, now in the Louvre as a bequest of Edgar Stern.

Most belonged to the so-called decorative arts of the French 18th century, but objects which exhibit such perfection in proportion, respect for the essence of wood and the chiseling of gilded bronze are beyond the realm of the purely utilitarian. One feels that a table such as the Riesener, now in the Frick Collection, or a delicately conceived bit of bronze and enamel such as the Veil-Picard chandelier, now in the Louvre, deserve special cases, like bibelots, to preserve what they reveal of a civilization which attained for a few years a pinnacle of refinement.

All the great cabinet-makers were represented: Riesener, Oeben, Weisweiler, Saunier, and Martin Carlin in pieces of furniture so perfect architecturally that they remind one of the glorious buildings of a Gabriel or a Mansard, yet so delicate in texture that the hand longs to stroke them. Here, too, were the *bureau du roi*, which my father later gave to the Metropolitan Museum; sets of furniture upholstered in tapestries designed by Casanova and Le Prince; busts by Houdon; drawings and gouaches and paintings by Nattier, Lancret, Boucher, Prud'hon; all sorts of documentary drawings, including those ordered by Louis-Philippe as models for the engraver who recorded the historical paintings which the King had gathered for the Chateau of Versailles. Among the most impressive of the sculptures were the Coysevox busts of the Grand Dauphin and the Duc d'Orleans, which must certainly have adorned Versailles. They are now a part of the Samuel H. Kress Foundation in the National Gallery at Washington.

Robert Cecil, Assistant Keeper of the Wallace Collection at Hertford House, has been much interested in trying to establish an inventory of the complete holdings of the Hertfords and Sir Richard Wallace. That he has succeeded remarkably in this difficult research task is attested by the series of articles on the subject which appeared in the *Burlington Magazine,* and I would like here to acknowledge gratefully the assistance he has given me in the preparation of this chapter.

Due to the 1940 loss of the Seligmann records, a complete recapitulation of the Wallace-Bagatelle Collection will probably never be possible. However, it is much nearer realization than seemed likely when this book was begun, for I have recently found a copy of an inventory made a few weeks after the death of Sir John Murray Scott. French law requires that every legal action be taken through a *notaire,* and such records are never destroyed. Through luck I discovered the proper *notaire.* This inventory, dated February 16, 1912, was made at the behest of Douglas Alexander Scott, apparently before his brother's will, leaving the collection to Lady Sackville, had been located. It is definitely not the list which my father had, for that was handwritten and Scott's is a typed legal document. Anyway it is hardly likely that the Scott family would have made it available to Lady Sackville or her prospective purchaser. While this inventory is almost as sparing of detail as the other, it does give an occasional indication of artist and a certain amount of description. For the sake of the record, and for those specialists interested in such documentation, a resumé of the inventory has been included in the appendix, along with as complete a record as I have been able to make of the present whereabouts of major items of the collection.

The first private collector to see this collection while it was still at rue Laffitte was Henry C. Frick, who came straight from the golf course, dressed in plus-fours and a plaid cap. With him came Elsie de Wolfe, who was advising him in purchases for his new home. A selection was made on the spot, neither of them being at all disconcerted by the untidiness, the junkshop atmosphere of the cluttered rooms. Miss de Wolfe's recollection of this episode in her book, *After All,* is faulty on several points. She states that it was Lady Sackville who approached Jacques Seligmann, which may be true, and that the arrangement was for the selling rights to the collection in return for financing her lawsuit, which is not true. The deal was an outright purchase. Nor could Miss de Wolfe, as she relates, have gone with my father to the rue Laffitte house while it was still under seal. The seals had been placed by the courts for the protection of all parties concerned and were not lifted until the ownership of the collection had been definitely decided by the court. I stress this because the extraordinary feature of this huge transaction was the fact that my father was willing to pay a remarkably large sum for a collection he had never seen.

A few days after Frick's visit, the entire collection was moved to Sagan. There it was installed in the new building on the far side of the garden. The exhibition was the sensation of the season, with collectors coming from North and South America, and from all over Europe, to admire and to buy.

Sadly, it was one of the last international gatherings in Paris for many years to come, for the year was 1914 and the month was June. On August 2, France mobilized, and for four years, Europe abandoned the enjoyment of art for grimmer pursuits.

CHAPTER X

The War Years, 1914-1918

Within hours of the mobilization order, I was in uniform, a second lieutenant of infantry, far from the art world, and my activities for the next few years have no place in the story except as they affected my future life. My father was not in Paris at the time of my departure, but an incident concerning him remains in my mind. He had given specific instructions to the office manager that in the event of a sudden call to arms in his absence, I was to be given a thousand gold francs to take with me. I protested strongly, but my father's orders were law, and for many months of muddy trench life, I was burdened with my useless gold francs. I had to buy a heavy leather belt to hold them, which was stiff and uncomfortable. It was only on my first leave, almost a year later, that I could convince my father that a lowly tin of sardines, which no amount of money could have bought, would have been much more useful.

Business in Paris came to a standstill; by mid-September the galleries were closed and the Palais Sagan was turned over to the Red Cross. On that first leave I found the once neat and elegant courtyard filled with temporary wooden shacks and vehicles of all sorts, and Sagan itself busy with the activities of a hundred or so women, sewing, rolling bandages, all working toward the same end: aid to the wounded returning to the city. Paris was never far from the fighting front; at one time the fortified positions were only about sixty miles away, and while the atmosphere of the great city was still that of the rear, this closeness gave it special stimulation.

When later leaves brought me back to the city, my father sometimes made the pretense of a business call to some old and valued

104

friend and client, asking me to accompany him. Since no real business talk ever developed out of these visits, I have a suspicion that their true purpose was to show off his officer son. I especially treasure a visit to Arthur Veil-Picard, a great collector and a delightful man. With all his wealth, his art treasures, his shrewd knowledge of men, he remained simple, pleasant, and even affectionate.

Veil-Picard was a sort of Balzacian character; his big house on the rue de Courcelles, near the Parc Monceau, presented an imposing façade, but past its elegant foyer, confusion and profusion reigned. Here were hung, with no discernible plan, row upon row of the most precious creations of France's great 18th century artists. He always claimed that they were disposed with a definite decorative purpose and according to a chronological scheme, but I was never able to make it out. It looked as if someone had finally convinced him that the paintings really should be hung on the walls rather than stacked about on the floor, and to have peace he had answered, "Well, all right, all right, over there is an empty space; hang them up!"

This interpretation was in some measure borne out by the man himself. He had a short, powerfully-built body, as rugged as the Jura Mountains under whose shadow he was born, and he spoke with the earthy accent of his native region. His vast fortune was begun early in life, shortly after the Franco-Prussian War in 1871. He had inherited a small banking business in his native Besançon and one day was called upon for funds and advice by the owner of the Pernod distillery, then a small, undeveloped enterprise. Realizing the potentialities of the business, he sold his assets, purchased the company, and turned his financial acumen and energy into making it successful. His achievement, however, made of him neither a snob nor a society man. Dress was the least of his preoccupations. Callers, regardless of rank or quality, always found him in the same attire, a business suit, probably ready-made and already of some age, its trousers loosely held up by a belt, and a distinctive white stock tie, also ready-made and often not too fresh, hanging slightly askew about his neck. At home he usually wore slippers of soft leather with the broken counters folded under his heels. When he went out, he changed these for old-fashioned black buttoned shoes.

He had but two passions in his later years. One was for art of the French 18th century and the other was for race horses. He owned a fine stud farm and a racing stable, and was as well known a figure on the turf as he was in the galleries. In fact, so completely was his life divided between these two hobbies that each indicated where he could be found at any hour. In the morning he was at home unless there were races outside Paris. In the afternoon he went to the race course, to his farm, to an exhibition or to an art dealer. My father never made an appointment (in fact, Veil-Picard had no telephone except the one in the porter's lodge) but just dropped in on him. Careless, frugal and even parsimonious about the smaller amenities of life, Veil-Picard had such high standards in his collecting that to find another exquisite gouache or pastel to please him was truly difficult; but he never hesitated to buy when he found one. Whatever the price, the account was always settled immediately, in cash, from the apparently unlimited supply which always seemed to be at hand in a drawer of his desk.

He kept no invoices and, of course, no catalogue, but he had an amazing memory for the details of every object he owned. He could name all the successive owners, the dates, and the amounts involved in the longest pedigree. He probably could do the same for his race horses. Not only was he posted about the provenances of his own possessions, but there was scarcely a great work of art from the French 18th century which he did not know in the same detail.

The last time I saw him, in 1938, he was thrilled and excited by two new "children," two gouaches by Lavreince which he had just acquired from the Mortimer L. Schiff sale in London, *L'Assemblée au Salon* and *L'Assemblée au Concert*. I had made the arrangements for the Schiff sale, and when I told Veil-Picard so and how delighted I was that the two exquisite Lavreinces had found such an appreciative owner, he reproached me for not having notified him before they went to auction. He said he would have bought them immediately from me in New York, without even seeing them. He had known them and wanted them for years, and he recounted their provenances to me.

The art world held no secrets for him. Besides keeping in touch with the leading dealers, he had several intermediaries constantly on the scent of new treasures. He was a shrewd bargainer and apparently felt that a purchase commission to an intermediary represented less than a profit to a dealer, a reasoning not always correct. Arthur Veil-Picard assembled in his lifetime an almost unequalled collection in his chosen field; sumptuous series of pastels by La Tour and Perron-

106

neau, of gouaches by Lavreince, Moreau, and Dugourc; paintings and drawings by Fragonard and Hubert Robert; marble sculptures by Houdon; and small objets d'art of surpassing quality. Among these was an exquisite small gilt-bronze chandelier, ornamented with enamel of an unusual blue-gray tone, and appliquéd with fine gold. It was made in the Regency period by some unknown craftsman of great talent, and was formerly in the Wallace-Bagatelle Collection. Veil-Picard rightly kept it under glass. His daughter has since presented it to the Louvre. His delightful portrait of Mademoiselle Duthé, the celebrated actress, also came from the Wallace-Bagatelle Collection. It had been commissioned from Vestier by the Comte d'Artois for his Folie de Bagatelle and was said to have ornamented, appropriately enough, his *salle de bain,* for it depicts the charming lady stepping daintily from a woodland pool.

Veil-Picard was, in fact, one of the first to visit the Wallace-Bagatelle Collection after my father bought it. Two other outstanding items he acquired were souvenirs of Marie-Antoinette, one of them a touching and intimate memento. It is a small notebook, a *Carnet de Bal* perhaps, of only a few leaves between covers of chased gold and green *galuchat;* on one side is a portrait of the Queen herself, while on the other are the two children of her brother-in-law, the Comte d'Artois, held in the arms of their mother, and the Comtesse de Provence. These miniatures, attributed to Dumont, represent the Queen and the two countesses in the full bloom of their youth and beauty. Inside, in a childish writing, perhaps done with the tiny gold and ivory pencil which accompanies it, are these words, "Charles à été mechant" and "Charles sans friandises." Charles was the familiar name of the little Dauphin, the Duc de Normandie, and it is likely that he scrawled the words himself. Little is known of the book's history except that Lord Hertford acquired it in 1868 and that it had once belonged to the Clermont-Tonnerre family. A truly royal bed made by the famous Jacob, also said to have belonged to the ill-fated Queen, still carrying its superb draperies of embroidered silk designed by Philippe de La Salle, always held a place of honor in the Veil-Picard salon during the old gentleman's time. It is one of the few items which has left the possession of the family; it is now in the Cleveland Museum. Also from the Wallace-Bagatelle Collection were the pair of superb Riesener commodes which graced the salon, as well as several exquisite small tables and a *bureau de dame.*

Arthur Veil-Picard's greatest love, however, was undoubtedly Fragonard, an impressive group of whose paintings and drawings he already possessed when shortly before the war he added the crowning jewel, the smaller version of the *Fête à Saint Cloud,* formerly in the Goldschmidt and Count Pastré Collections. Perhaps next in his affections was Hubert Robert. His Roberts were of a type rarely encountered; they belong to the period of the artist's maturity when architectural detail gave way to a broader expression in open spaces and sparkling bodies of water. In addition, Veil-Picard owned part of a unique group of true portraits which Robert painted for Madame Geoffrin, a field into which the artist seldom ventured, but then with what charm and grace.

Surrounded by the 18th century, Arthur Veil-Picard's knowledge of the history of France in that period was detailed and intimate and completely self-taught.

His son inherited his father's love for the beautiful, along with the rue de Courcelles house and a share of its treasures. When faced with the necessity of rearranging his home after some works of art went to other heirs, he set about displaying the remainder in an appropriate manner. Today, the house no longer has a Balzacian character, but has acquired dignity and style. Young Veil-Picard has broken away from the typically French reticence which kept his father from responding as generously as he might have to requests for loans to exhibitions. With modern civic spirit, he feels an obligation to share the enjoyment of his riches.

My reason for recalling with pleasure this wartime visit to the elder Arthur Veil-Picard had nothing to do with works of art. It must have been in late 1916, after the heavy fighting around Verdun, when a regrouping of troops, in order to give us a respite, had sent me to a large, so-called quiet sector in Alsace and a temporary assignment to General Staff. Naturally, my experiences and duties interested Veil-Picard and my father. I mentioned that because of the extensive length of the front, even the infantry officers (I was now a First Lieutenant) had taken to horseback and I sorely missed my own excellent mount which had been commandeered at the beginning of the war. Veil-Picard insisted that I come immediately to choose one from his stables, any one I wished. I was much too fond of horses to submit a delicately bred animal to the rigors of a front-line division, and I told him that I felt it would be wrong to accept. He said that it would be waiting for me when I came back. He could not have made a kindlier gesture and I was greatly touched by it, for he loved his horses as he did his works of art.

Such interludes for me in those years, however, were exceptional. As the war dragged on, the Allies' materiel rapidly diminished and the staggering human losses continued to mount. Of the fifty-odd officers in my regiment, only three were alive in 1916. Three battalion commanders and three successive company commanders under whom I served were dead. Civilian and military morale was at its lowest ebb that year. For Jacques Seligmann, it was one more year of daily anguish for his country and for his son at the front, heightened by the knowledge that his second son, my brother André, still under training, would also shortly join a fighting unit. He had practically given up business, but for a man of his character, idleness was unthinkable and he was eager to do something which would put his energies and his intelligence to use. Then, in January, 1917, he was requested by the French government to undertake a special mission to the United States. My father never said much about the real nature of his mission. I gathered in later years that it had a dual purpose—diplomatic and financial. I do not have a clear picture of the diplomatic part of the trip, other than that he was to explain the French situation to leading New York newspapermen and influential people and to get their advice on means of correcting American misunderstandings. This was one of those times when the delicate balance of international affairs made it expedient for a government to entrust such a mission to an independent businessman who would be unhampered by official regulations and diplomatic commitments.

The financial part of the mission resulted from government concern about the drain of French gold and French-held American dollars. Any activity which might put dollars at the disposition of France was vigorously encouraged. Jacques Seligmann, and a number of other firms doing business in New York, were requested to reactivate their New York offices. It was not an easy assignment. Shipping works of art through enemy submarines was risky; gathering a group of objects of sufficient importance to tempt a wartime American market was difficult. The voyage itself meant personal danger for my father.

It was for none of these reasons, however, as I know from a letter I received at the front, that acceptance of the mission cost my father something in mental stress. He was afraid that his departure from

France at so crucial a moment might be misunderstood, that he might be accused of "business as usual." In addition, there was the anxiety he felt at putting an even greater distance between himself and news of his son at the front.

Nevertheless, armed with a diplomatic passport, he embarked under the dubious protection of a neutral Spanish ship. Reticent though he was about the achievements of the mission, he was voluble and caustic about the crossing, not so much about its dreariness and its physical discomfort, which must have caused some pain to a man used to peacetime luxury liners, as about the type and quality of his fellow passengers. The United States was still neutral and this was a neutral ship. For the first time in three years my father heard German spoken about him. It must have been difficult indeed for a man of his temperament to hold his tongue. Too, it was necessary to keep in mind that espionage went on under the most innocent guises and a chance remark might prove costly. It was with great relief that he landed in New York and found that the shipment of art had also arrived safely.

The *Morning Herald* of January 22, 1917, reported his arrival under a headline, "Jacques Seligmann here with canvases to help stop France's gold outflow." It also quoted him as predicting that America would soon be the art center of the world. The *Art News, The New York Times,* and other journals carried notices of his activities during the two-month stay. I can report little of the intangible diplomatic results, but I can affirm that the tangible financial ones were spectacular. He cleared more than a million dollars. An unusually precise record of sales was kept and, fortunately, retained by the New York office.

The first entry records the purchase of five superb Fragonard drawings by Mortimer L. Schiff, whose name appeared again two weeks later when his prize was a unique Clodion group, a child riding on a griffon. There must have been rivalry between him and Henry Walters over this exquisite little sculpture, as it was the period which Mr. Walters admired. Apparently, however, Walters was consoled by the four large representations of the *Four Continents* by Bertos. William Salomon added a famous Riccio incense burner to his already fine collection of early Italian bronzes and Clarence Mackay carried off a bust by Leone Leoni and a 16th century *Flying Mercury*. Between them they spent more than sixty thousand dollars. Senator W. A.

110

Clark acquired a lovely portrait of *Elizabeth of France* by Vigée Lebrun. Jules Bache bought a gold-woven tapestry panel representing a *Head of Christ;* Edwin S. Bayer, a Flemish 15th century *Virgin in Glory.* Stanley Mortimer added to his group of majolicas; Mrs. B. N. Duke to her collection of water colors.

Such sales inevitably were reported, often erroneously. One art journal said *La Frileuse,* the lovely Houdon bronze from the Wallace-Bagatelle Collection, was sold to an undisclosed collector for one hundred and seventy thousand dollars; in a later edition it carried the headline, "Frick gets *La Frileuse*," and the story had the price at two hundred and seventy thousand dollars. Both amounts were wrong and the purchaser was not Frick, but Henry P. Davison. The same paper announced the sale of a bronze *Hercules and Antaeus* by Giovanni da Bologna to Henry E. Huntington, which was correct, but the figure paid, while high, was not the reported sixty-two thousand dollars.

One side of my father's ledger indicates art sales, while a separate column shows a series of often equally generous figures representing sums donated to the Paris Red Cross, the war orphans, the mutilated, and the blind. The American collectors not only were willing to spend lavishly on their hobbies and their enjoyments; most of them knew and loved France and were anxious to help alleviate the suffering which had overtaken the French people. My father was exceedingly impressed and profoundly touched by the spontaneity of the response and the bounty of the gifts, evidence of a great American trait which he had not before had an opportunity to discover.

November of 1918 found me passing my second dreary month in the Russian hospital in Athens. I had come to Greece in early September at the request of General Gramat, who had been commanding Colonel of my original regiment in 1914. He was now military advisor to the Greek king, and I, as a Captain, had spent the last year and a half as liaison officer with the A.E.F. I left France reluctantly, as the final big push was about to begin, but the Balkan area also promised important action in the attack about to be launched against the "soft underbelly," and aide-de-camp to the General was an exciting post. Actually I saw nothing of the Greek action and very little of Greece, for a particularly virulent type of malaria struck me almost upon my arrival and thus put me in the Russian hospital. The only

111

precise, and certainly only pleasant, memories I have of the whole Greek episode are of two or three early morning rides to the Parthenon in the green light of the Aegean dawn and, two months later, the sound of the distant battleship guns in the harbor of Piraeus, announcing the Armistice. The cease-fire arrived just in time; now I could be moved to Paris for the proper care and treatment needed to save my life.

Since I was one of the younger and unmarried men in the army, it was almost another year before I was discharged. After a convalescent leave, I was given a desk job in Paris, and so, though still in uniform, I was on hand to take part in a second international mission entrusted to my father, this time in his capacity of art expert.

One of the great questions of the peace negotiations, of course, was reparations—how much, and of what, should be claimed from the vanquished nations, who had caused this catastrophic upheaval. Gold stocks, railroads, customs receipts, and some of the means of industrial production were the obvious sources for payment. Other sources were also suggested, among them works of art, not as the loot of war, but after due expertization and evaluation. The sums so reached would then be credited to assessments made against the defeated countries, and the works of art would be prorated among the allied nations, chiefly France, England, and Italy. The idea was at first well received. In the heat of the still burning resentment at destruction of human life and national sustenance, it seemed only just that the hated nations be made to pay with everything they owned and be dispossessed of their most treasured assets. The procedure would have a purpose beyond the strictly material; it would be a moral reminder that war endangers the spiritual heritage of a nation as well as its territorial holdings.

This principle of the dispossession of the vanquished was made somewhat more palatable by the fact that the objects in question were not, in most cases, to be taken from the common property of the nation, but rather from the personal possessions of the former reigning houses. The paintings by Watteau at Potsdam, for instance, had been assembled by Frederic the Great of Prussia and had remained the property of the Hohenzollern family. A large part, if not all, the treasures at the Hofburg in Vienna and the Castle of Schoenbrunn were Hapsburg heirlooms. Furthermore, was not a part of this aesthetic treasure the result of earlier lootings? Would there not be a sort of inherent justice in removing works of art which had come from the plunderings of the past? Such considerations seemed to justify the plan.

My father was called in by Philippe Berthelot, the permanent Secretary of Foreign Affairs, and, after several conferences, was requested to establish an inventory of the Hapsburg tapestries in Vienna. Unless my memory has gone amiss, in the general scheme these tapestries were destined for France, who never got them. The paintings were to be claimed by Italy, some of which she actually received.

The remnants of the railroads across Europe were still in the hands of the army, and no civilian could travel into Austria except on special mission. My father, with his credentials, and I, still in uniform but on special leave, had no difficulty in obtaining priority seats. But official status could do little to make the journey pleasant. The train was slow and unheated, the once-luxurious wagon-lit was in dismal condition. The only food we had was from cans we brought with us. After four years of front-line life, the trip was comfortable enough for me; but it was a definite hardship for my father. More than that, though, he was opposed to the plan of impounding great works of art to pay for war damage and was going to Vienna only out of a sense of duty.

We started to work immediately after arrival. It required more than presenting credentials in the proper quarter; it meant moving the poor devils in charge of the collections, who were apathetic under the triple weight of malnutrition, the depression of defeat, and an understandable reluctance to cooperate in the alienation of cherished treasures.

The tapestry collections of the Austrian and Spanish Hapsburgs together comprise the greatest group in the world. Both derive from a common 16th century source, the Emperor Charles V. I have not seen the Madrid tapestries, but it would be hard to conceive of anything finer than those in Vienna. After several visits to museum officials, many of whom my father had known well before 1914 and dealt with often, it became apparent that the chief obstacle was with the officials of the Hofburg, the former Imperial Palace. We had understood that all the tapestries were stored there, and we did find some exceptional ones, but so few that another repository must exist. After several days of polite lack of cooperation, it took threat of military action to discover it in the Castle of Schönbrunn just outside the

113

city. Once accomplished, every facility for carrying out the task was afforded us.

No complete catalogue of the tapestries existed; I doubt that one had ever been published. There was not even an inventory in the Austrian archives. (When the art treasures of Vienna were exhibited in New York in 1950, it was explained that the tapestries had achieved the status of a national collection only after the dissolution of the monarchy in 1918; previously they had been part of an Imperial "depot" from which individual items could be withdrawn for wall decoration as court occasion or ceremony demanded.) For several days we were shown the fabulous fabrics, carefully rolled, and in a dazzling state of preservation; they glittered with gold and silver threads. Except for a few superb 18th century examples they all belonged to that period of the Renaissance when emperors, princes, and prelates were the Maecenases of art, and their wall-hangings had to rival the richness of their gilded or enameled suits of armor and the brilliance of their jewels. Series after series was unrolled, one more brilliant than another—series of two, of four, of six—all with magnificent borders bearing crests, crowns, initials, or fleur de lys, according to the status of their owners. One particularly handsome set was woven on a red background, and it must have been blinding in its brilliance when made; now the tarnished gold, glinting darkly against the blood-red background, gave it an almost sinister beauty.

The cartoons had come from the greatest ateliers of the day; designs by Raphael similar to those in the Vatican, others by artists then little known, like Vermeyen, who accompanied Charles V on his military campaigns, and Etienne Delaune. The weavers, too, were the best—William Pannemaker of Brussels, Pieter Coecke van Aelst, Henri de Nèves. The subjects were as diverse—military, religious, allegorical—some familiar, others unique. All were in pristine condition; many had never been hung on a wall.

Despite his long experience and foreknowledge of what to expect, my father was deeply impressed. Slowly he dictated to me the titles of the series, the subject of each tapestry, the weaving atelier, the size and condition, and any special data. There were almost nine hundred items. At the end of each day, my father asked me to make a formal longhand copy of the notes; they were too confidential to entrust to anyone else.

The monumental job was never finished. Philippe Berthelot arrived in Vienna and called my father to a meeting of those in charge of the project. The import of the brief conference left an indelible impression on my memory.

After hearing a succinct report by my father on the type and number of tapestries examined, Berthelot explained that France was in no financial position to maintain so valuable a collection. While a few examples in French museums would be of great aesthetic value, it would serve no purpose to keep hundreds. In view of this, if the collection were awarded to France as part of the reparations, the only reasonable course would be to convert it into money. Turning to my father, he asked, "Mr. Seligmann, can you give us a rough valuation of the collection?"

"I regret that I could not do so within any reasonable margin," he replied.

"Then let me put it this way," said Berthelot. "At what price would you be willing to purchase the whole collection?"

My father smiled and replied that it was indeed a flattering question, but even if he had the means to close such a deal, he would still hesitate to commit himself. It would take a great many years to dispose effectively of so many tapestries.

"Would you, then," continued Philippe Berthelot, "consider acting as selling agent for the Government, and, if so, would you venture an estimate of how much credit France might count upon to be charged against reparations?"

My father understood the implication of Berthelot's question. It was public knowledge that in 1917, Jack Morgan had sold a number of his father's gold and silver woven tapestries to a syndicate of private collectors and dealers and that several had since been resold at extremely high prices, rumored to be as much as three to five hundred thousand dollars. Was it not possible, therefore, to similarly evaluate those in Vienna, even taking as a basis one-half of the figures obtained in the Morgan sale in New York? My father realized that he would have to explain the delicate mechanism of supply and demand in the art world.

"Contrary to the laws of arithmetic," he said, "were we to give a valuation of even one hundred thousand dollars apiece, three hundred of them would not add up to thirty million dollars. The financial value of a work of art is computed not only in terms of its aesthetic merit, but also in terms of its rarity. Were three hundred paintings

115

by Rembrandt suddenly to be offered on the market, we would be faced with the same condition. There might be three hundred collectors eager to buy a Rembrandt, but they would not pay for one of three hundred the price any one would bring if offered alone. The only solution for the tapestries, and a very unsatisfactory one, I will admit, would be to stagger the sales over a period of perhaps ten years. Even then it would be necessary to keep secret from the buying public the knowledge of regular offerings to come—a difficult thing to do."

That ended the meeting. Eventually, the whole idea of assigning works of art in payment of reparations was discarded, much to the relief of all concerned. Philippe Berthelot was, I feel sure, opposed on the same moral grounds as my father to the principle of the scheme. So was I. But I would give a lot to know what became of my notes.

CHAPTER XI

End of an Era

The trip to Austria, and the leisure afforded by the un-exacting duties of my army desk job, gave me an opportunity to return gradually to the activities of the art world. By that time, Sagan was reopened, the temporary wooden barracks were removed, and to all outward appearances everything was as it was before the war. When I was finally officially discharged, all I had to do, or so it seemed, was to start civilian life where it stopped in August, 1914. This illusion was quickly dispelled. The war had wrought changes in the art world just as it had in everything else. Collectors were different; some older ones had died and new ones were developing; tastes in collecting were changing; the problems of buying were new; economic problems were vastly different, for the balance of money power had passed to the New World; even I, as I was to find out, was not the same.

Awareness of these changes naturally did not come at once, and it was not until my first postwar trip to America in early 1920 that some of them began to impress me. That journey more or less directly precipitated the only two real differences of opinion which ever arose between my father and me during the too few years of active partnership that were left to us. These differences resulted from some of the postwar changes which I believed affected matters of policy of tremendous significance for the future of the firm.

The first discussion had to do with my desire to spend the greater part of my time in the United States, whereas my father wished me to remain in Paris. My arguments were based on sound business considerations, but, I realize now, my determination resulted from wartime changes in my own point of view.

In 1917, as a Captain after three years of heavy fighting all along the front, I became the first French officer assigned to the first American combat unit to land on French soil, appropriately, the First Division, Major General William L. Sibert commanding. As an officer in the operations branch of the Division's General Staff, I was responsible for all liaison, not only with French divisions but with the different elements of the American division as well. I had, temporarily, all the prerogatives of an American officer and worked directly with all members of the front line units, from Commanding General to privates. The First Division was an elite unit; the best officers, both regulars and reserves, had been eager to be a part of it. George C. Marshall, U. S. Chief of Staff in World War II, was a Captain in G3; Major Theodore Roosevelt, Jr., later a Brigadier General, was in command of an infantry batallion. For over a year I lived with Americans of all kinds under very trying circumstances. Except for the fact that we spoke English instead of French, they might have been my own countrymen. I appreciated the comradeship they offered me, their enthusiasm, their eagerness, their courage.

And it was not only my personal reaction; I saw the response of the French peasants in villages where we were billeted to the easy-going, friendly spirit of the American soldiers, always ready to give a hand or to play with a child, their good sportsmanship, their will to understand a situation and act accordingly. During three years of fighting, from the north of France to the Swiss border, I had had many opportunities to watch other foreign troops mingle with the civilian population in relationships which had not always been so smooth. Other foreigners came to France and held on to their specific traits and customs. The American succeeded in adapting himself to a new environment.

Only years after did I realize how closely, even then, I had subconsciously identified myself with America and Americans. When later I made the decision to choose New York as the home of my own firm, there was no emotional wrench, for the transposition had long since been achieved.

The arguments I presented to my father in 1920, however, were more immediate and less personal. They were based on the conviction that one of us must devote the greater part of the year to the American business, or we should give it up. My few weeks in New York had convinced me that no halfway program of short visits would work

118

under the new conditions. For five years, the American firm, dependent as it was upon Paris for its inventory, had been virtually closed; Eugene Glaenzer, our American representative and partner, had had little choice except to conduct a sort of holding operation. My father had crossed the Atlantic only once in those years, on the government mission in 1917. In the meantime a very different business climate had developed in the United States.

My father's former powerful clients were now mostly of advanced age. Several of them, notably Morgan, Altman, and Frick, had already died, and a new group of collectors with new fortunes had grown up. It seemed plain to me that if we were to build up a new clientele in the United States, one of us would have to be there, and I was the logical choice. I did not believe that we could do this by conducting the New York business as we had in the past, with a few weeks of hectic activity a couple of times a year. The art business is based essentially on personality, and if new American clients were to be my responsibility, I did not feel that a young man just beginning his career could expect, on short visits, the indulgence accorded to Jacques Seligmann. I felt the only alternative to nearly full-time activity in New York would be to remain in Paris entirely.

To entertain ideas which I knew were not in keeping with those of my father was such a new experience that I kept telling myself that it must be I who was deficient in judgment. Further, my father was extremely sensitive, under his outward brusqueness, particularly when it appeared that his feeling toward his children was being misunderstood. I would have given up the whole idea rather than hurt my father; yet I felt that the issue had to be raised.

To complicate the situation, a second and corollary issue of equal importance simultaneously presented itself. Those same first weeks in postwar America had convinced me of another great change—the growing interest in, and insatiable demand for, paintings among American collectors. Should we remain out of this lucrative field as we had in the past, or should we develop a greater interest in paintings commensurate with the importance of the firm? My father had become more or less convinced of the justice of my reasoning about the New York office. But on paintings he was adamant; it remained the only issue which ever really clouded the affectionate and sympathetic relationship between my father and myself.

Today the question of paintings seems academic, but my father's position reflected his own years in the art business. The section of the great Paris Exposition Universelle of 1900 devoted to works of art before 1800 contained more than four thousand items; only sixty were paintings. Even at the time I was arguing my conviction, many collectors still spent fortunes on collections which did not include a single painting. This was not a question of cost; paintings were not more expensive than other objects. Exceptional Sevres porcelains often fetched fifty or seventy-five thousand dollars; marble sculptures of the Renaissance vied in price with those of the French 18th century; and rare early Gothic tapestries often brought a hundred thousand dollars or more. It was simply another day and another taste.

As far as the Paris firm was concerned the question had not yet become a serious one, for there was still a lively, diversified European market, just as there is today. Even new collectors, spending newly made fortunes, still looked upon paintings as just one phase of collecting.

Jacques Seligmann was himself something of a traditionalist, and it was only natural that the clients coming to Sagan sought the type of object for which the firm had long been renowned. During my first weeks in the New York office, things seemed much the same as at Sagan, as Eugene Glaenzer, a man of my father's generation, took me about among the firm's clients and introduced me to his friends. Few of them talked about paintings. It was only when I began to get about on my own, meeting people and acquainting myself with the American art world, that I began to understand that the collecting field had enlarged considerably, and the majority of the newcomers coveted paintings above all other works of art.

Jacques Seligmann, of course, had bought and sold paintings in the past, usually important examples from well-known collections, such as the Isenbrandt from the Lippmann sale (now in the Metropolitan Museum), a Gerard David, a Crivelli, and a Flemish primitive from the Dollfus sale (all of which went to George Blumenthal and are also in the Metropolitan), a Goya portrait from Jacques Doucet, and a Rembrandt in the Yerkes auction (now in the De Young Museum in San Francisco). He owned an impressive group of Fragonard water colors and drawings, and he even made one foray into the modern field when he acquired seventy-one paintings, pastels, and drawings by Degas in the sales of the *Atelier Degas* of 1918. These

120

were intended for his private collection; other paintings hung on our walls at home as well. Yet, when he bought the Wallace-Bagatelle Collection in 1913, he disposed of a large part of the paintings to Roland Knoedler, en bloc, rather than bother with them.

In 1920, the year we had our most serious discussions on the subject, an auction came up in Amsterdam in which there was an extremely rare and important painting from the Borger collection, a *Donor with Saint John the Baptist,* by Hugo van der Goes. I was eager to have it and after much imploring, my father was finally persuaded to buy it. It was almost immediately acquired by Henry Walters and is today one of the glories of the Walters Gallery in Baltimore. The success of that venture emboldened me to try again when the Villeroy Collection came up for sale in Paris in 1922 with two paintings about which I was very keen. One was an adorable profile portrait of an unnamed woman, attributed only to an unknown artist of the Italian 15th century; the other, also in profile, purported to be a portrait of Marie de Bourgogne, but it, too, was unbaptised, and simply called Flemish, 15th century.

Again, after considerable persuasion, my father let himself be convinced on the Flemish painting, but on the so-called Italian portrait he was immovable, and it went to Duveen Brothers, who promptly sold it to Clarence Mackay as a Pisanello. It may now be seen in the National Gallery, via the Mellon Collection, and the attribution, the last I knew, read "Unknown French artist of the international style." I still consider it one of the most delightful paintings I know.

As for the portrait of Marie de Bourgogne, which we did buy, I was dismayed to learn, on my return from a trip to the States, that my father had sold it almost at once, for an extremely small profit, to one of our competitors, who in turn sold it to Philip Lehman. It is today in the collection of his son, Robert Lehman, and was exhibited in Paris in 1957 under the title "Portrait Posthume de Marie de Bourgogne, attribué à Hans Maler," a Swabian painter of the early 16th century. I was distressed that my father had sold the Marie de Bourgogne so summarily in my absence, but I was encouraged that he had been willing to buy it at all.

It certainly could not be said that Jacques Seligmann disliked paintings or did not appreciate their aesthetic qualities. His knowledge of works of art was an eclectic one, and he refused to specialize in any particular field, believing that specialization led to a limitation of one's understanding of beauty and quality. When it came to a judgment upon objet d'art or a sculpture, he would not hesitate to oppose the opinions of recognized scholars, whether Wilhelm von Bode of the Kaisier Friedrich Museum or a curator of the Louvre. When the Berlin museum purchased the famous Flora bust and the Louvre the equally famous Tiara of Saitaphernes, he was among the first to speak his mind about their genuineness, and he was right in both cases. In our old files I came across not long ago an invoice made out by my father which carried the notation: "A marble bust of a youth. Guaranteed Italian work of the 15th century." This was followed by another, underlined: "In spite of Dr. von Bode's attribution of this bust to another Italian artist of the same period, I consider it beyond doubt the work of Donatello." Having taken the time and the trouble—it probably meant a trip to Germany—to consult Bode about a work of art, it was only to disagree with him. Moreover, the client was evidently satisfied. A dealer making such a statement today would immediately be requested to obtain the opinions of two or three other art experts, who would probably not agree with one another. And therein, I believe, lies the answer to my father's reluctance to delve wholeheartedly into the field of paintings—the growing preoccupation of the new collector with names and opinions.

To the European collector of my father's generation, the question of the authorship of a work of art or of its exact date was a comparatively unimportant factor in his decision to buy or not to buy. Works of art were either genuine or forgeries and quality was the paramount issue. While it is true that French collectors of that time were chiefly interested in objects of a type which are apt to be anonymous, even when they collected paintings, the name of the artist was less important to them than the quality of the work; to know school and period sufficed. Certainly there was then, as there is today, concern for authenticity and state of restoration. Beyond this, scholarly arguments interested the collector very little.

As far as my father was concerned, his reputation for connoisseurship was such that it would have been somewhat daring of a collector to consult anyone else, implying a doubt of my father's word. Jacques Seligmann did not consider himself infallible; he did claim that if, in the enthusiasm of making a purchase, his eye betrayed him, he would detect his error within a few hours of contemplation. He always kept a new purchase in his office for a while, and between the time of its arrival and the moment when he might wish to show it to a client, if it were not right, it would have lost the *sui generis* quality which it first appeared to have. The treasure which had lost its luster would be thrown into a corner and its cost marked off to education. I can remember only a few such incidents, but I remember them well, for my father insisted that I study them as he considered these errors an important part of the training of the eye. The spurious work of art has a remarkable faculty to grow increasingly dull, almost unbearably so, to the sensitive eye when observed long enough in comparison with a genuine treasure.

Moreover, collectors like Le Breton of Rouen, Bardac, Dormeuil, Chalandon were brilliantly knowledgeable men who had seen and handled almost as many works of art as had my father. Their keenness and love for the objects they collected had developed in them an extra sense which made them react almost instantaneously, and their judgment was rarely at fault. For them collecting was a true passion sometimes carrying them far beyond their financial means. They preferred to do without some essential of elementary comfort than to forego the acquisition of an object which stirred them deeply.

The relationship between such collectors and the dealer was of a rather special nature. The collector was grateful when his attention was called to a specific work of art, and he took his time in examining it. If he was elated at first sight of it, he compared it with other examples he already owned and consulted the dealer as an advisor. If convinced, then the question of price was broached. But it was almost a secondary matter; he could afford it or he could not, in which case he might ask for time in which to settle, but have it he must.

The true amateur's aesthetic appreciation was as great as the historian's, but the details of art history with its minutiae of schools, dates, and related information were of little import to him. Certainly they did not influence his buying. He was pleased to have his collection admired by the learned men, but their opinions were not a primary concern. Certain collectors used to say, in fact, that the academicians had wide book knowledge and useful memories, but that few of them had eyes.

In those circumstances it can readily be understood that the specialist as we have grown to know him in recent years was little needed by either collector or dealer and outside academic circles the art historian played a comparatively small role.

This should not be taken to mean that the dealer of my father's time scorned the advice of an independent expert or museum man—it was simply sought on a different level. My own introduction to the art historian in his capacity of consultant came long before World War I, when my father took me to Berlin to call upon the great German savant, Wilhelm von Bode, head of the Kaiser Friedrich Museum, advisor to Kaiser Wilhelm II, as he had been to his mother, the Kaiserin Victoria, and recipient of all the available honors, including knighthood. Jacques Seligmann and Bode were on the friendliest terms. There was even a measure of deference in the scholar's manner toward my father, as there was in my father's toward him. When later it was my turn to call upon Bode, I have to admit, somewhat shamefacedly, that I found it difficult to respond as warmly to his cordiality as I really wanted, and for quite an unobjective reason. It had nothing to do with his rather brusque and categorical way of speaking or with any doubt of his knowledge. It was simply because he always reminded me of Bismarck!

Though Bode was a great expert on paintings, particularly of the Dutch schools—his works on Rembrandt and Frans Hals are still basic references—it was in Italian sculpture of the Renaissance that his influence was most felt, and it was usually upon this subject that my father consulted him. Certainly there was much work to be done in this field, a lot of clearing and pruning, and probably no one outside Italy has done as much toward a rational study of Italian art as have the German scholars, from Burckhardt to Bode and his followers. The vast amount of research done since Bode's time dates some of his works, and the younger generation, prone to criticize its elders, has had a tendency to make light of his publications. However, the correctness of the general lines of his classifications must be recognized. If names such as Donatello or Verrocchio became generic terms embracing whole schools, it was still no mean achievement to have established the characteristics which enabled him to gather so many previously anonymous works under one head.

Around Bode at the Kaiser Friedrich Museum were several other men whom we occasionally consulted. Otto von Falke, later Director of the Kunstgewerbe Museum in Berlin, who wrote one of the definitive works on Italian textiles, was also a great connoisseur of early medieval works of art. He was always willing to discuss problems of attribution, period, and country, particularly in his favorite field of early cloisonné and champlevé enamels. For works of the 10th and 11th centuries, we might ask the learned opinion of the delightful Professor Adolph Goldschmidt, a great savant with a prodigious knowledge and an equally prodigious memory. Later I used to see him off and on in New York, particularly at the Morgan Library, for Belle Greene admired him greatly. However, to me he always seemed professorial in his explanations and I had the impression that he was more archaeologist than aesthetician. The importance he immediately gave to stylistic details irked me, as it was in direct opposition to the teachings I had received—always to go from the general to the particular, to let the details only confirm or disprove the first impression.

The opinions of such specialists were always of great interest to my father, but the consulting expert had never been indispensable to his business. It was with the advent of a new type of collector, particularly new American collectors, too busy or without a sufficiently deep interest to train the eye or the sensibilities, that the art historian became a guiding authority for the collector and thus important to the dealer.

Art scholarship, however, was still in its infancy. There had not yet been time to delve into the bypaths, nor means to develop the scientific methods we know today. As the passion for names grew along with the demand for paintings, attributions to the great masters were made, so to speak, in generic terms. A great many canvases were called Rembrandt, for instance, simply because they were close to the master's technique; and anyway Rembrandt was an awfully good name. The man who had no informed opinion of his own, yet could not bring himself, sometimes wisely, to rely entirely upon the word of a dealer, had recourse to the services of a third party—the professional expert, the art historian, or the consulting connoisseur. This was particularly true of the new collector of paintings to whom names were more important than the work of art and such attributions as "anonymous artist of the 15th century" or "school of" were anathema. Thus the consultant became indispensable to the dealer for he could usually supply a name, as well as the detailed data which the client demanded.

Although Jacques Seligmann could hear new clients dismiss objets d'art as "decorative arts," giving the term a pejorative connotation, he was just not sufficiently interested to expand the firm's painting department if selling paintings meant seeking a name to sell with the canvas. The issue between my father and me, then, was simply the different outlooks of different generations. My father had done his best to train me to be both a connoisseur and an art historian. Paintings interested me, and I was willing to put my knowledge to the test.

I was doubly pleased that same year when we acquired a handsome Venetian altarpiece of the late 15th century and my father consented to show it to Bernard Berenson. It was my first meeting with the great B. B., though my father had known him for many years.

If Wilhelm von Bode was the final authority on questions of Italian sculpture, B. B. was supreme on Italian painting. Undoubtedly the world-wide reputations of these two dynamic and vivid personalities had much to do with the rise to prominence of the consulting art historian. In fact, I would say that no man has played a more influential role in the art world generally than Bernard Berenson, been more revered, or more surely captured the imagination of all, for the aura surrounding Berenson affected even those who never met him. Many who wished to meet him never had that opportunity for, as he had every right to be, he was difficult to approach and impatient with callers who came for no particular purpose. To those who interested him, however, or those who visited him on pertinent and legitimate errands, he was the gracious and entertaining host par excellence. I never think of Berenson without also thinking of Voltaire; both sharp of wit, quick of repartee, exquisite in sarcasm, and fearless in opinion, but also deep in understanding of human nature and compassionate with its weaknesses. B. B., like Voltaire, had a globe-circling correspondence and a host of acquaintances who consulted the oracle of I Tatti as an older generation consulted the oracle of Ferney.

He was at home in the capitals of the world, speaking Italian, French, and German as fluently and as elegantly as English. His knowledge of backgrounds and intrigues in political and social circles was as all-embracing as his knowledge of those of the art world. There can be little doubt that had he lived in the Renaissance he would have been a Vasari or a Castiglione, advisor to the great in their pursuits of art treasures, all the while keeping them posted on the undercurrents and rumors of the political world. He began his career, while still in Florence, as advisor to Isabella Gardner, a true descendant of the Renaissance, in the assembling of one of the first comprehensive

126

private collections in the United States. We are indebted to him for a prodigious number of the paintings, particularly of the Italian school, which now grace American collections, both public and private.

I still remember that first encounter with the small, delicate-looking man—his expressive hands, his delightful manner, his soft, well-modulated voice, pronouncing decisions that one felt were beyond appeal. Fortunately, the big Venetian altarpiece which he had come to see met his approval, and he immediately pronounced it the work of Cima da Conegliano, but added that he believed the landscape background to be by a lesser master, Santa Croce. With all due respect to the great expert, the name of Santa Croce just might have been mentioned to soften the price, for a few days later, Lord d'Abernon (later Ambassador in Berlin) came to purchase the painting at Mr. Berenson's suggestion, presenting just that argument for a lowering of the quoted figure. Nor have I ever been quite certain whether the altarpiece was actually intended to enrich d'Abernon's own collection; within a comparatively short time the painting had come into the hands of a well-known firm, from which it entered the Mellon Collection, and eventually the National Gallery.

A second meeting with Berenson was to come only a few months later when he came again to see a recently acquired painting, this time by a rare Flemish master of the 15th century, Joos van Gent. Berenson's interest was universal, and if his judgment was less quick in the northern than Italian schools, it was no less sure. Works by Joos van Gent are scarce indeed, and he needed time for a study of comparative material, but again he confirmed the attribution, and his decision has never been contested.

With these two successes behind me, I began to hope that my father was gradually being won to my point of view about painting, as he had seemed to be about our New York office. I truly believe he might have been, but time was running short, too short for the full cooperation that would have grown over the years between a father and a son so closely linked.

These differences of opinion between my father and myself never turned into an important personal feud, or even violent disagreement. Neither did I feel personal triumph when I proved to be right and he wrong. I recount them only for what they reveal of the evolutions of the world of collecting. My devotion to my father far exceeded business considerations. I owed to him the gift of appreciation and enjoyment of man's most beautiful creations, a gift in itself beyond price and one I have cherished throughout my life.

In the summer of 1923, my father motored to Italy where I joined him for a few days of vacation before returning to New York. One evening, as we walked along the banks of beautiful Lake Varese, I found myself trying, awkwardly enough, to express to him something of that sense of gratitude. Neither he nor I were prone to talk so intimately, and we rarely expressed our emotions fully, though I had long guessed his sensitivity and how much such words could mean to him. Premonition? Perhaps. It was the last time I saw him. A few weeks later, on the 30th of October, he died, a victim of pneumonia, while I was racing from Chicago to New York, trying to reach the first steamer to take me back to him.

CHAPTER XII

Some Collectors

When I reached my office in New York after that hurried trip from Chicago, I found Thomas Fortune Ryan waiting for me. It was not yet nine o'clock in the morning, but he had come in the hope of catching me before I sailed. I was truly moved by the warmth of his sympathy and the spontaneity of the gesture, the assurance it brought me that he mourned the loss of a friend as well as of an advisor whose opinion he valued and trusted. His visit, and the many others, the messages from friends both here and abroad, were a real source of solace, evidence that great and small recognized the mettle of the man. Especially was it important to me that these mighty businessmen, many also self-made, understood the courage, daring, and energy it had taken to achieve Jacques Seligmann's success.

Inevitably the first months after my father's death were much occupied with the immediate problems which confront a family suddenly bereft of the head of the house. The legal formalities attendant upon the settlement of the estate, difficult enough anywhere, but in France often confusion compounded, were made more complicated by the necessity of reorganizing the financial structure of the firm itself. Certain members of the family wished to retain their interests, others, including my brother André who had already established a gallery of his own in Paris, did not. Meanwhile, of course, the business had to be conducted at the Palais de Sagan, at the rue de la Paix gallery, and in New York. My father's death had followed by only a few months the demise of Eugene Glaenzer, our American partner and manager, so that office was without a resident director. In 1924 I began a veritable commuter's life which in the next fifteen years was to entail more than a hundred and twenty-five crossings of the Atlantic. Since a crossing took a week—the airplane was not yet available—I figure that more than two years of my life were spent on shipboard.

Fortunately, the Paris firm was well-staffed with a number of men who had been with my father for many years and who could be relied upon during my absences. Albert L. Meyer was particularly valuable for his sound knowledge of the 18th century and his exquisite taste. His name still gives eclat today to the drawings which he gathered for his personal collection. René Seligmann, my first cousin, the eldest son of my Uncle Simon, had come into the business immediately after his war service. His charm, sunny nature, genuine liking for people, and active social life made him an ideal associate in the building of a new clientele. We were almost of an age, and I found in him a valuable ally both in Paris and New York when I wished to launch the firm into the new direction which collecting was taking, particularly in the United States.

Any son of a successful father who is suddenly called upon to assume that father's functions as head of an important firm is bound to feel a sense of his own inadequacy, no matter how well prepared he may be by years of training. Though I was thirty when my father died, my years of actual business experience had been curtailed by eight years of military service. To my father's employees and associates, as well as to his competitors, I was still "young Germain" who had yet to prove his ability. If I was able to surmount these problems and to weather the inflationary storms of the turbulent twenties and the depression doldrums of the thirties, a good measure of the credit must go to the encouragement I received from my father's loyal and affectionate friends among the great collectors, both French and American.

One I shall always recall with deep affection and gratitude is Henry Walters, who by a simple and generous act gave a badly needed lift to my morale at a crucial moment. Mr. Walters had been a valued friend and client of my father since the turn of the century. Though I had met him a number of times, circumstances had somehow always prevented the ripening of a real friendship, and I had an unreasoned feeling that I should probably never see him again, at least as a client. I was therefore doubly pleased when he appeared at Sagan one afternoon in the spring of 1924, unheralded, as was his custom.

After the amenities of greeting were over, I took him into the room reserved for showing the most precious works of art. As soon as we were alone, without preamble he said to me:

"Young man, I have just come from your competitor, Mr. X, who said, 'I feel so sorry about young Germain Seligmann. I am very fond of him; if his father had only lived a few years longer, he would have been able to keep up the business; but now, so young, what will he be able to do!' "

Then, before I could reply, he added, "I am repeating this to you because I feel you should know what you are up against. As for me, I am not interested in what other people tell me. I have eyes of my own. If you keep up your father's traditions, you have nothing to fear. It is up to you."

No man could have been kinder, no words could better have given me the encouragement I needed at that time, and his frankness moved me deeply. I was so touched that I stood speechless for a few seconds. Then he said, "Well, now, what have you got to show me?"

Before he left Sagan that day, I had made my first sale to Henry Walters, and a very important one, too. He never mentioned the topic again, nor did I; but if he forgot it, I never have.

Henry Walters with his short, round figure, his white hair, mustache and goatee, always personified to me the typical Southern gentleman of whom I had read. His father, William T. Walters, founder of the Atlantic Coast Line Railroad, was himself a collector who, between 1850 and his death in 1894, had filled the big Baltimore home with paintings and objets d'art typical of his era. He was also an anti-secessionist and when the Civil War broke out, disturbed by the political situation in the United States, he dispatched young Henry to Paris. There he attended the Lycée with young Durand-Ruel, who became his fast friend, and acquainted himself with the art of France.

This experience, coupled with his father's tutelage (he used to assign essay topics on art to his son), apparently served to nurture and expand an inherent feeling for works of art. By the time of his father's death, collecting had become a true passion with Henry Walters. Even during the days of the railroad battles when he had to fight to complete and develop the Atlantic Coast Line, he always found time to indulge in his avocation. By 1907 his collection had so increased that it was necessary to erect a gallery building, connected

131

to the family home by a "bridge of sighs" over the intervening alley, to house it. Until Henry Walters' death in 1931, this building was opened to the public from time to time, with a fifty-cent charge for the benefit of the Family Welfare Association.

Henry Walters was already past middle age at the time of the Sagan visit of which I speak and had recently married the charming Sadie Green Jones, widow of Pembroke Jones. They were living in New York in the house which was hers on East 61st Street. When deciding upon a purchase, he would indicate whether it was intended for his home or for "the museum," meaning the family mansion in Baltimore. Once when he referred thus to "the museum," I questioned him about it and was delighted when he offered to meet me in Baltimore and show it to me.

Though I had no preconceived notion of what to expect, beyond a knowledge of the objects he had acquired from my father or from me, the reality, when I entered the vast and gloomy hall of the marble building, was a shock. There was a wilderness of cases filled with objects of every description with a typical Victorian disregard for method, value, aesthetic merit, or period. Seeing my dismay, Mr. Walters explained that this was largely the collection which his father had left him, that he had added much to it, but had had no time to arrange or catalogue it. At least this way, he said, the objects were stored in a measure of safety.

Walking around, I immediately became aware of certain objects which were either copies or out-and-out fakes. Somewhat disappointed, I decided that the only thing to do was to ignore them, and so passed without comment to the wealth of truly fine things about which I could be genuinely enthusiastic. But Mr. Walters, unnoticed by me, must have been watching my reactions keenly. He kept taking me back to some of the things which I had so carefully avoided, asking for my opinion. I was decidedly embarrassed and tried to turn him aside with some inoffensive remark, but he repeated his questions until I finally decided there was nothing to do but take a stand and speak my mind.

Henry Walters then said calmly, "My boy, that is just what I wanted to hear. I know they are fakes, but since they were bought by my father, they will remain here as long as I live. Meantime it gives me a good test of other people's knowledge."

The fakes were the least of the surprises offered by the Walters

132

house. After going through several rooms where a few of his latest purchases were visible—one could hardly say exhibited—I inquired about a particular sculpture which he had acquired from me the previous year and of which I was especially fond, a lovely *Saint John the Baptist* by Sansovino from the collection of the Empress Frederick, mother of Kaiser William II. Mr. Walters replied that it was still in its packing box, and marking my astonishment, he chuckled and asked if I wanted to see the cases. We then walked through a maze of hallways where unopened cases by the dozens were piled on top of each other.

"I probably won't live to see them all opened," he said, "but you can imagine the surprise of those who will unpack them after I am gone."

I know now that there were two hundred and forty-three of those unopened cases, and from the accounts of those who took part in the opening and classifying, I gather that Mr. Walters' prediction was a mild understatement. Here, never unpacked, were the rare and exceptional objects which I knew he owned, purchased from my father, from me, and from a host of others. Curiously enough, almost no one in the art world at that time seemed to know anything about this treasure trove, not even the museum men. I seldom found anyone, until after Mr. Walters' death, who had the least conception of the fantastic importance of this collection or the broad range it covered from Archaic to 19th century, from the Far East to America.

This experience throws a revealing light on the character of Henry Walters. He was always pleasant to casual acquaintances, but he was, nevertheless, a very reserved man, modest in his behavior, and an arch enemy of personal publicity. In the very beginning of our relationship, in the days when the daily papers were anxious to publish information about great art purchases, he told me that if I gave out any such data, our association would end. It was said that he had been offered the presidency of the Board of Trustees of the Metropolitan Museum and had repeatedly rejected it, though he served the museum as vice-president for many years.

Quietly, unassumingly, over a period of years Henry Walters built a private museum almost unequalled in variety and quality. There was no thought of enhancing his social position or of seeing his name in large letters over the portal of a fine building. He even deprived himself of the joy of handling those beloved and precious objects left carefully packed in the museum storage rooms. Yet he was truly a lover of the beautiful. Often I have seen him actually caress a work of art, and occasionally he could not resist temptation and would tell me, "I think this should go to Baltimore, but send it home first so I can enjoy the sight and the feel of it."

Usually, however, the objects sent to his home in New York were presents made to Mrs. Walters, who always accompanied him on his visits. Her one purpose seemed to be to please him in each of his whims, and when at times he turned to her questioningly, her answer was always, "If you like it, dear, buy it. I think it's lovely." Mrs. Walters was already elderly when I first met her, but she must have been a great beauty. She was still charming and gracious, and completely devoted to her husband.

Walters' attitude toward the money he spent on works of art was consistent with his whole character. One morning in New York he called me on the telephone, full of good humor, requesting that I drop by his office to add up the invoices he had received from me. Later in his modest office, without bothering to call a secretary or an accountant, he added up the invoices himself, asked me whether we agreed on the total, and wrote a check. Then he picked up a pair of large scissors and began cutting the invoices. I was horrified and tried to stop him from destroying the documents over which I had labored hard, as they contained complete descriptions and pedigrees, a point on which he was very particular. Laughing at my dismay, he explained that he was only cutting off the prices. "I don't want anybody in later years to talk of my collection in terms of money spent," he said. "That is my business; they'll have the works of art and their pedigrees." And indeed they do have the works of art, of a diversity and quality which few museums can equal. They do not always have all the pedigrees, however, as I have since learned from members of the Walters Gallery staff. If the invoice was a long one, the material often extended to the back of the page; thus in cutting off the price, which was placed last on the right-hand side, he deleted part of the pedigree.

Henry Walters belonged to the generation of men who, having acquired millions, understood the profit motive and did not begrudge it to others. At the sale of the Octave Homberg Collection in Paris, I bought a pair of beautiful small paintings by Boucher and had barely

Plate 65
Pierre-Auguste Renoir (1841–1919). "Le Bal à Bougival," 1883, 5' 10⅝" x 3'
1¾". Acquired by the Museum of Fine Arts, Boston, 1937.

Plate 66b
Paul Gauguin (1848–1903). "The Queen of the Aréois," 1892, 36" x 28½".
Acquired by William S. Paley, New York, 1936.

Plate 66a
Paul Gauguin (1848–1903). "Tehura," 1893, 30" x 21½".
From the Daniel de Monfreid Collection, Paris. Acquired by
Chauncey McCormick, Chicago, 1937. Present collection:
Mrs. Chauncey McCormick, Chicago.

Plate 67
Paul Cezanne (1839–1906). "L'Estaque," 30¾" x 38¼". From the Michel
Monet Collection, Giverny. Acquired by William S. Paley, New York, 1935.

Plate 68
Pablo Picasso (1881–   ). "Les Demoiselles d'Avignon," 1907,
8′ x 7′ 8″. From the Jacques Doucet Collection, Paris. Acquired by
the Museum of Modern Art, New York (Lillie P. Bliss Bequest), 1937.

Plate 69
Pablo Picasso (1881–   ). "La Vie," 1903, 6′ 5⅜″ x 4′ 2⅞″. Acquired by
the Cleveland Museum of Art. Gift of Hanna Fund, 1945.

Plate 70a
Georges Braque (1882–   ). "Le Jour,"
1911, 13¾" x 9½". From the Jacques Doucet
Collection, Paris. Acquired by Mrs. George
F. Porter, Ojai, California, 1937.

Plate 70b
Georges Braque (1882–   ). "Le Gueridon,"
1926, 5' 10" x 2' 4½". Acquired by the Museum of
Modern Art, New York, 1941.

Plate 71a
Honoré Daumier (1808–1879). "L'Amateur
d'Estampes," 15¾" x 13". From the Jacques
Doucet Collection, Paris. Acquired by Marshall
Field, Chicago, 1938. Present collection: The
Art Institute of Chicago, Gift of the Estate of
Marshall Field.

Plate 71b
Honoré Daumier (1808–1879). "Les Deux
Confrères," watercolor, 11½" x 8⅛". From the
Esnault-Pelterie Collection, Paris. Acquired by
Emil Bührle, Zurich, 1953.

Plate 72
Edgar Degas (1834–1917). "L'Essayage chez la Modiste," pastel, 27″ x 27″. Acquired by Mrs. David M. Levy, New York, 1938. Present collection: The Museum of Modern Art, New York. Gift o Mrs. David M. Levy.

Plate 73
Georges Seurat (1859–1891). "The Beach at Le Crotoy," 1889, 27½" x 34".
Acquired by Edward G. Robinson, Beverly Hills, California, 1938.

Plate 75a
Edgar Degas (1834–1917).
"La Grande Danseuse,"
bronze, height 39". Acquired
by Edward G. Robinson, Beverly Hills, California, 1938.

Plate 75b
Pierre-Auguste Renoir (1841–
1919). "Venus Victrix," 1916,
bronze, height 5' 11". Acquired by Museu de Arte,
São Paulo, Brazil, 1951.

Plate 76a
Edgar Degas (1834–1917). "Portrait of Diego Martelli," 1879, 29½″ x 45¾″. Acquired by Museo Nacional de Bellas Artes, Buenos Aires, 1939. (Reproduced courtesy of the Asociación Amigos del Museo.)

Plate 76b
Edgar Degas (1834–1917). "Chevaux de Courses," pastel, 22″ x 25½″. Acquired by Leonard C. Hanna, Jr., Cleveland, 1939. Present collection: The Cleveland Museum of Art. Bequest of Leonard C. Hanna, Jr.

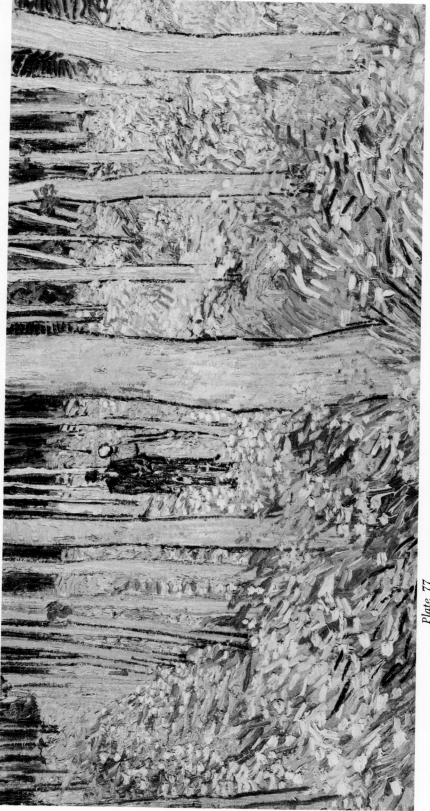

Plate 77

Vincent Van Gogh (1853–1890). "Sous Bois," 1890, 19⅝" x 39½". From the collections of V. W. Van Gogh, Amsterdam; Mme J. Van Gogh-Bonger, Amsterdam; and Gilbert Fuller, Boston. Acquired by private collection, Cincinnati, 1944.

Plate 78
J. A. D. Ingres (1780–1867). "Portrait of Madame Moitessier," 1856, 47¼" x 36¼". Acquired by the National Gallery, London, 1936. (Reproduced by courtesy of the Trustees.)

Plate 79
Jacques-Louis David (1748–1825). "Bonaparte, First Consul," 1798, 31⅞″ x 25⅛″. Acquired by Carlos de Beistegui, Paris, 1938. Present collection: The Louvre, Paris, Bequest of Carlos de Beistegui.

Plate 80
J. A. D. Ingres (1780–1867). "Odalisque en Grisaille," 32¾" x 43".
From the collection of Mme. Emmanuel Riant, the artist's niece.

Plate 81
Francisco de Goya (1746–1828). "Portrait of the Architect Don Juan Antonio Cuervo," 1819, 47¼" x 34¼". From the collection of Godfrey S. Rockefeller, Greenwich, Connecticut. Acquired by the Cleveland Museum of Art, Mr. and Mrs. William H. Marlatt Collection, 1943.

Plate 82
German (probably Nuremberg School), 15th century. Baptismal font, 1483, bronze, height 3′ 7″. From the collections of Baron Achille Seillière, Château de Mello, and Clarence H. Mackay, New York. Acquired by the Museum of Fine Arts, Boston, 1941.

Plate 83
French, c. 1550. Parade armor of King
Henri II, embossed, damascened and
gilded. Later presented by King Louis
XIII to Bernhard von Weimar. From the
collections of the Archdukes of Saxe-
Weimar-Eisenach, and Clarence H.
Mackay, New York. Acquired by the
Metropolitan Museum of Art, Dick Fund,
1939.

Plate 84
French (Burgundian), 15th century. Two
Mourners from the tombs of the Dukes of
Burgundy, Chartreuse de Champmol, mar-
ble, height 16¼". From the collections of
Baron Arthur de Schickler, Martinvast, and
Clarence H. Mackay, New York. Acquired
by the Cleveland Museum of Art, J. H. Wade
Collection, 1940.

Plate 85
Giovanni Battista Tiepolo (1696–1770). "The Martyrdom of Saint Sebastian," 1739,
21″ x 12½″. Modello for the altarpiece in the monastery church of Diessen. Acquired
by the Cleveland Museum of Art, Holden Collection, 1946.

Plate 86
Neroccio de' Landi (1447–1500). "The Rapalano Altar," 5′ 2″ x 4′ 7¼″. From the Arthur Sac[hler?]
Collection, New York. Acquired by the Samuel H. Kress Foundation, 1943. Present collection: N[a]-
tional Gallery of Art, Washington, D.C., Samuel H. Kress Collection.

Plate 87
Jacopo Tintoretto (1518–1594). "Christ at the Sea of Galilee," 46″ x 66″. From the
Arthur Sachs Collection, New York. Acquired by the Samuel H. Kress Foundation, 1943.
Present collection: National Gallery of Art, Washington, D.C., Samuel H. Kress Collection.

Plate 88
Italian, second half of 14th century. "The Holy Family Leaving Nazareth," drawing, 10¾″ x 10
after the fresco attributed to Giotto in the Church of Saint Francis, Assisi. Acquired by the Pie
pont Morgan Library, New York, 1939.

Plate 89

Hans Memling (1430/35–1494). "Madonna and Child Enthroned," 28½″ x 19½″. From the Mortimer L. Schiff Collection, New York. Acquired by the Nelson Gallery-Atkins Museum (Nelson Fund), Kansas City, Missouri, 1944.

Plate 90
Gustave Courbet (1819–1877). "La Grand-Mère," 1862, 36″ x 28¾″. Acquired by the Minneapoli
Institute of Arts, the William H. Dunwoody Fund, 1940.

aude Monet (1840–1926). "Madame Paul, Patissière à Pourville," 1881, 25¾″ x 21½″. Acquired
Mrs. Maurice Wertheim, New York, 1955. Present collection: The Fogg Art Museum, Harvard
niversity. Maurice Wertheim Bequest.

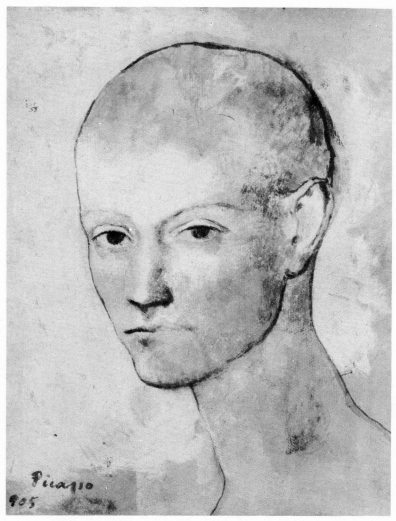

Plate 92
Pablo Picasso (1881–   ). "Head of a Boy," 1905, 12³⁄₁₆″ x 9½″. From the collection of Gertru
Stein. Acquired by Leonard C. Hanna, Jr., Cleveland, 1937. Present collection: The Clevela
Museum of Art. Bequest of Leonard C. Hanna, Jr.

te 93

rre-Auguste Renoir (1841–1919). "Portrait of Mademoiselle Lacaux," 1864, 31⅞″ x 25½″. Ac-
red by the Cleveland Museum of Art. Gift of Hanna Fund, 1942.

Plate 94a
Pablo Picasso (1881–   ). "Cubist Composition," 1911, 29¼" x 37⅞". From the collection of former Governor and Mrs. W. Averell Harriman, New York. Acquired by private collection, Cincinnati, 1944.

Plate 94b
Juan Gris (1887–1927). "Portrait of casso," 1912, 36¼" x 28¾". Acquired Leigh B. Block, Chicago, 1949. Prese collection: The Art Institute of Chicag Gift of Leigh B. Block.

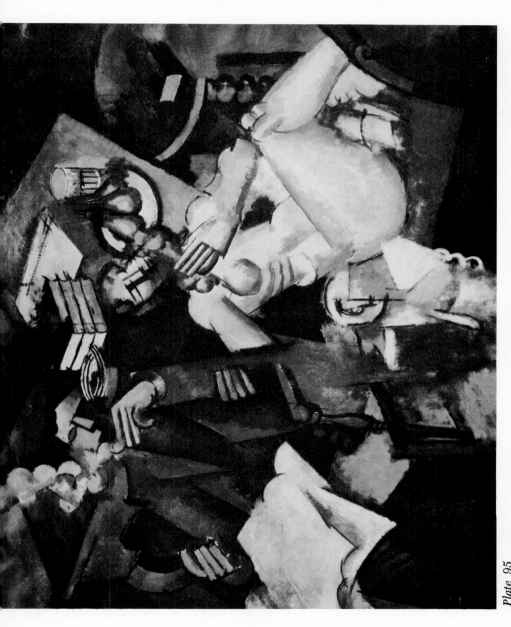

Plate 95
Roger de La Fresnaye (1885–1925). "La Vie Conjugale," 1912, 38″ x 46¼″. Acquired by Leigh B. Block, Chicago, 1948. Present collection: The Minneapolis Institute of Arts. Gift of the John R. Van Derlip Fund.

Plate 96a
Henri Matisse (1869–1954). "Carnaval de Nice," 25¾" x 39¼".
Acquired by Emil Bührle, Zurich, 1951.

Plate 96b
Raoul Dufy (1877–1953). "Port du Havre," 1906, 23½" x 28¾". Acquired by the Art Gallery of Toronto. Gift of the Woman's Committee Fund to commemorate the Golden Jubilee of the Art Gallery of Toronto, 1953.

received them at my gallery when Walters walked in. Immediately enchanted with them, he asked for the price.

"I've only just bought them, Mr. Walters, and I find them particularly lovely. I'll tell you what I paid for them, but," I added jokingly, "I do want a big profit."

Whereupon he offered me, spontaneously, a larger sum than I would have asked.

On another occasion, in 1928, I had just reacquired the famous *Triumph of Amphitrite*, also by Boucher, which had originally been in the Wallace-Bagatelle Collection. Its purchaser then was Baron Eugene de Rothschild of Vienna who had come to Paris to live after the war and found his charming house in Passy too small to do justice to this monumental canvas. Thus, it was once more available in the place from whence it had come fourteen years earlier. Though carried out in a somewhat sketchier manner than the Bouchers of Hertford House in London, it must have been originally a part of this same series, and its unachieved character gives an interesting insight into the artist's technique. Opulent and impressive, it is a painting which personifies the lavish life of the 18th century and the sumptuous homes of Boucher's patrons.

The painting had been at Sagan but a few weeks, when I received the visit of Henry Walters. I realized that it was too large for a private house, so it was in his capacity of Trustee of the Metropolitan Museum that I showed it to him. A painting of its unique and superb quality should go, I felt, to a museum.

He was obviously stirred by the painting, but after a few minutes of hesitation, he said that in view of his knowledge of available funds he did not think he could recommend the purchase; the museum could not afford it, and the price was too high.

He let me absorb this disappointing and unexpected statement, for he seldom questioned prices and the sum asked was not out of line considering the merit of the painting. Then, with a twinkle in his eye, he added, "But if the Trustees will accept it, I'll *give* it to the museum." This was typical, both of his sometimes teasing sense of humor and of his generous civic spirit. I was so impressed that I in turn felt called upon to make a gesture. Since I had a partner in the ownership of the painting, I could not reduce the selling price, but instead I asked to be allowed to make my own personal contribu-

135

tion to the gift. When the picture was accepted by the museum, Henry Walters saw to it that my name also appeared as a donor and benefactor, a delicate gesture typical of him.

If he was capable of such beaux gestes, he could also be realistic about the art world, as I learned through another encounter. The news had been bruited about Paris that the famous Gustave Dreyfus Collection of Italian sculptures, which I had known and admired since my student days, could now be bought. I, of course, was intensely interested. After some inquiries, a price was indicated to me, and while it was considerable, it was not beyond the value of so exceptional a collection. But, alas, it was definitely beyond the funds I then had available. In accordance with my father's principle of never borrowing, I realized that there was no hope of my acquiring it alone. Was there not some other way of financing the transaction? If, for instance, I could find an immediate buyer for a part of the collection, could I not with those funds swing the rest?

It was with such a thought in mind that I called upon Henry Walters at the Hotel Ritz and explained my problem to him. He knew the collection well and understood my eagerness, for there were many collectors and museums who would compete for certain of the rare and beautiful pieces.

"But if you don't have the funds and don't want to borrow, how do you propose to finance the purchase?" he asked.

"It is for that I have come to you, Mr. Walters," I said, "With your help, it might be feasible to get together two or three museums, giving them first choice . . ." I went on to explain the details of my plan.

He heard me through, then said, "My boy, keen as I am to see the Dreyfus Collection come to the States, don't ask me to get several museums together with any expectation of their agreeing on anything. It can't be done; I've tried it before, and it just won't work."

Thus, having no more ideas, I had to forget the Dreyfus Collection.

Paris in the late spring was the time and place for Henry Walters to devote himself to collecting. Then he was relaxed and carefree, a combination he seldom enjoyed in New York. Talking recently with one of my long-time associates, I was amused to find that his principal recollection of Henry Walters was that Thanksgiving Day was traditionally devoted to showing him works of art in the New York gallery. I used to drop in occasionally at the Walters' home on Sunday morning after church or in the afternoon for tea and a chat with the two of

136

them. He would sit back and reminisce, especially about his sojourn in Paris as a young man when he had seen the Empress Eugénie in full regalia and beauty. What days, what evolutions and revolutions he had seen, and with what serenity and happiness he enjoyed the sunset.

One of the first things I did upon my return to New York from Paris after my father's death was to telephone Thomas Fortune Ryan to ask if I might return his call. I was invited to breakfast at eight, a favorite appointment hour with him, as with a number of business-men-collectors. We chatted about my plans, and he seemed pleased to hear that I intended to continue the business along the old lines, keeping Sagan and the New York gallery. He had almost ceased to collect, though he did purchase a few items from me, notably a rare, large Limoges plate *à paillons* from the collection of the Duke of Saxe-Weimar which he particularly cherished.

Quite aside from business, I enjoyed these breakfast chats with Ryan for their own sake, and the light which they threw on the man. One such morning, having noticed in the evening paper of the day before an article about some new development in the tobacco industry, I asked his reaction to it. His reply was to laugh heartily and to say, "Don't go believing everything printed in the daily papers. News can be inspired, you know." From which I gathered that he was probably the inspiration.

However, on another occasion when I commented on a news item about sugar in Cuba, he surprised me by seeming to have forgotten his previous warning and discussed the matter with apparent trust in the newspaper account. It was strange, I thought, that even men of his experience sometimes failed to apply to other fields the rules which held good in their own.

I always found tremendously interesting the stories told me from time to time by these builders of gigantic industrial empires in the America of the late 19th century. Listening to them was like hearing a fantastic novel given added intensity and color by the excitement of their voices as they recalled experiences of earlier days. Most of them were still physically and mentally powerful despite advancing years, and I could understand how and why they had been so successful in their earlier years. Nothing, it seemed to me, could have resisted such indomitable men.

None of the giants I knew rivaled Henry E. Huntington: the word describes him literally as well as figuratively. He was as tall as Thomas F. Ryan, many inches over six feet, but was broad of shoulder and massive in build, whereas Ryan was lean and slender. The last time I saw Huntington was in the course of a visit to California in 1926, when I called on him at his magnificent home in San Marino, now the museum. He was already a very sick man and was abed when I arrived; but he knew that I was to be in Los Angeles for only a few hours and insisted upon keeping the appointment, though his nurse told me I must not stay long. His bedroom on the second floor was as simple and unadorned as the ground floor was sumptuous. The bedroom windows opened on a sea of palm trees through which drifted the scent of orange and lemon. This was my first visit to California, and it seemed truly an Eden where the beauty of nature vied with the aesthetic creations of man. I told Huntington of my amazement at the beauty of California, of my trip to Mount Shasta, of my delight in San Francisco, and spoke of the places I hoped to see on my way back to New York. The conversation came around to the subject of railroads, and then Huntington became animated, despite his illness. In connection with one stop I had made, he said that it was where he had his first experience at breaking a strike.

He grew excited by the memory as he lapsed into railroad vernacular, punctuating his account with colorful expletives. The incident took place when he was twenty. He had arrived early one morning at the office of the station master to find a crowd of men shouting and gesticulating, the leader declaring belligerently that "No train leaves this station today!"

" 'Is that so?' says I," Huntington said, "and I pulled out the two pistols I carried and, says I, 'I'll take this train out of here myself, and the first s.o.b. who tries to stop me is a dead man.' And I got on the engine and took that bankety-blank train out of the station!"

By this time Huntington's voice was a roar, his eyes flashing as he relived the scene. It seemed to me then that H. E. Huntington at twenty, with or without pistols, must surely have been a man with whom no one would have cared to fight.

Arabella Huntington, who had married Henry Huntington some years after the death of her first husband, Collis P. Huntington (Henry's uncle), had died before my California visit. Shortly before her death she had called at Sagan. She had just dropped in to say hello, she said, as she was no longer in a buying mood and had everything she wanted to own. She was almost seventy by that time, but still carried her unusual height with a splendid bearing. I seated her in one of the rooms opening onto the garden where we chatted for a while and then, with no thought other than to please her, I showed her a number of objects of a type which I knew she enjoyed, among them a delightful little marble Venus by Falconet.

Looking at me somewhat reproachfully through thick-lensed glasses, she said, "You really shouldn't go to so much trouble for me. You know my sight has become so bad that I can hardly see anything." Whereupon she leaned forward for a closer view of the little figure, not a foot high over all, and exclaimed, "What a lovely thing. Isn't it a shame that the little finger on the left hand is broken!"

I couldn't help bursting into laughter, as I congratulated her on her bad eyesight, for the whole hand was certainly not over a half inch long. Almost before I did, she threw her head back in a hearty laugh. Then she asked what I wanted for it, adding quickly that, of course, she was not buying, but liked to keep up with these things. When I named a figure, she bought it.

D. David-Weill, head of one of the leading private banks of Europe, the internationally known firm of Lazard Frères, had been a long-time friend and client of my father. From my early days I remember calling with my father, usually on Sunday morning, at his classically beautiful Louis XVI house in its well-ordered garden setting. Its very location was in the tradition, just beyond the gates of Paris, which still existed then, not far from the Bois de Boulogne in that lovely quarter of Neuilly which was a favorite location for the *folies* of the past. The entrance was through a sober white stone hall, ornamented by only a few sculptures whose proportions were in scale with its great height, its severity relieved by the warmth of a rich Savonnerie carpet which ran the length of the hall and up the splendid stairway. One of the sculptures was the *Grande Vestale* of Clodion which came from my father, as did the bronze portrait bust of the architect, Robert de Cotte, by Coysevox. Another was the beautiful marble bust of the Marquise de Jaucourt by Houdon. The reception rooms on the ground floor opened to the garden by full-length windows. Here were the choicest items of the collection—the Fragonards (among them one of his most beloved and best known portraits, the *Boy with the*

Cherries, also from my father), the Bouchers, and the Perronneaus—a veritable museum enhanced by human life and living. Later, a recess was built onto the dining room to display the all-but-unique collection of French silver which included not only precious examples of the 18th century, but even more rare, superb pieces from the 17th century.

David-Weill's appreciation was tactile as well as visual, and he was especially fond of the precious bibelots of gold, silver, and bronze in which the 18th century artisans so excelled, the tiny boxes for every conceivable purpose to delight the heart of man or woman. The most precious of them were displayed in two fine Louis XVI vitrines in the drawing room, but upstairs in the *petites appartements,* others were within easy reach of the caressing hand. Here the furniture was exquisitely scaled to the smaller rooms, and the warm old boiseries set off to perfection the delightful drawings and gouaches by the *petits maîtres,* all of surpassing quality.

To collectors like David-Weill, 18th century French art was more than just a tradition, evidenced today only by what remains of its great architecture, painting, and sculpture; it was a symbol of classical training in the humanities. They reacted not only to the outward manifestations of sheer plastic beauty, but also to the inward meaning of the 18th century genius—its literature, its philosophy, its code of manners—an appeal in which they could lose themselves at will.

David-Weill never allowed this absorption with tradition to blind him to the beauties of other periods and other countries. An exhibition held in homage to him after his death in 1952 numbered almost a thousand objects which he had either given to or helped to buy for the museums of France. They were by no means all French or all 18th century. He was one of the first Western collectors to discover the sober beauty of Chinese archaic bronzes and potteries, building up a superb collection which now enriches the Musée Guimet. And it was he who prompted and organized in 1928 the first exhibition of Pre-Columbian art to be held in Paris.

A fact of considerable interest in the evolution of collection is that David-Weill eventually deserted the 18th century to turn toward French painting of the 19th. This was a departure, indeed, for a man so steeped in tradition and explains the breaking up of his great collection from which many items found their way to museums and private collections in the United States. He never went all the way

140

to a clean sweep, as had Jacques Doucet, and although some of the Fragonards, the Bouchers, and the Perronneaus gave way to Renoir, Degas, and even Cézanne, his home contained until his death evidences of his first love.

I saw more of David-Weill during my father's lifetime than in later years, and I never felt that I really knew him as a person, only as a collector. Aside from the fact that I was spending a great deal of time in the States, I feel sure that this was partly my own fault. David-Weill was a man of considerable reserve, perhaps even of innate shyness; I, as the son taking over the position of a dynamic father, undoubtedly also felt a certain diffidence. Thus with reserve meeting reserve, I seemed never able to draw forth the warmth of feeling and enthusiasm which I am sure was there. One does not collect great works of art without it. Nevertheless, the firm was always on his calling list for occasional drop-ins and if I telephoned or wrote him of some object or exhibition which I felt would interest him, he invariably replied or came within a day or so. Over the years he continued to acquire works of art from me which I was happy to see again at Neuilly on occasional visits.

I recall particularly his visit to Sagan at the time of the exhibition of the Philippe Wiener Collection. He went around slowly, carefully examining the paintings, the drawings, and the exquisite bibelots, made his choice, asked for the prices and simply said that he wished to have them. There was no bargaining, no discussion, and the purchase was concluded with few words. He recognized the interest of the pieces he had chosen, and I realized that it would make little sense for me to try to impress him with the quality of those he had neglected.

It may have been that this seeming austerity was the defense of a naturally retiring man faced with many public demands. Though he played an important role in finance of the period, particularly during the crisis following World War I, his name seldom appeared in the public press. He was from early life a dedicated philanthropist and actively continued the foundation for low-cost housing for workers which his parents had begun. He founded, with André Honnorat, the great international housing project for foreign students known as the Cité Universitaire. In addition, he was for twenty-two years the hard-working, progressive president of the Committee of French Museums, a member of the *Institut,* and a *Grand Officier* of

141

the Legion of Honor. It was only after his death that the general public realized the full extent of his gifts to the nation. He was truly one who believed that the pleasure and privilege of possessing money and works of art carries with it the pleasure and duty of sharing them. His son, Pierre, who follows his father as a partner of Lazard Frères, has kept up the tradition of philanthropy and, among other activities, is an energetic trustee of the Cité Universitaire. His other son, Jean, on the other hand, has perhaps inherited more of his father's interest in aesthetic matters, and is Curator of Near Eastern Art at the Louvre and a professor at the Ecole du Louvre.

George Blumenthal, an American partner of Lazard Frères, had been since early youth a close friend of my father, and the warmth of that affection was a heritage passed on to me. Whatever his engagements, he always found time to see me, either at my galleries or at his home. I rarely visited his downtown office, unless the matter was urgent. He liked to make his appointments with me for nine or nine-fifteen in the morning, and kept one eye on the clock throughout. The time ordinarily allotted me was about fifteen minutes, and if I knew that the topic I wished to discuss might take longer, I would tell him in advance, since his appointments were always carefully planned. But these were business meetings, and it was often my privilege to be in the Blumenthal home simply as a friend.

By 1920, the house on which Florence Blumenthal had been working for several years with such love and care was completed. The rather austere, almost forbidding, Italian Renaissance structure at the southwest corner of 70th Street and Park Avenue revealed little to the passerby. Once inside, the impression of austerity was replaced by a world of the imagination, far from the material bustle of New York. It was a dreamlike oasis of beauty, complete with melodious sound from the running water of the patio fountain, often the only sound of greeting. At dusk, the light from a table-lamp opposite the entrance gave to the high, wide court a quality at once eerie and intimate, as it reduced the proportions and picked up the warmth of blooming flowers, green plants, and colorful oriental rugs. It is difficult to explain how so sumptuous and impressive a house could be so intimate; this was but one of the achievements of an extraordinary woman.

The first and second floors were devoted to formal reception rooms.

From the patio, with its royal pair of Pannemaker tapestries, one passed into the ballroom, a later addition built only after a complete set of 18th century flower-strewn tapestries had been found to cover its long walls. The focal point of the long axis was a marble *Orpheus* by Francheville, since attributed to Cristofano da Bracciano and believed to be part of a group made for the Palazzo Corsi.

On the floor above was the great Gothic hall, built specifically for three great works of art: the magnificently simple fireplace which determined the proportions of the whole; a gay and secular 15th century *mille fleurs* tapestry depicting a hawking party on the opposite wall; and a marble *Virgin and Child* by Pisano which occupied a special niche in the linen-fold paneling of the smaller wall. On the same floor was a larger Renaissance salon whose velvet-hung walls served as a background for most of the paintings of earlier date. Here, too, were the monumental Venetian bronze andirons from the Spitzer and Taylor Collections. The formal dining room, where the magnificent *Charlemagne* tapestry was the pièce de resistance, was also on the second floor, with a smaller family dining room on the third floor. There, with the exception of George Blumenthal's den, the decoration was entirely of the 18th century, reminiscent, in its charm and intimacy, of the *petits appartements* of a French royal chateau.

There was perfection in each detail of the house, a perfection which went beyond the works of art. Every bouquet of flowers or potted plant, appropriate in color, size, and kind, was chosen for its appointed place; service was at the elbow before a wish was expressed, but so unobtrusive as to be almost invisible. The food, the wines, the linens, the table service were flawless. It, of course, took an enormous amount of concentration and work to maintain such perfection, but this never intruded on the enjoyment of it.

Florence Blumenthal moved about like a fairy-tale princess, small and dainty, with delicate hands and feet. In the evening, she often wore Renaissance velvet gowns, in dark jewel-like colors which not only enhanced her beauty but gave her an air of having been born to this superb environment where every work of art seemed timelessly at home. She actually lived among the treasures, as it had been intended one should; while seated in one of the low, comfortable chairs, she could let a hand stroke the cool marble of a small sculptured head or the sharp edges of an ivory diptych on a nearby table. They were there to be touched, and if an occasional piece like the

Hispano-Moresque plate, one of the earliest known, remained under glass, the rest were simply there, as by happy accident.

This superb aesthetic efflorescence had had its birth in tragedy. Florence and George Blumenthal had lost their only child, George, when he was eleven. The shock of his death, added to the knowledge that she could never bear another child, left Mrs. Blumenthal in such despair that every means was employed to create new interests for her. Chief among them was travel, with long stays in Italy and France. Gradually her innate taste and love of beauty was reawakened. Guided by special tutors, she plunged into a serious study of the history of art. By the time she began to develop her ideas for the New York house, she had acquired real knowledge to complement a natural bent.

Mrs. Blumenthal diffused about her a sense of refinement which made natural for her a setting which might have seemed theatrical for another. It inspired her visitors. Talk was never high-pitched, and the subject of conversation was apt to be in keeping with the atmosphere, serious and scholarly, or gay and witty. The company was always stimulating and never banal.

Florence's interests, however, were not limited to the world of the past. She took an active part in the development of new talents, creating in Paris a series of scholarships for gifted and promising young artists in need of the financial and moral encouragement her patronage could give. She had hardly completed the Park Avenue house, when she started another in Paris; but grandiose as was the New York mansion, correspondingly small and intimate was the French home. It recalled the charming *folies* built about 18th century Paris by ladies and gentlemen of the court. The drawing room of the Paris house, with full-length windows facing the park on two sides, was designed to contain a Louis XVI *boiserie*. The furnishings were on the same scale, blending in tone and proportion. As befitted the atmosphere, the walls were hung with drawings, water colors, and small oils. Where chaste white lilies were the flowers becoming the Gothic room in New York, in Paris there were bowls filled with roses and spring flowers—still perfection, but of a more intimate kind.

Though he would never have admitted it later, I believe that George Blumenthal did not feel, initially, the same enthusiasm as did Florence for these aesthetic extravagances. But it was not long until he, too, was infected by the atmosphere. How could a man of sensi-

144

tivity and education resist such an environment, especially when praise and recognition came to him from all directions? His study on the top floor, overlooking the corner of Park Avenue and 70th Street, was an indication of his own interest and appreciation. Its walls were adorned with one of the most precious gold and silver woven tapestries of the early 16th century, a great *Crucifixion* which, like Morgan's, had come from the collection of the Dukes of Berwick and Alba; with two exquisite French Renaissance masculine portraits by Corneille de Lyon; with a painting by El Greco and another by Cima da Conegliano. Behind his desk, on a shelf above his books and records, were precious ivories, Renaissance bronzes, and small, early, exquisite wood carvings.

His first important purchase for me, after my father's death, was the famous *Adoration of the Magi* by Joos van Gent, which had come from the Chapel of the Dukes of Frias, near Burgos in Spain, and is the most important composition in America by this exceedingly rare master. It hung in the patio on the ground floor, which was not an ideal place for it, and Florence always promised to move it; but unfortunately failing health in her later years prevented her from giving her usual assiduous attention to details. Nor had she many years to enjoy the splendors she had created, for she passed away in 1930.

George Blumenthal became President of the Board of Trustees of the Metropolitan Museum in 1934, after having served as a member of that Board since 1909. He was not a man to accept so great a responsibility without planning to give it all necessary time and devotion, which he did superbly for seven years. This was a side of his life which might be considered an indulgence of personal taste, but he also served on the Board of Mount Sinai hospital for forty-six years, twenty-seven of them as its President. After his retirement from business in 1925, he devoted half of his day to each of his two beloved projects. His philanthropies to Mount Sinai are well known; less so is the personal interest he took in deserving individuals who stood in need of assistance. He remained a hard worker until a few weeks before his death in 1941, and he brooked no laxity in fellow-members of the boards he directed, unequivocally reminding late-comers that it was a business meeting and not a social gathering.

A man of daring in business, and a highly successful banker, he was, like so many men of his kind, difficult to argue with, and had little

145

inclination to waste time listening to all sorts of stories. I had grown to know, however, from association with great collectors, that they often purposely adopted a negative attitude. They reasoned that should a man be keen enough about his subject, an unresponsive audience would not discourage him; it would rather make him extend himself to reinforce his position and convince his listener. This trait of the collector I sometimes found trying. It was not that these men doubted my word or good faith; it was simply that on that particular day at that particular moment, resentful perhaps at the thought of being believed a pushover, which none of them ever was, they had to be sold, even though the object in question might have interested them from the start.

It was not easy, however, to persist when faced by men of this caliber, especially when the tone of voice and its implied finality offered so little encouragement. Because their collecting was a diversion and a pleasure, rather than a business, I think they sometimes took an especial joy in applying these tactics to art matters. I still recall vividly an encounter of this kind with George Blumenthal.

It was in connection with a superb French Gothic marble sculpture of the 14th century which I had succeeded in acquiring from a German museum only after many months of negotiation and a number of journeys, involving a great deal of time, patience, and expense. The piece had just arrived in the United States, and the risks of transport across the ocean for so fragile a thing had added their share of anxiety to the considerable nervous energy already expended. Moreover, it was an acquisition which not only filled me with pride, but was a work of art about which I was personally enthusiastic. Thus, it was definitely a shock when George Blumenthal, to whom I showed it first, told me rather brusquely that he would not be interested, as he did not think it would add much to his collection. I was so unprepared for this answer, and so hurt (it was like having a dearly beloved child slighted) that I answered rather sharply. I, of course, regretted it at once, for not only did I value his friendship highly, but he was a much older man. I told him that he certainly had nothing like it in his collection and, what was more, there was nothing like it in the Metropolitan. After further discussion, he somewhat grudgingly agreed to consider it, and did eventually buy it, not for himself but for the Museum. Several months later when paying a visit to the former Musée de Sculpture Comparée in the Trocadero (now called the

Musée des Monuments Français), I discovered, among the casts of great French monuments in that marvelous study collection, one of this very statue and with it the information that it had originally come from a church near Rheims. This, of course, added considerable interest to the statue, and when I reported it to George Blumenthal, he remembered our argument, and confessed that he had admired it immediately, but just wanted to see to what extent I was enthusiastic about it.

From the start, dealings between George Blumenthal and myself had been put on a simple basis—there was to be no bargaining. I would name a price at once, whether he had evinced an interest or not; should he be tempted and find the price justified, he would purchase it; if he thought it too high, he would leave it. I cannot recall a single instance in which there was any discussion about price, even though at times I had to admit that I might have paid too much for a certain object which I had been unable to resist.

Already in 1927, George Blumenthal had established a fund of a million dollars for the Metropolitan Museum, and in his will he left to that institution all the works of art in his collection which dated from before 1720. It had been his intention to bequeath his house, as it stood, to the museum, to be kept intact as an auxiliary branch. But his years of Trusteeship had given him a thorough understanding of the maintenance problems involved in the running of a modern museum, and he changed his mind. Instead, the house was ordered dismantled and sold for the benefit of the museum, with the patio, the *boiseries,* stained glass, and all such architectural features to be retained by the museum, and installed when and how it saw fit. Outside of a request that the collection be exhibited together for a few months, there were no restrictions placed on the museum's use of them, showing an understanding rare among such benefactors.

George Blumenthal was among the group of clients and old friends who lent from their collections to a major exhibition of religious art in the spring of 1927. Organized for the benefit of the Basilica of the Sacré Coeur in Paris and sponsored by Their Eminences Louis Cardinal Dubois, Archbishop of Paris, and Patrick Cardinal Hayes, Archbishop of New York, it was one of the most beautiful exhibitions we ever held. Among the treasured objects which contributed to its success was Arthur Sach's lovely 14th century *Annunciation* panel,

Clarence Mackay's beautiful Verrocchio *Madonna and Child* and great Mantegna *Adoration* which is now in the Metropolitan; and Mortimer Schiff, Harold Pratt, and Blumenthal lent their rarest tapestries and a stunning group of enamels. Among the sculptures, one of the most beautiful, a moving French Gothic stone head of the Sorrowing Christ, came not from one of the firm's old friends, but from a new one, Grenville L. Winthrop. I was especially touched at his decision to lend it because it was his firmly established policy never to lend to an exhibition.

Grenville Winthrop was one of a small group of collectors whom I have always classified in my mind as "perfectionists," using that word in its most complimentary sense. The first time I visited him, he was still living on East 37th Street, not far from the J. P. Morgan home. I had written to him, asking if I might call. His reply came within forty-eight hours and was written in longhand. During many years of a most pleasant relationship, neither I, personally, nor my firm ever received from him a typewritten note, although he was an exceedingly busy attorney. I understand that the Fogg Museum, to which he eventually left his collection, has a large file of correspondence from him, not one letter of which is typewritten. He was a gentleman of the old school and to him collecting was not a business matter, but a pleasure.

Beauty, perfection, and learning constituted the credo by which he collected. He was as fastidious about the matting and framing of his superb water colors and drawings and their appearance on his walls as he was about their quality. And he was indeed particular about this, for quality was his primary concern. I have never known a man quite like him. There was no field of art which failed to interest him. His knowledge embraced all countries and periods with a seemingly equal enthusiasm, yet I doubt if he ever bought a work of art solely because he himself liked it; each was destined to fill a lacuna in a sequence essentially pertinent to a specific school or artist. He was by no means cold to the beauty and humanity of great works of art. It was rather that he collected with a rare combination of aesthetic and didactic purpose. From an educational point of view, his collection constitutes a unique ensemble of unique series, each composed of perfect and representative examples. I learned only much later that he had a definite goal and had gathered his treasures with the

148

intent of eventually presenting them to some great public institution.

In what field Grenville Winthrop began his collecting, I am not sure, but probably among the Italian primitives, some of which were not up to the standard of later acquisitions. I do know that the group of Blake water colors and drawings, the magnificent paintings and drawings by Ingres, unique in quality and number on this side of the ocean, as well as the series of paintings by Chasseriau and Bonington, two rare artists, were built up simultaneously. The first painting he purchased from my firm was a portrait of *Napoleon in Coronation Robes,* Jacques Louis David's preliminary study for the larger version, from the Wallace-Bagatelle Collection. He later added to his group of Ingres subjects the magnificent drawing of the *Family of Lucien Bonaparte.* The pedigree of the latter, by the way, is a fascinating attestation of the international character of works of art. My firm acquired this French drawing from a Danish client, who had chanced on it in a Swedish collection, whence it had come from its original owners, the family of the Italian architect, Charles Bonaparte Primoli. Now it has found its permanent home in an American museum.

When Winthrop moved to 81st Street, he organized his large house into a veritable private museum, but it was one in which students and art lovers were always welcome. The great surprise which he always reserved for the climax of a first tour was the collection of Pre-Raphaelite paintings, unequalled outside England and little known in this country. He took great delight in showing them, and one realized anew the high degree of knowledge and understanding of this extraordinary collector. With the Pre-Raphaelites as with the Blakes, the literary association was very important to him, for it rounded out a cultural pattern.

Current fashions in collecting carried no weight with Grenville Winthrop, though one might except the *Portrait of Choquet* by Renoir. Even this was only a half-exception, however, for in the background of the portrait is a painting by Delacroix, thus establishing a link with the past through the admiration of the great Impressionist for the great Romanticist—again teaching value. The fact that the works of a certain artist might temporarily be neglected failed to influence him. Witness his devotion to the almost forgotten Pre-Raphaelites and his acquisition from me of the luxuriously big and colorful Gustave Moreau which he proudly displayed on his stairway.

Nor could pressure be exerted. So much could be said in favor of a work of art, but no more. One could explain one's point of view as to its value to his collection, but if Greenville Winthrop's interest was not stirred by the object itself—and one could always tell—it was unwise to add another word. He knew precisely what he wanted and his taste and knowledge supported him abundantly.

CHAPTER XIII

Evolutions of the Twenties

M y visits to the United States in the early twenties had revealed a further evolution in collecting. The new trend was not only toward paintings in general, but more and more toward French paintings of the late 19th century, the Impressionists and Post-Impressionists and, in the mid-twenties, toward the contemporary movements, the Fauves, the Cubists, the whole School of Paris, with all its new and exciting creativity.

The trend had begun to manifest itself in both France and America before World War I. As early as 1910 some of the first-rank French collectors, not just youngsters whose immature enthusiasm might be held responsible for so radical a change, began to take an active interest in the so-called moderns. No less a collector than Jacques Doucet, the internationally known couturier who had spent several decades amassing a superb collection of French 18th century art objects, suddenly disposed of it at auction in 1912. The catalogue of the sale of paintings, drawings, sculptures, and furniture is still a guide to what is best in that period and a memorial to his exquisite taste. The news of the approaching auction caused a sensation in Paris and started all sorts of rumors about the reasons for it and what he intended to do with the reported two million dollars of profit. The public was not long left in doubt. Jacques Doucet, pillar of tradition, was buying "modern" paintings.

Further, just to make a clean sweep, he moved from his formal house with its beautiful old *boiseries,* to a newly built one in Neuilly which he decorated with his customary taste to fit the new collection. In the more traditional rooms on the ground floor he hung the Daumiers, Manets, Degases, Van Goghs, and Cézannes. Then he con-

structed a long gallery especially for the more important of the contemporaries, with the powerful *Demoiselles d'Avignon* of Picasso
occupying the place of honor on a small landing approach, set off by
a wrought-iron framework. In the gallery itself, the big *Charmeuse
de Serpents* of Douanier Rousseau held the center wall with the
smaller works ranged about it. Pierre Legrain, who designed the iron-
work, arranged the lighting and decorated the gallery, was by then
generally recognized as one of Paris's finest *artiste-decorateurs,*
thanks in large part to Doucet's unerring eye for young talent. In
Legrain's leaner days, Doucet had entrusted to him the binding of
his entire library. The exquisite results in tooled and gilded leathers
are now collector's items.

Thus, in one remarkable step, Jacques Doucet encompassed two
full cycles of the evolution of painting, from the Impressionists to the
Cubists. It was the more astounding if one considers that he was well
along in years; in fact, he died too soon to witness the full public acclaim and official recognition which came to the artists whose talents
he had so correctly gauged.

Nor was Doucet a solitary example. There was Count Isaac de
Camondo, whose collection, now in the Louvre, was somewhat flor-
idly described in a Paris art journal as a symphony, with French 18th
century as *allegro,* the medieval as *adagio,* the Orient as *scherzo,* and
the modern, "by turns feverish and dreamy," the finale. Still another case was that of Auguste Pellerin who began by assembling a
superb group of thirty paintings by Manet. Then, feeling that he
had outgrown his taste for this artist, who was still considered quite
advanced in many circles, Pellerin sold them in 1910 and began
to devote himself exclusively to Cézanne, at that time a most controversial artist.

These departures from the collecting traditions are particularly
startling if one understands at all the psychology of the Frenchman,
at once a conservative and a realist, an individualist and a traditionalist. Due to his background and education, he has a far greater interest
in the art of his proud past than in the art of his present. Revolutions
of this type were rare. France was actually sadly remiss in both public
and official recognition of her geniuses of the 19th and early 20th centuries. The examples of a Doucet, a Pellerin, or an Isaac de Camondo
do not prove the foresight of the French collector; they serve only to

point out how strong the new movements were in making headway even in France, essentially so conservative.

When the French today plead the impossibility of competing with American dollars to excuse the relative dearth of Impressionist and Post-Impressionist works in their public collections, they are anxious to forget the right of priority they actually had. In the years before World War I, when French collectors and French museums might have had these treasures almost for the asking, a small but persistent group of American collectors, actively aided and abetted by a smaller and even more persistent group of American artists, were purchasing the paintings which form the basis of the great American public collections of today. Mrs. Potter Palmer in Chicago and Mrs. Henry O. Havemeyer in New York, both spurred on by Mary Cassatt, already had made enviable collections of Impressionist paintings before the turn of the century, and they did not cease to buy during the ensuing years. John Quinn, the brilliant attorney, began his championship of contemporary artists and writers in the early years of the century. At his death in 1924, his collection contained some fifty Picassos, and it is thanks to his will that the Louvre has its only major work of Seurat, the great *Circus*. A. E. Gallatin and Walter Arensberg whose collections are now in the Philadelphia Museum; John T. Spalding in Boston; Frederic Clay Bartlett and Martin Ryerson in Chicago; Miss Katherine Dreier, who formed the Societé Anonyme in 1917, had already been buying for a number of years. The irascible Dr. Albert C. Barnes in Philadelphia, Duncan Phillips in Washington, and Miss Lillie P. Bliss whose collection was to form the nucleus of the Museum of Modern Art, all began their collecting before 1920, many before 1910.

If this roster is impressive, it should be remembered, lest we become too smug about American perceptivity, that these were the exceptions, truly the avant garde, and that there were degrees of daring even among them. Actually, in the evolution of collecting taste in the United States, the average buyer before 1914 did not venture far. A press note of 1910 announced that a group of "modern" paintings had been left to the Metropolitan Museum; they consisted entirely of works by Barbizon painters and 19th century academicians. Daumier was perhaps eligible to the slightly less conventional collectors, along with the romanticists, Delacroix and Géricault, or even the realist,

Courbet (Mrs. Havemeyer acquired the two great nudes of the Metropolitan in the 1890's). Boudin and Manet were still more advanced, while the typical Impressionists—Monet, Sisley, and Pissarro—were positively daring, though a Monet exhibition at Durand-Ruel in 1910 was a definite success. From there it was not too difficult a step to Renoir (but not the late ones) and Degas, but a new barrier was raised before Cézanne, Lautrec (largely on the grounds of subject), Gauguin, Van Gogh, and Seurat. The Carnegie International of 1911, the Fifteenth, contained not a single Post-Impressionist, no Picasso, and no Matisse.

The great landmark for the introduction of the Post-Impressionists and the 20th century French artists to the American public was, of course, the fabled Armory Show of 1913, undoubtedly one of the most exciting events in the annals of art history. Yet, despite the tremendous crowds, the enormous publicity, and the profound influence it had on the future of American artistic production, there was still a large segment of the public, not to mention the critics, who remained unconvinced, even about Impressionism, much less the later movements. An exhibition of Post-Impressionist paintings at the Metropolitan Museum in 1921, prompted by the prodding of John Quinn, Mrs. Havemeyer, and Miss Bliss, who lent most of the paintings, drew an excellent audience, but also critical letters to the press about degenerate art and Bolshevik propaganda.

During the next twenty years it was a sort of relay race as the leaders of the succeeding movements were recognized one by one, not so much for their own achievements, but because each in turn looked gentle and conservative beside the succeeding revolution of style and color. If the tempo quickened in the forties and fifties and public taste has come more nearly abreast of artistic creation, there are still today collectors who acquire only contemporary paintings of a certain traditionalism and who have considerable difficulty adjusting to the great abstract paintings of forty years ago, the Picassos and Braques of 1910 to 1912, for instance.

Nor can the dealers claim a much better record of pre-1914 conviction. If in Paris the Impressionists had their Durand-Ruel, the Post-Impressionists their Vollard, and the Cubists their Kahnweiler, these were the exceptions. By 1914 there was a lively international market for the Impressionists and Post-Impressionists (the German dealers and collectors were particularly active), but there was still only a handful of galleries where one could see or buy works by the younger men of the new movements. London had its first exhibition of Post-Impressionists at the Grafton Gallery in 1910. In New York there had been sporadic exhibitions of both Impressionists and Post-Impressionists and one could see representative works at a number of galleries, but until the Armory Show, Alfred Stieglitz's Photo-Secession Gallery was almost the sole exhibitor of the more revolutionary movements of the 20th century. From then on the pattern of the dealer's interest followed much the same evolution as that of the collector—sometimes leading, sometimes following—with the early believers making the pioneer efforts and the rest joining the procession as they conquered their conservatism and were genuinely converted or as they realized the potential of the rapidly growing demand.

My personal introduction to the so-called modern art came, curiously enough, through the family dentist, who was Dr. Georges Viau. His office, like that of most French professional men, was in his home. As a youngster awaiting my turn, I could take my mind off the unpleasant moments ahead by studying the Manets, Degases, Renoirs, and Cézannes which lined the walls of his waiting room. While I admired them tremendously, I would have been much astonished to be told that twenty-odd years later I would be the purchaser of a number of fine paintings from the estate of this great collector. I also had access to the collection of Count Isaac de Camondo, where I could admire the Manets, the Monets, and the superb Degases which are now at the Jeu de Paume. As for the controversial younger artists, the Fauves and the Cubists, I was only thirteen when Picasso painted *Les Demoiselles d'Avignon,* often called the first Cubist painting. When he and Braque were turning out their beautiful almost monochromatic abstractions of the 1910–1912 period, I was collecting photographs of the 19th century minor academicians. If I heard of Picasso, Braque, and Matisse or saw any of their work in the years before World War I, they made absolutely no impression on me. It was only after the war that I began to take a serious interest in either the Impressionists or their successors, an interest in part stimulated by the beautiful series of seventy-one Degases which my father had bought in the sales of the *Atelier Degas* in 1918. The results when he put them up at auction in New York through the American Art Association in January, 1921, were not such as to encourage him further along this line. The sale was not a financial triumph although the collection contained such important paintings as *La Fille de Jepthé* which is now in the Smith College Museum and the beautiful early *Mlle. Fiocre dans le ballet de "La Source"* in the Brooklyn Museum. Nevertheless, my own interest was growing, and I spent as much time as I could at exhibitions and in increasing my knowledge of the field.

When, in 1926, the New York firm was obliged to seek new quarters because the E. H. Harriman house at 705 Fifth Avenue was to be razed to make way for an office building, the house we took at 3 East 51st Street was large enough to give us display rooms for a variety of periods. I determined to enter the fray on the side of the moderns. However, the tradition of the firm had always rested on the art of the past and since other members of the family, still silent partners, were opposed to any change in this policy, I decided to set up a separate organization on my own for this purpose. The new company, entirely financed by my personal funds, was incorporated as De Hauke & Company and headed by Cesar M. de Hauke, then a young man who had come into the firm through his friendship with my cousin, René. De Hauke had (and still has) very real interest in modern art and excellent taste, of which I had seen convincing evidence in the works he had chosen for his Paris home. The devotion he brought to his task was a great factor in the success of the new venture, for succeed it did, to such a point that the doubters of the family withdrew their opposition to modern painting. Within a few years De Hauke & Company was integrated into the New York firm of Jacques Seligmann & Company.

We began at once to buy and to exhibit the "new" art. Two exhibitions held in 1927 included the whole roster of French paintings of the late 19th and early 20th centuries from Manet to Matisse. In April, 1928, we held the first American exhibition of paintings by Pierre Bonnard. In 1929, we were the first gallery in the United States to hold a major showing of the works of Modigliani.

We were all, my cousin, René, and my associates, Cesar de Hauke, Clyfford Trevor, Hans Waegen, and Robert Leylan, comparatively young men who shared an enthusiasm for pioneering, but it was not yet upon modern art that the firm could depend for its profits. We continued to be active in the fields which had made the firm's name, except that paintings began to bulk larger and larger in the inven-

156

tory and gradually to account for a bigger percentage of the profits. Before long we could boast a painting inventory which ran from 15th century primitives through Bellini, Titian, Fragonard, Raeburn, David, Ingres, Delacroix, and Boudin, to Renoir, Cézanne, Van Gogh, and Seurat.

CHAPTER XIV

The Unreal Years—the 1920's and the Aftermath

The decade of the 1920's with its frenetic political, social and economic movements, affecting the art world no less than any other, will always have an unreal quality for me. This unreality first began to manifest itself in the economic life of Europe, where, in spite of the monstrous destruction of wealth and manpower during World War I and the heavy taxation which followed it, in spite of the slow but steady flow of gold to America and the loss of the immense markets which had been represented by Russia, Germany, and Austria, the West had somehow managed to talk itself into a transitory, abnormal prosperity. It was a prosperity based on speculation, with all its attendant evils of false value.

The first wave of speculation had come with the war itself, engineered by men, largely from the so-called neutrals, who sold arms and food to the belligerents indiscriminately. Then this first greedy crew was displaced in the twenties by a second lot who, in their turn, waxed fat on the manipulation of the fluctuating postwar currencies. They brought problems to the art world for which it was wholly unprepared, chief among them being a completely new type of client. For the first time we found coming to Sagan men whose names and faces were unknown to us, a situation hitherto rare in our business, where a man is usually well-known in some other activity before he becomes a collector. Moreover, few of these newcomers were genuine art lovers; they were buying works of art purely as a speculative venture.

The Unreal Years—the 1920's and the Aftermath

There is nothing reprehensible about buying works of art to hold for an anticipated rise in price, if this is based on an expected enhancement in the value of the object itself or on a belief in the general betterment of business conditions. In Europe during the twenties, however, such deals were only too often premised on out-and-out currency speculation, involving deferred payments to be made after a predicted, or maneuvered, currency devaluation. We learned about this variety of swindle through the collapse of several German art dealers whose vaunted big deals turned out to have been based on installment payments to be made in marks. By the time payment was received, the mark had lost its value, and the German dealer had lost his works of art—and often his business.

The French had at first considered the rapid drop in the value of the mark as only a natural outcome of the war. It was not until later, too late for some, that it became plain that the devaluation was encouraged, even purposely and willfully managed, by the Germans in power. By selling its marks abroad, Germany fraudulently acquired foreign currencies, and simultaneously depreciated her internal debt, war bonds, pensions, and the like, at the cost of ruin for her own people as well as for foreign investors. Before the French really grasped the full implications of the fall of the mark, it became apparent that the franc, which had already lost much of its 1914 value through the outflow of gold and an enormous foreign debt, was also dropping in the international money market at a faster-than-reasonable rate. The world speculators, whose appetites had been whetted on the mark, were now gnawing at the franc.

The principal raider of the franc was rumored to be a huge syndicate headed by Fritz Mannheimer, a German, whose meteoric career was extraordinarily brilliant, if not exactly exemplary. After a splendid record as a law student, Mannheimer had entered the banking business in Paris where he proved himself so able that, upon his return to Germany in 1914, he was sent by the Reichsbank to Amsterdam in neutral Holland. After the war, he became associated with the highly respected firm of Mendelssohn & Company, where his acumen and dynamism quickly gained him a partnership and the direction of that firm's Amsterdam branch. Under his influence, the old firm lost its conservative character and several partners resigned, leaving Mannheimer in full control. The Amsterdam office then became headquarters for a quasi-official organization, whose activities were condoned,

159

if not encouraged, by the German minister of finance, in charge of selling marks short. The success of this operation led to raids on the franc and, no doubt, on other shaky currencies.

The staggering returns from these activities enabled Fritz Mannheimer to indulge lavishly in his avocation, the collecting of works of art. His taste ran chiefly to objets d'art of the Renaissance and to Dutch paintings, which he had ample opportunity and funds to acquire in Holland, but he also owned some excellent Gothic tapestries, superb Dresden porcelains, and a sprinkling of French 18th century paintings and drawings. Whatever his moral sense, Mannheimer had a real love and understanding of the objects he chose.

Mannheimer was not a client of my firm, but we did have an experience with a member of his syndicate which is amusing, if only in retrospect. On my return from New York in the late summer of 1926, I was met at the Paris station by my cousin, René, and my associate Albert Meyer, both much concerned about the visit the day before from a Herr Drucker of Vienna. Drucker had spent several hours looking at a considerable list of works of art and then had made an offer for the whole lot, an offer which Meyer would have accepted under ordinary circumstances, as it was close to the total of the individual prices quoted. Drucker, however, was completely unknown to us and the offer, in francs, had been rather vague as to terms of payment. In view, therefore, of my imminent arrival, the deal had been left open and Drucker was told that as soon as Meyer had conferred with me, he would hear from us.

Rumors had already reached me of the colossal pressure being brought on the French franc, and I immediately told Meyer that I did not care much for Drucker's offer. On the other hand, it involved an important sum which we could not turn down without trying, at least, to conclude the deal with the necessary protection against a further decline of the franc. Above all, of course, we would not give a bill of sale to Drucker until the terms of payment had been satisfactorily settled. Such precautions had heretofore been completely unknown to us.

We drove straight from the station to the Ritz where the manager, an old friend, told us that Drucker, of whom he knew little, had been occupying one of the most luxurious suites and had paid his bills promptly; but he had left, unexpectedly, a few hours before for Vienna. He had left a note for Albert Meyer advising him that he

160

could be reached at the Hotel Imperial in Vienna, if necessary, but would be back within four or five days at the Ritz in any event. Ordinarily, the matter would simply have been tabled to await Drucker's return, but two of the most valuable items he had chosen were also among those I intended showing to an important New York collector due to arrive shortly. Obviously, I could not do so while the Drucker deal hung fire, so this uncertainty, coupled with our natural interest in a major sale, influenced us to go to Vienna. On arrival, we went immediately to the Hotel Imperial and announced ourselves. Much to our annoyance, word came down through a secretary that Drucker was extremely sorry but, because of the press of business, he could not receive us. He would be back in Paris within two or three days, and meanwhile we were, of course, free to reject his offer. Which seemed to be that, for the moment anyway.

As we stood in the lobby discussing this development, our attention was caught by a group of men who emerged from the elevator, talking earnestly together. We recognized Fritz Mannheimer as the center of the group, but attached no particular significance to the incident since we had understood Drucker to be associated with him. As for us there seemed to be nothing to do but return to Paris.

Back on the train, sitting somewhat glumly in the dining car after crossing the French border, we noted a group of excited Frenchmen talking and gesticulating at once. In the hubbub, I could not gather what they were discussing, only that it must be momentous. There was an unmistakable air of stirring public events about them, so we stopped one of them and inquired what it was all about.

"Don't you know, haven't you seen the papers? Poincaré has caught the shorts. The franc went up fifteen points in a few hours last night and is still advancing."

Albert Meyer and I looked at each other; we needed no further explanation. Not only did we never hear from Drucker again, he never returned to Paris and seemed, even in Vienna, to have disappeared as swiftly as he had come. He was a victim of Poincaré's stabilization of the franc in 1926, which settled at about twenty-five to the dollar; it was fifty-three when Drucker just dropped in.

Later in the thirties when even solidly based firms could no longer weather the storm, Fritz Mannheimer's firm, Mendelssohn & Company, geared to a bull market and unprepared for the inevitable reversal, went under with a mighty crash. I understand that its creditors were later substantially reimbursed, but Mannheimer himself committed suicide in 1939 just two days before the outbreak of World War II.

The Drucker incident is worth telling largely for what it reveals of conditions about which, up to that point, my firm had known little. Other similar occurrences were to come, and for a while we looked upon every newcomer with a certain suspicion. Ivar Kreuger, the Swedish match king, also committed suicide, in Paris in 1932, after having spent a sizable part of his fortune on works of art. I feel fortunate in never having known or done business with him.

Alfred Lowenstein of Brussels, whose activities were similarly connected with money manipulation, we did do business with, however. His sumptuous house in Brussels contained beautiful things, among them the famous set of Beauvais tapestry chairs and hangings after designs of Casanova from the Wallace-Bagatelle Collection, the only complete such set I have ever known. His paintings, drawings, and water colors, including several by Fragonard, were of equally high standard. In true European taste, there was a homogeneity in his house and its scale, with the furniture, the high candelabra on pedestals flanking the tapestries, the clocks and mounted vases on the mantelpieces, all enhancing one another to the advantage of the whole. Lowenstein, too, ended his own life, by the rather spectacular expedient of leaping from his private plane into the English channel.

A third wave of new fortunes, which began in the twenties and reached its peak in the thirties, was based not on speculation in money, but, equally unpalatable to the French, upon speculation in a future war and the rearmament program of Germany. To it belonged Ottmar Strauss and Otto Wolff who, like Hugo Stines and his son, had established huge cartels of coal and steel and had built great houses along the Rhine. Among these men, certainly the most striking personality I encountered was the steel magnate, Fritz Thyssen.

I recall vividly his first visit to Sagan in 1928. His name meant little to me then, but I remarked quickly that he understood a good deal about art and particularly about French art of the 18th century. In fact, I truly believe that he is the only German I ever knew who gauged that period according to its true merit, seeing in it the grandeur, the elegance, and the balance which are its basic characteristics, rather than mere prettiness and sensuality. Thyssen looked at a number of objects with interest and after some discussion, decided upon

162

the purchase of a painting by Fragonard and a delightful small canvas by Boilly, representing a little girl carrying her baby brother on her shoulders. The Fragonard, by the way, was the charming small version of the *Dîtes, donc, s'il vous plaît* which Baron Edmond de Rothschild rejected because of its varnish smell.

Our business concluded, and the day pleasant, I suggested that he stop for a cup of tea on the terrace, for I was interested in what was going on in Germany. I was also curious about this obviously cultured and well-informed individual. Thyssen accepted and, sensing my interest, developed in leisurely fashion his ideas about the necessity of re-educating the German masses, especially the young. It sounded rational and reasonable, without anything I could later connect with the horrors of the Hitler regime. That Fritz Thyssen contributed financially to the Hitler movement has been established beyond doubt. How much of it was done willingly, and to what extent he actually shared in the extreme views of Nazism, are questions I cannot answer. I have always felt that it must have gone against his inner feelings and against his background of education and refinement.

Ten years later, in 1938, after Hitler had been unmistakably revealed for what he was, I wrote to Thyssen about the Mortimer L. Schiff collection, a part of which was coming up for sale in London. In his reply, which remained in the files of the Paris firm until they were destroyed, Thyssen deprecated the narrow-mindedness of Hitler and the savagery of a regime which would not allow him to take advantage of the exceptional opportunity offered by this sale. When one considers the dangers such a letter involved in Germany, where all mail was censored, it evidenced conviction and courage. Certainly I have no desire to depict this man as better than he was, nor to relieve him of responsibility for the earlier successes of Hitler which in turn meant increased activity for Thyssen's vast industries, but I doubt whether he foresaw or desired the war and the atrocities which followed. That was my one and only meeting with Fritz Thyssen, although he came to Sagan a number of times in my absence and invited me to call on him in Germany, but during those brief years when I still had any desire to set foot on German soil, something always prevented my seeing him.

Fortunately, the inter-war period also bred newcomers of constructive ability, and a new generation of hardworking businessmen-collectors grew up in every country—France, England, Switzerland, even in the short-lived independent states, such as Czechoslovakia, created by the Versailles Treaty. In Prague, for instance, the various members of the Petschek and Gellert families, with whom the firm entertained cordial personal and business relationships, developed into refined and discriminating collectors. I often wonder what has become of the sumptuous homes they built and furnished in the French 18th century manner and whether, behind the Iron Curtain, they still live and continue to collect.

One of the most interesting of the new French collectors was François Coty, who started with nothing and, during the early twenties, built up a great cosmetic industry. When he came to Sagan the first time, while my father was still alive, Coty had already acquired the charming house which had been George Kessler's in the Bois de Boulogne district and the lovely Pavilion of Madame du Barry at Louveciennes and was busy perfecting their arrangement in 18th century taste. To these he had now added the handsome Château du Puy d'Artigny at Montbazon on the Loire and there, in a vast room especially decorated for the purpose, he proposed to hang one of the most remarkable sets of gold and silver woven tapestries I have ever seen.

Unique is a word often too lightly used in the art world, but this set, which my father had bought from the estate of the late Baron de Hirsch, merits the adjective in its strictest sense. Contrary to the usual practice which allowed tapestry cartoons, even when made by great artists, to be repeated as long as they were in vogue and commissioned by any wealthy patron who fancied them, these were executed but once. They were a royal command—a gift to the Comte de Toulouse, natural son of Louis XIV, from his mother, the Marquise de Montespan. Designed by Berain, they were woven at Beauvais about 1703 for a particular room of the Hôtel de la Vrillière. Since the addition of gold and silver threads is essentially a technique of the Renaissance and was seldom used in the 17th and 18th centuries, this rich embellishment adds another touch of rarity to the set. The Comte de Toulouse, being a Grand Admiral of the Fleet, chose, appropriately, the Divinities of the Sea, Amphitrite, Venus, Eurus, and Thetis as the central motifs of the four hangings. The lower section of each represents the sea itself, and when hung low on the wall, the beholder has an illusion of being at water-level,

164

part of an exceptional seascape. This effect is heightened by wide borders of fanciful architecture or curious rocks, so that one has the further sense of being inside a grotto, looking out into the sparkling daylight. In the lower corners are coats-of-arms bearing the blazon of France and the *barre sinistre* of the bastard line, with anchors to denote the office of the Comte.

Whether François Coty ever actually hung them on the walls at Montbazon, I do not know. I hope he had that pleasure and satisfaction before misfortune caught up with him a few years later, for in matters purely aesthetic, he was a man of vision as well as great ambition.

Upon Coty's death and the sale of his collection, in 1936, the tapestries, curiously enough, returned once more to the great house for which they had been woven, the Hotel de la Vrillière, now the headquarters of the Banque de France.

In the United States during the same period, we had been going through our own particular brand of speculation, based on the belief that the stock market was a sure road to riches without work. As the decade drew to its close and the unreality of the economic structure began to make itself apparent, art prices fluctuated along with the stock market. The stabilizing factors which steadied the one were equally important for the other, and these factors had vanished. When the money market came down in crashing disaster, the art market also collapsed.

October 1929 is still too vivid in the minds of my generation to be recalled without shivers. For younger men who have grown up in the shadow of its economic effect but for whom the actuality is only legend, it must be difficult to conceive that we could drop from one day to the next, from a sky-is-the-limit economy into what appeared to be a bottomless abyss. Neither great nor small was spared—the bank president and the messenger boy who imitated him; the master of a great household and the butler who acted upon the tips garnered about his table; the difference was only in proportion. Respected names became involved in official investigations and others which had been synonymous with fortune and honor went down to ignominy and disgrace. Collectors of works of art were no exception.

For the art dealer, the credit side of the ledger soon had little meaning. If he borrowed against his accounts receivable or committed himself to purchase on the strength of them, he, too, was in immediate jeopardy. Added to these troubles of a type shared with all business-men, was one which is special to the art business. If circumstances oblige a collector to sell, he is astonished and hurt that the dealer does not jump at the chance to buy back (at a profit to the collector, of course) the object previously sold him. In boom times this might, in fact does, happen, but many a collector seems to feel that it should be equally true when the bottom drops out. The same collector may understand that no other capital asset can be sold under such terms, that a stock bought on a rising market must be sold at a loss on a falling one, even though it represents an enterprise which is as sound as ever; but for some inexplicable reason, he feels unable to apply the same logic to works of art.

In a way, of course, he is right. A fine work of art never "goes off the board" as did stocks in the early thirties; it always has a value. Nevertheless, the dealer who sold it was entitled to a profit on the risk he had taken; the purchaser meanwhile had the enjoyment of the object; and, more important, the same economic condition which forces the collector to sell, also affects the dealer.

A man of considerable means who had managed to hang on to a goodly share of his assets, but who like everyone was short on cash, had made a purchase from me in more prosperous days for which special terms of payment were arranged. The larger part had already been paid when he came to me, asking that I cancel the deal and take the painting back at what he had paid for it. With conditions as they were, and my own need to husband my cash, I could only refuse. He became so annoyed and so insistent that I finally offered, to show my good will, to buy the painting back at a slight loss to him. This he in turn refused and, moreover, he never forgave me. I learned later that he had wanted the money to invest in certain stocks then very low which he felt were bound to come back. In his mind there was no link between the one transaction and the other.

Nor was he the only one. Some were harder to refuse because I realized that they were really desperate. I remember well the despair on the face of a young and attractive Philadelphia woman, as she pleaded with me to take back several paintings which her husband had purchased a few weeks before the crash, and for which he had not yet paid. She told me that the mink coat she wore was one of their last assets; that they were closing their house, the servants had already been dismissed, and if I were to press my claim, it would ruin them. She added, of course, that they would be eternally grateful to me and as soon as conditions had straightened out, I would be the first dealer to whom they would return. We were able to work out some sort of arrangement, and they did resume their collecting some years later, but I have never seen either of them again.

One collector who owed my firm a considerable amount, committed suicide and a compromise had to be reached with his estate. Another entered into voluntary bankruptcy, and his account was settled in payments extending over a period of ten years. There were others whose actions were less honorable. My largest debtor claimed that his purchases had been made upon my recommendation and he held me responsible for the fact that he could neither pay for them nor sell them. What an easy way out for a man of mature years, a great manufacturer who owned a fine New York house and still had sufficient money to maintain it and to lavish jewels on his wife. In this case, there was no reason to give in and I did not, although I did have to agree to an extension of the payment period.

Thanks to my father's precept, I had neither borrowed nor pledged my credit to buy works of art during the seemingly endlessly rising market. I had limited my purchases that summer of 1929 rather strictly and so was able to weather the storm. Even more fortunately, there were still a few clients left like the great lady of Chicago who, to my astonishment, came in one day expressly to buy a painting which she knew I owned. "My stocks are bringing me nothing, my rental properties are eating themselves up," she explained. "My works of art are the only assets I own which I know will still have a value and the only investment worth making just now."

This is an attitude that is much less usual in America than in Europe where works of art have always been held in higher esteem from the standpoint of capital assets, and not just among collectors. During the depression, a group of Berlin bankers had been approached by a Viennese collector for a loan of considerable size, and he offered his works of art as collateral. Should an expert appraisal show their value to be near the amount requested, the loan would be made; should he fail to repay the debt within the period of the loan—which seemed altogether likely—his collection would be sold by the bank. I was called, not only to act as expert for the bankers, but, in the event of the collector's failure to repay the loan, as the prospective selling agent.

I had called upon this Viennese gentleman in happier times. His collection, which he had amassed in a relatively short time, had not impressed me to the extent of the millions of Renten marks (then the new German currency) he was seeking to borrow. Nevertheless, should the figures not be too far apart, the proposition was a tempting one, for my firm would have no investment to make and the publicity would be considerable. Furthermore, business was dull in Europe and worse in the United States. Yet could I conscientiously encourage a risky deal? On the other hand, if I turned it down, might not a less scrupulous competitor be glad to take it on, even though I had been assured in Berlin that the syndicate would either work with me or drop it?

It was a diversified collection, including well-known paintings by Rembrandt, several Tiepolos, Italian sculptures and bronzes, majolicas, tapestries, and some furniture. It was a case made to order for the training game that my father used to make me play: in a rapid survey of the whole to try to determine within minutes which works of art, qualitatively speaking, are the most important, those which bring an immediate reaction and stand out among the many. If the total value of these objects does not approximate the expected total figure, there is no need to go any further. Exceptional works of art are never difficult to sell, it is the average items in a collection which take time and effort and in the end seldom bring enough to balance the account. I had allowed myself two or three days to study the situation, but at the end of five or six hours, I knew the answer. I wired Berlin that I considered the business unacceptable to the syndicate and to my firm.

The bankers involved in the proposed loan were all successful, hard-headed businessmen, yet they did not hesitate to entertain the idea of accepting works of art as collateral for a business loan. Such a proposition would still be difficult, if not impossible, to put across in the United States. If in this case they turned down the loan, it was not because of the nature of the collateral, but because of its lack of quality.

CHAPTER XV

Moscow, 1928

The wild speculation of the twenties and the financial crises which beset individuals and governments alike in the depression had perhaps its most bizarre manifestation in the sale by a major country of its art masterpieces in order to obtain hard money. The country was the Soviet Union. In 1930, press reports, followed by official denials, told of the purchase by Andrew Mellon for two million dollars of great works from the Hermitage Museum in Leningrad. No matter what the circumstances, it was hard to believe that a government would part with treasures from its own national museum. When at last, in 1933, the sale was confirmed, I could only look back on my own role in the events that preceded that sale as the most exciting and most frustrating adventure of that whole strange period.

One day in Paris in the fall of 1927 I received a group of Russians representing what they termed a "commercial venture" controlled, naturally, by the Soviet Government. After considerable hedging, they finally came to the point: they were inviting me to go to Moscow where they hoped we might be able to work out a satisfactory deal. My firm had been approached first, they said, because of its pre-revolutionary reputation in Russia. Although I pressed for more specific information and further details, they remained vague. Plans were still incomplete, but they were sure that if I were interested in the works of art I would see in Moscow, a deal could certainly be arranged. I requested a few days to think over so unexpected a proposal, and they went away assuring me that should I accept, as they hoped, the matter of visas could be settled in no time, a matter of a fortnight at most. This was at a time when a visa to Russia, if issued at all, was delayed for months, as I assume it still can be.

Of course I was tremendously excited and curious, with visions before my eyes of the great works of art which I had seen in Russia years before. But as tempting as this new adventure sounded, I was very hesitant. Russia at that period was almost an unknown quantity, and the little I did know about it, I did not like. I knew from experience that the journey would be cold and uncomfortable. I was no longer eighteen and youthfully venturesome, and my schedule of travel between New York and Paris was already a heavy tax on my time and strength. However, I was duly conscious that no decision of mine would matter if the project were disapproved by the French government, so I decided to leave the whole matter in the hands of the Office of Foreign Affairs. A few hours after my talk with the Russians I was in conference with Philippe Berthelot, permanent secretary at the Quai d'Orsay with the rank of Ambassador, an old friend of my father, as well as a collector and art lover. He became quite excited and declared, "But, of course, you're going; you can't refuse. You know very well that the greatest collections of French 18th century art outside France are in Russia; it's a matter of tremendous interest to France. I shall give immediate instructions for your passports [my associate, Albert Meyer, was to accompany me if I went] and provide you with special letters to our Chargé d'Affaires there and the ambassadors along the way." Thus my mind was made up for me.

The political geography of the long ride to the Russian border was very different from that of 1911; new states had been created or re-activated—Estonia, Latvia, and Lithuania, and the Polish Corridor, which had to be crossed in sealed cars. When the train reached the Russian frontier, orders had evidently preceded us, for we were greeted like ambassadors. A pleasant young officer, with two men to carry our baggage, presented himself. We were passed through customs without formalities, our passports only glanced at. In no time at all, we were back in our train compartment, on our way as fast as a Russian train allowed. Whatever political changes we might find in Moscow, the Russian landscape was still as vast as I remembered it, the cold was as paralyzing, and so was the tedium of the journey.

When at long last we arrived in Moscow, we were conducted at once to rooms at the Hotel Savoy and there duly provided with an interpreter who would attend us throughout our stay. It was he who suggested that we would wish, of course, to visit the tomb of Lenin before going to our first appointment next morning. Far from "of course," nothing could actually have been further from our thoughts, but the waiting expectancy and the matter-of-fact manner of our guide left us in no doubt; this was accepted procedure, and we dared not refuse. Thus, we had the honor of descending into the mausoleum with the relieving guard for a private view, while a long line of shivering people waited patiently outside for admittance. It was indeed an impressive place in its solemn simplicity, for the original, rather bare, wooden structure had not yet been replaced by the grandiose shrine of today, and there was none of the pomp which has since, I understand, been added. Even the uniforms of the officer guards were as plain as those of privates. We were a little worried about what was expected of us, but our decision simply to doff our hats and stand at reverent attention was apparently the right one.

This ritual over, without faux pas on our part, we were conducted to an office for our appointment. After a few minutes of preliminary talk with a functionary, we were shown into a vast hall filled with rows of immense wooden trestle tables on which was spread the nationalized property of the revolution. It comprised, essentially, trinkets of a personal character—writing sets, toilet sets, and boxes of all sorts for snuff, cosmetics and a hundred uses, some of silver or silver-gilt, others set with stones or decorated with enamel. Here and there were a few works of art of mediocre quality. Initials, coats-of-arms, and crests on the majority of the objects would have made it easy to identify the previous owners, but this was no concern of ours.

I tried to make it clear to our cicerone that such personal items were of no interest to us, but I quickly realized that there was a gulf between us; to these people, fine metal and precious or semiprecious stones seemed of great value. And, indeed, they did, in the aggregate, represent a considerable amount of money; but they were not the class of object which we had come all the way to Russia to see. In spite of all my explanations, it took another two or three days of going over more of the same, literally thousands of items, before I finally told our guides, in terms which left no room for doubt, that unless they were willing to show us true works of art, we should return to Paris. As pleasant as their hospitality was, we were definitely wasting our time and theirs.

Finally, we were granted an interview with the Commissar in

charge, a cultivated and pleasant gentleman whose name I no longer recall, who asked me first in which language, French or English, both of which he spoke fluently, I preferred to converse. To my surprise, he proved to be remarkably well-posted on art questions, and when I expressed disappointment in the quality of the items we had seen, he countered by showing me reports of auction sales in New York and California where similar objects had obtained what he considered good prices. Though I am certain that he understood my point at once, he tried to argue his. The government was anxious, and rightly so, to dispose first of the lesser items, and only later, perhaps, of the important ones. Again and again I had to explain that my firm did not handle this type of material, and that he should deal directly with auction rooms.

Realizing at last that we were adamant, orders were given to have us shown the "Reserves," where I recognized immediately treasures I had seen in private collections on my previous Russian visit. Here were the type of things we had come to see—the paintings, the sculpture, the fine furniture, the precious objets d'art. At the same time it was made clear to us that showing them was not to be interpreted as expressing the Soviet government's willingness to part with them. One room was an extraordinary sight—a vast hall which gave the impression of being a great cave of ormolu and gilt-bronze, with stalactites and stalagmites of gold and crystal. Hanging from the ceiling, standing on the floor or on tables, was an incredible array of chandeliers and candelabra, small, large, or huge, all glittering, for they seemed to have been well cared for, with gilded ornament and glass or crystal pendants. Nor were the tables they stood on less resplendent, with ormolu ornaments and tops of marble, onyx, agate, or that vivid green malachite of which Russians are so fond.

We spent a few more days visiting these Reserves, and then had a final talk with the Commissar in which I, once again, made my point perfectly clear. If the fine objects in the great Reserves were not to be sold, there was no proposition I could make. I expressed our thanks for the many courtesies extended us: we had been taken through the sumptuous and formidable Kremlin, shown some of the building developments, and, most exciting, had been allowed to see a part of the fabulous Morosoff and Chtchoukine Collections of Impressionist and Post-Impressionist paintings. And we departed, feeling that the long journey had netted us little but an unusual experience.

172

In Paris, I reported to Philippe Berthelot the details of the trip and my disappointment at its outcome. Berthelot, however, was far from being as pessimistic as I. My visit, in his opinion, must have been just as disappointing to the Soviet government, since it had dashed their first hopes; but he believed they would come to my point of view later.

When I returned to Paris from New York the next spring, I again received a visit from the Soviet emissaries, with a proposition so staggering I could hardly take it in. They wanted me to take charge of the sale not only of all the works of art I had seen, but of all those we had not been shown. It would be up to me to plan all the arrangements. They were sure my terms would be agreeable to them, and as soon as I accepted, we would immediately sit down and work out the details.

When I had caught my breath, I expressed my pleasure at the confidence in me shown by the Soviet government, but tried to make two points clear at once: first, I had to receive the approval, official or unofficial, of the French government; and, second, in view of the tremendous number of items to be sold, it would be necessary to enlist the services of the Parisian auctioneers for a number of public sales. Since I was not an auctioneer, I could see no advantage to be gained by my intervention. They replied that they understood all this; I was to have a free hand to make whatever arrangements I deemed necessary, determine what to sell through my own firm and what to put up at public auction. It would even be up to me, they said, to decide the composition of the different *trainloads* and the order in which they would come. I was speechless. Again I had to ask for a couple of days to think things over, and, of course, to consult the Office of Foreign Affairs.

I rushed to Philippe Berthelot who was exasperated that I had not accepted forthwith. "Don't you see what it will mean for France," he began, "to be able to show these art treasures, many of which went directly to Russia from the artists' hands in the 18th century. The stupendous exhibitions you can organize, the visitors they will bring." His excitement was as great as mine. A couple of times I tried to interrupt, to point out the difficulty of protecting such nationalized works of art, as many of the original owners were still alive. He brushed this objection aside with, "We will do all that's necessary." He telephoned the *Jurisconsulte* of Foreign Affairs, introducing me by telephone, announcing my immediate visit, and emphasizing that everything possible should be done to make the plan a reality.

While France had recognized the Soviet government *de jure,* and exchanged ambassadors, in the fall of 1924, the long involved negotiations, concerning debts, trade, the rights of nationals, were still dragging on. Diplomatic relations had been particularly strained that winter and at one stage came near the breaking point.

It was decided in our case that affording official protection to the Soviet government offered too many diplomatic and legal difficulties. In 1928 there were a great many emigré Russians in France and just imagining the legal confusion as they all tried to make claim to their nationalized possessions must have given the *Jurisconsulte* a *crise de nerfs.* As recently as 1954, when works of Picasso were lent by the Soviet government to a Paris exhibition, Madame Chtchoukine charged that thirty-seven of the paintings had been confiscated from her father in 1918 and asked the French court to impound them pending legal action for recovery. The French court refused to take such action, but the nervous Soviet authorities nevertheless withdrew the paintings from the exhibition and hurried them to the Soviet embassy.

The *Jurisconsulte's* decision was a great disappointment both to Philippe Berthelot and to me, but my personal chagrin was somewhat tempered by the realization that I had been spared what would have been a nerve-wracking amount of work, lasting over a period of many months or even years. Later, as auction sales of Russian collections were announced in Germany and Austria and I began to hear rumors of fabulous private sales to some of the leading international art firms, I realized that I should have kept in touch with the Soviet authorities rather than let the entire matter drop.

From 1930 through 1932 a series of auctions took place in Berlin, in Leipzig, and at the Dorotheum in Vienna, sometimes under the name of a single former Russian collector-owner, sometimes with objects from several collections together. The first of these, in the spring of 1930, immediately set loose the rumor that not only were nationalized works of art being auctioned, but paintings from the Hermitage Museum in Leningrad were leaving Russia by private sale. Then the rumors became more specific, culminating in the one involving Andrew Mellon. A news item in *The New York Times* of September 25, 1930, carried an emphatic denial, first by the Soviet embassy, second by the unnamed dealer, and, third by Mr. Mellon. As no hint had been given me in my various interviews with Soviet officials of the possibility of selling Hermitage paintings, I was inclined to believe the denials.

The most spectacular of the auctions was that of the Stroganoff Collection in Berlin on May 12 and 13, 1931. The collection had been formed largely in the 18th century by Alexander Sergejevitsch Stroganoff and contained paintings and objets d'art of first quality. In spite of the withdrawal of several paintings, notably two fine Bouchers, because they did not reach the reserve prices, the sale brought more than half a million dollars—a large sum in the early days of the depression. Surviving members of the Stroganoff family attempted to stop the sale, but were unable to do so.

New York shared in the excitement when a syndicate of German dealers, operating under the name of the Import Antique Company, brought over a group of about five hundred minor objets d'art, which they had bought in Germany, for sale at public auction. The wide advertising of "property of the late Czar" provoked a court injunction to stop the sale on behalf of two of the Grand Duchesses, sisters of the Czar. This only effected a delay, however, since they failed to post the necessary $25,000 bond asked by the court pending legal action. The objects were of little importance and when the auction took place, a week or so later, the sales amounted to only some $69,000, according to the newspaper accounts.

In 1932, as the depression deepened and art prices dropped, the Soviet public sales began to taper off and I doubt that all of those contemplated took place, in view of the bad returns from the last few. Despite repeated denials, rumors continued, however, about important private sales of extremely valuable objects from the Hermitage. By 1931 it was common knowledge in the art trade, though officially unconfirmed, that paintings had been sold, most of them in the United States.

It must be pointed out that in selling paintings from the Hermitage, the Soviet government would not be disposing of confiscated or nationalized property of private citizens. While most of the objects had originally been Imperial property, the Hermitage had long been Russia's national museum. As such, the new regime had every legal, if perhaps not moral, right to dispose of them. Nevertheless, it was a shock to the art world when the news was finally confirmed, in the fall of 1933, that the Soviet government had sold some of its finest masterpieces. The sums, while large, could have been only a thumb in the dike of their financial crisis. Russia's loss was, of course, our gain. Twenty-one of the paintings were bought, through Knoedler & Company, by Andrew Mellon and are now a part of our own national treasure in the National Gallery in Washington, while the two famous Van Eyck panels went to the Metropolitan Museum.

While it is flattering to be considered of sufficient reputation as an art expert to be called upon by foreign governments, it can also have its uncomfortable aspects. In the early years of Mussolini's accession to power, when the world was still gauging his success in terms of the efficiency of his railroads, a lamentable ignorance of Italian politics led me unwittingly into a role I should have preferred not to play in one of Il Duce's minor dramas. I was approached one day by an Italian friend with a discreet inquiry as to whether I expected to be in Rome in the near future. The oblique approach is characteristic of the prospective seller of works of art, but I soon learned that where political ramifications are involved, it becomes even more acute. Since I made such trips practically on schedule, I could readily answer in the affirmative. My friend then indicated that his question was inspired by certain actions the new administration was contemplating in connection with a well-known collection. He did not wish to elaborate, but, if I were willing, I would be called on to act as art expert for the Italian government for an appropriate fee.

Naturally, I was interested, but respecting certain basic ethics, I insisted on knowing whose collection I was to judge and for what purpose. I did not wish to act against my conscience, either as expert or as a possible friend of the collector or those who might have advised him. It was here that my ignorance of Mussolini's methods led me astray. Although I was firmly assured that my opinion was sought only because the collection was coming to the Italian nation as a gift, I learned, too late, that the "gift" was actually a confiscation, collateral against a political fine imposed on the collector. Had I been told the truth, I should certainly have foregone this dubious honor. I had no wish to give even an indirect hand to the drastic policies of the Fascist government and certainly none to injure a collector who, while unknown to me personally, enjoyed a high reputation in the art world.

176

CHAPTER XVI

The Thirties, New York

It is interesting to consider, in retrospect, the evolutions that were taking place in the collector's taste while the art dealing world was struggling to keep itself alive in these worst years of the depression. The New York art market had never been more active than it was in the mid-twenties, when new fortunes were made. But the new money was too ephemeral to develop many true collectors. The lavish spending having brought a relaxation in standards of quality, the bad sold along with the good and the prices paid for mediocre works of art were as high as those paid a few years earlier for the best. No form of plastic art was unsalable in those free-spending days, but paintings nevertheless accounted for the bulk of the financial return, as higher prices were asked and received for everything from Italian primitives to English 18th century portraits, with the latter particularly expensive. When the 1929 crash came, even the most sought-after paintings, along with the sculptures, the coveted Sèvres porcelains, and the fine furniture, went begging in dealers' storerooms.

Then, as the economic picture brightened and life began to resume a more normal course, with former collectors or new ones in a position to pursue their hobbies, it was apparent that the interest had changed once more. The big demand was still for paintings, but not those of the same periods. Certain schools, the cherished English portrait, for example, once a fundamental of American tradition, suffered an almost total eclipse. Certain others began a slow recovery, but the collector demanded greater quality for his now hard-earned money, and the paintings of lesser merit fell into their proper perspective. As for the traditional decorative arts, they were almost as hard hit as English paintings. Tapestries which had sold for upwards of a hundred thousand dollars could not find American buyers at any price, as, in addition to the change of taste, both the old families and the newly rich had become apartment dwellers, relinquishing the spacious private dwellings to charitable and educational institutions, or to the wreckers.

But even paintings made only a dilatory recovery, with one remarkable exception. The new interest was in the works of the Impressionists and Post-Impressionists. Their prices had begun to rise in the years following World War I and though, of course, they had fallen in proportion to the rest, they now bounced back with alacrity and new vigor, to resume a steady upward climb toward today's vertiginous and almost frightening heights. Not only had the trend toward the "moderns" accelerated, but the demand for the almost-old-master Monets, Renoirs, Cézannes, and Van Goghs, was sweeping along in its train the whole roster of French contemporary artists. The public as a whole had, and to some extent still has, a tendency to catalogue everything since Impressionism under the general heading of Modern Art, and this is indeed an oversimplification of that complex series of new ideas which made early 20th century painting so exciting.

The firm of Seligmann, and its associate, De Hauke & Company, had already taken a stand for the late 19th and early 20th century works during the late twenties. Our first big exhibition of 1930 was planned for the autumn with a return engagement of the beautiful and colorful canvases of Pierre Bonnard. An extra dividend of its success was to be my acquaintance with that gentle and dedicated artist.

The firm owned a number of Bonnard's paintings, purchased in the open market, but in order to reveal his true talent to a public which knew little of him, it was necessary to obtain more. I particularly wanted to exhibit those canvases which Bonnard himself considered his best. Further, I was anxious to have the artist's official endorsement of the exhibition. So while it was still in the planning stage, I called upon him in his Paris studio. When I explained the purpose of my visit, Bonnard answered at once that I was, of course, free to act as I wished, but if I wanted his endorsement, he would insist upon my including the work of his two old friends, Vuillard and Roussel. I was decidedly taken aback, for while I am a great admirer of Vuillard's paintings, particularly of the period before 1905, I lacked enthusiasm for Roussel. Moreover, this had been intended as a one-man show and two more artists meant considerable added expense, not to mention work. Bonnard, however, was quietly and politely adamant in his loyalty. I finally had to agree to his condition and the exhibition was duly held as Bonnard, Vuillard, and Roussel.

When I asked Bonnard's advice about which paintings I should borrow from collectors and what prices should be asked for the few which would be available for sale, he answered that he really did not know. In the first place he did not know where his paintings were, and about prices he had no idea at all. Courteous and gentle as he was, it was evident that what he most wanted was for me to be on my way and let him get back to his painting. Painting was his passion and his sole interest. Recognition seemed to leave him thoroughly indifferent, and if he was flattered to learn that one of his works was in a famous collection in New York and another in Washington, he gave no inkling of it. He was one of the few truly dedicated artists of our time.

A few years later I made one of the firm's most important acquisitions in the field of modern art—two groups of paintings from the estate of the late Jacques Doucet, whose devotion to the contemporary artists had so startled Paris a few years earlier. My purchase consisted of two groups, one including the *Amateur d'Estampes* by Daumier and the famous *Irises* of Van Gogh, the other a fantastic array of Picassos. Among the Picassos were his epochal *Demoiselles d'Avignon,* a *Tête d'Harlequin* from his sensitive and delicate Blue Period, and a whole series of abstract compositions. For some years before Doucet's death in 1929 there had been a certain coolness between him and Picasso, for reasons I do not know. As a result, the artist had not seen any of the Doucet paintings in a good many years. Thinking that he might like to look at them again, particularly his great masterpiece of 1907, the *Demoiselles,* I sent him a note saying that the paintings would be at my Paris galleries on a certain date, if he cared to call. Picasso was there almost before they were unloaded from the truck.

He examined the *Demoiselles* with eagerness, remarked on its perfect condition and how well it had stood the test of time, both technically and as a key to the revolutionary movement it instituted. Then he went on to the rest of the group, all of which, with the exception

179

of the Blue Period head, belonged to the years between 1910 and 1914 when Cubism reached its most austere, classical, almost mono-chromatic style. Picasso had some interesting comment about each—when, and under what circumstances he had painted it, what his in-tention was—remembering them all perfectly with one exception, a small oval canvas in the typical white-through-browns-to-black range. He returned to that one several times in puzzlement.

By now the paintings were strewn about the room, leaning against walls or furniture, and Picasso sat down to contemplate quietly this exceptional assemblage of his early work. Suddenly, still bothered by the painting he could not place, he asked if he might turn it around. Without waiting for my reply, he jumped up and looked at the back of the canvas, exclaiming with satisfaction, "Aha, just as I thought; it's Braque!" There was no doubt about it, there on the back was the distinctive signature.

I offer this story respectfully to those whom I have heard claim an infallible ability to differentiate at once between the work of these two great artists in that particular period when they worked so closely together, a feat which I have often found difficult.

I have never had as much personal satisfaction from any other exhibitions as from the two Picasso showings which grew largely out of this Doucet purchase, the "Blue and Rose Period" in 1936 and the "Twenty Years in the Evolution of Picasso" in 1937, because they filled my galleries with the youth of the entire vicinity. Every day after school and all day Saturday, they came in swarms; some settled on the floor; others ran back and forth from one painting to another, and then back again to the first. They had to be put out with the lights at closing time. Picasso's work was certainly not unknown in New York at that time, but neither had he been recognized with the acclaim later accorded him. For many it was a rare opportunity to see paintings of which they had heard much but seen little.

The star of the 1937 exhibition was, of course, *Les Demoiselles d'Avignon* and it was with much satisfaction that we saw it go, at the close of the exhibition, to its new permanent home, the Museum of Modern Art. That pioneering institution, thanks to the persistence of a few courageous collectors, had opened its doors in November of 1929, despite the stock-market collapse. By 1932 it was forced to move to larger quarters to accommodate its growing collection and its mounting attendance. More remarkable, in exactly ten depression-ridden years, it prospered sufficiently to move into its own handsome new building. There is no doubt that the series of exhibitions which the museum held, the remarkable catalogues it issued, and the educational program it launched had much to do with the growth of public appreciation of the modern schools. I like to think that the art dealer, too, had a hand in it.

The art dealer, no less than the teaching institution and the museum, undertakes a program of public education when he plans an exhibition of a new artist, a new movement, or even a neglected artist or period of the past.

Among our contemporary exhibitions in the twenties was what might be described as a festival of French decorative arts. Much of the summer of 1925 was devoted to the selection in Paris, and it was late in the year before the shipments had arrived, cleared, and the exhibition set up in one of the large rooms in our building across from the St. Regis Hotel. The show was probably the most comprehensive to have been organized, including as it did the work of the talented Pierre Legrain, the master leather-worker and designer; Ruhlman and Leleu, the furniture makers; Puiforcat, Serrière, and Dunand, the silver and enamel craftsmen; and the rich and colorful glass of Marinot, as well as individually made creations of Lalique who had not yet turned to the more lucrative commercialization of his abilities. The exhibition was designed more as a museum display than a sales project, the beautiful objects being placed in glass cases to protect them from handling. The public was intrigued, anxious to see what new trend was arousing such interest, and it definitely was a succès d'estime, at least.

As is often true when a new phase of art is introduced, the financial return is likely to be more in the realm of future hopes than present reality. I would venture to say that it is rare for such exhibitions to pay actual expenses, much less the investment, within the period of the show. Beside the tangible costs of shipment, insurance, framing, advertising, and the publishing of a catalogue there are the intangibles. How can one put into figures the hours of research and correspondence involved, much less offset them against sales? The results, too, may be spread over a long period. The man who comes in today to buy a painting may do so as the result of an interest kindled at an exhibition five years earlier. To be willing to invest in the future this way, the dealer must have a complete conviction about what he is promoting. By the same token he offers the most convincing evidence of his faith in what he has to sell.

Some firms, of course, operate largely on a consignment basis; they do not own the works of art they show, but sell them on commission, thus limiting the risk. This has always been contrary to the Seligmann policy, instituted by my father and one which I have followed. Of course, like all good rules, one may make exceptions for reason. In general, however, the firm has bought outright the works of art which it has handled. In the twenties and thirties, few French artists had American representation, that is, a gallery which acted as exhibiting and selling agent. The paintings, drawings, or sculptures we showed were acquired on the open market either here or abroad. It was only when we went into the contemporary American field in the mid-thirties that we undertook to operate as artists' agent, something entirely new for us.

It had always been my belief that American art firms should encourage and promote American contemporary artists, and I had made several efforts along this line at Sagan in the twenties. The most ambitious was an unjuried Salon, sponsored by the American Ambassador, Myron T. Herrick, and open to all American artists working in Paris.

About 1935, due to the presence in my firm of a remarkable young woman, Theresa Parker, whose belief in and sympathy for the American artist has never wavered or diminished in the thirty-six years I have known her, the New York gallery began to represent a limited number of American artists.

There are certain fundamental differences between handling the art of the past and dealing with the production of living artists, the most basic, of course, being the fact that one now has the added responsibility of treating with a sentient, creative human being. The staff which works with the artist has a full-time job and the larger the roster represented, the larger the staff required. Exhibitions by living painters and sculptors involve not only all the detail of any other show, but more promotion and a whole new set of psychological concepts, requiring patience.

We then established certain rules. First, and most important, the Seligmann galleries could never, under any circumstances or at any price, be rented by an artist for the display of his work. This left us independent to choose only what we believed to have merit, a freedom which is lost if one rents. The second had to do with the expenses which are chargeable to the artist. These were to be only the extras which pertained immediately to the promotion of his work—advertising and invitations to special openings, for example—and should in no way reflect the general running expenses of the firm, which would come out of the firm's earned commissions just as those for other works of art come out of the profits.

If a firm is to handle traditional works of art and at the same time promote contemporary artists, doing justice to both, it must have the space to store two types of inventory and sufficient personnel to run two schedules of exhibitions. During the thirties, when the firm still occupied the large house at 3 East 51st Street, we had both the space and the personnel to present well-known American painters like Sidney Laufman, Louis Guglielmi, Hobson Pittman, and Julian Levi in their first New York one-man shows, exhibit the works of Picasso, Leger, or Juan Gris, and, in another part of the house, carry on the more traditional activities of the firm.

CHAPTER XVII

The Thirties, Paris

The crash of 1929 and the subsequent depression did not affect business in Paris to the same extent as in New York, nor did collecting undergo as drastic a change of interest. Certainly Europe suffered financially in the thirties, but there continued to be a more or less active art market even in the depths of the depression. As in the United States, paintings had become our most important items, with the modern schools gaining ground all the time. But France has never lost her taste for her own 18th century decorative arts, and French collectors have always tended to be more eclectic in their interests. The exhibitions we held in Paris, then, were of a more varied, if more traditional, kind than those in New York.

The more important ones, as in New York, usually benefited some worthy cause, with most of the works of art lent by public institutions and private collectors. Parisians love exhibitions; people strolled through the big rooms at Sagan as they would at a social function or a private museum, just to enjoy the works of art, rather than as clients. New Yorkers also feel free to attend showings in the same way, but it is unfortunate how often out-of-town people confess a certain timidity about attending an exhibition in a dealer's gallery, believing that only buyers are welcome. Nothing could be more mistaken, of course.

I was always particularly interested by the number of men in official position who attended the Paris exhibitions. They were keenly interested in art, if not from an aesthetic view, then from a historical and literary viewpoint. In 1930 we held an exhibition of the works of L. L. Boilly, who is not one of France's leading artists, but one of the best of the *petits maîtres*, a remarkable draftsman, and a refined

184

painter. He recorded one of the most colorful periods of French history, the Revolution and the quarter century or so which followed it, in anecdotes of wit and vivacity which are precious social documents and a veritable history of the city of Paris. Thus it was fitting that the exhibition should benefit the Amis du Musée Carnavalet, the museum dedicated to the past of Paris, and that its committee of organization should be headed by Francois Boucher, the museum's curator. The President of the Amis du Musée Carnavalet was Maréchal Lyautey, the great hero of Morocco, who in the last years of his life was still surrounded with the glamor of his exploits. Lyautey's arrival at the opening was one of the exhibition's high moments. Tall, slender, and with a splendid bearing, he wore his dress uniform with full decorations. Over it was the white wool burnous of the African spahis. Accompanying him was a full retinue of aides-de-camp, staff officers, and their elegantly attired wives.

Naturally, his identification with the exhibition drew a large army audience. Even without this incentive the number of military and political figures, including generals and ex-premiers, who dropped in to the Palais de Sagan had always impressed me. Our location was a convenient one, just halfway between the Invalides, general headquarters of the army, and the Ministry of Foreign Affairs and the Chamber of Deputies. General Gouraud, who had lost an arm in the battle of the Dardanelles and was now military governor of Paris, General Weygand of the French cavalry, Chief of Staff under Marshall Foch, Louis Barthou, who shared the fate of Alexander of Yugoslavia in Marseilles in 1934, Philippe Berthelot, permanent secretary of Foreign Affairs, and Edouard Herriot, the great Socialist leader, were frequent visitors. It was a particular pleasure to accompany Herriot, himself a collector, writer and historian, through such an exhibition as the Boilly. To him the paintings and drawings represented living history, and as he had recently published a book on Madame Recamier, he had witty and penetrating comments on the personages portrayed. The army men were naturally more interested in the military scenes, but here, too, I was impressed with the overall knowledge that these career soldiers had, not only of the history of their country, but of its literature and its art. Nor did they feel it unmanly or unmilitary to take an interest in the purely aesthetic.

The exhibition that certainly drew the biggest attendance of any in this period at Sagan was the beautiful display in 1931 of drawings by Jean-Honoré Fragonard, organized for the benefit of the Maison de Santé du Gardien de la Paix and inaugurated by the President of the Republic, Gaston Doumergue. Strangely, there never had been an exhibition entirely consecrated to the drawings of this remarkable artist, one of France's greatest. For that reason, and thanks to the official patronage, we were privileged to show for the first time since they left France in the 18th century, the wonderful Fragonard drawings from the Albertina in Vienna. Louis Réau, the distinguished French art historian, headed the organizing committee and wrote the preface to the catalogue, which opens in this delightful fashion:

"The idea of enrolling Frago, who has left the reputation of being a somewhat naughty citizen, for the profit of the Hospital of the Guardians of the Peace may seem at first an audacious paradox and even somewhat piquant. But benevolence knows no laws and has been accustomed to receive from all hands. Moreover, all those who have made the turn of the works of Fragonard know that this versatile Provençal, who seems to have as many guises as Proteus, did not confine himself to *scènes galantes* and, under the influence of Diderot and Jean-Jacques, changed himself at times into a teacher of the virtues."

Mme. Edgar Stern, the wife of one of the lenders to the exhibition, would have agreed with the first premise rather than the second. Edgar Stern, the banker-collector, occasionally enjoyed adding to his collection of drawings those which treated of the lighter moods of the 18th century. Madame Stern was a strait-laced woman of strict principles, and when he bought one it had to go immediately to his private quarters, for she would not allow him to hang it in the reception rooms of their elegant house on the avenue Montaigne. The Frago which he acquired, *Les Jets d'Eau,* was a subject so popular in its time that the artist had to repeat it three or four times. There is really nothing wanton or lustful about it; what harm is there, after all, in enjoying the sight of disheveled young women startled from their beds by the streams of water which their teasing swains are directing through a trap door? But it was not for Madame Stern.

Edgar Stern himself was an example par excellence of the collector of the old school whose knowledge, empirically founded, equaled that of the best experts in his chosen field, the French 18th century. He owned a truly superb collection of drawings and water colors, but his greatest pride was his gold-enameled snuffboxes, and he was inordinately choosy about them. His reactions were instantaneous, and if they were adverse, no words or outside opinion could convince him differently. His keen glance needed no magnifying glass to detect at once the smallest defect, and his fingers, as he felt the thickness of the box, could discover if any part had been re-enameled or if the inside had been reinforced to accommodate a later addition. All these small technical details he knew both instinctively and empirically; he saw and he felt simultaneously. He knew the markings, the *poinçons,* by heart and not only could say immediately whether the little gold box was French or foreign—many were made in Germany or Russia by French artists engaged at these courts—but he could also detect with ease whether it was Parisian or provincial, a more subtle problem.

His decisions to purchase or reject were usually made on the spot, though occasionally he might pocket one of the precious boxes to take home for comparison with others in his cabinet, in which case it was returned within a few hours or he sent a check.

Stern had been one of my father's oldest clients, and as a young man I learned much from their encounters, as they never ceased to argue about the relative merits of some of the little gold boxes which Stern already owned or new ones he was considering. My father always stood his ground, feeding the discussion with new arguments, and Edgar Stern, who could be quite witty, even sarcastic, seemed to thoroughly enjoy the give and take of opinion freely expressed.

When the exhibition of the Wallace-Bagatelle Collection was opened, Stern was among the first to see this wonderful array of 18th century treasures which even his sophisticated taste and natural scepticism could not resist. He acquired one of the chief prizes, Houdon's penetrating marble portrait of Sophie Arnould. Her greatest roles were from Rameau and Gluck and it is as *Iphigénie en Aulide* that Houdon has depicted her. This lovely marble portrait is now in the Louvre as a bequest of Edgar Stern.

The exhibition with which we chose to inaugurate our newly rebuilt gallery on the rue de la Paix in 1934 featured the portraits of J. A. D. Ingres whose influence spanned so many decades of French artistic production. To emphasize this aspect of his genius, the exhibition, "Ingres et ses Élèves," included a number of his pupils, Chasseriau,

187

Granet, and others whose names are scarcely known in the United
States, like Flandrin, Girodet-Trioson, Amaury-Duval, and Mottez.
Again, the Guardians of the Peace were the beneficiaries, with the
President of France, Albert Lebrun, doing the opening honors and
Paul Jamot, Curator of Paintings at the Louvre, heading the organiz-
ing committee. Jamot also wrote the preface to the catalogue, in the
same elegant style which makes his studies on his cherished favorites,
Poussin and the Brothers Le Nain, such a joy to read.

A member of the committee was another curator in the Painting
Department of the Louvre, Jean Guiffrey, who had followed his
illustrious father, Jules-Joseph Guiffrey, late Director of the Gobelins,
in choosing a career in the arts. I knew Jean Guiffrey first during my
student days at the Louvre. Later, he went to the Boston Museum of
Fine Arts as Director, where he remained for several years before
returning to the Louvre. He was an indefatigable worker who undertook the prodigious task of cataloguing the vast French drawing collection of the Louvre, a work not yet completed. He also compiled a
remarkable catalogue raisonné of P. P. Prud'hon which is still the
definitive work on that refined 19th century artist.

Guiffrey was genial and stimulating, and, though he was capable
of being brusque if the occasion warranted, he was a man to whom
one could talk frankly. It was to Guiffrey that I once posed a problem
which was occupying my mind at the moment. It was not a problem
in which I was personally concerned, but one which I felt involved a
principle vital to both the art dealer and the museum man. A dealer
in a European city was fortunate enough to discover an extremely
important painting by a rare master. The dealer was not particularly
well-known, but he had a keen eye and was a real connoisseur. Thus,
when he called the attention of a trustee of the national museum to
the painting, the trustee, himself a collector, immediately communi-
cated the news to the Director, along with the price quoted, which
was considerable. The Director and two of his curators examined the
painting at the dealer's gallery, were patently impressed, and asked
to have it sent to the museum for further study. The painting was of
a period and a country in which the museum was particularly rich
and about which its curators were the leading experts. It would be to
them, in fact, that a private collector or a lesser museum might appeal for information about the artist and for an authentication of one
of his canvases. Thus, when the Director of the national museum rec-

188

ommended the purchase and the dealer was paid, the fact that the invoice carried the customary "to the best of my knowledge" guarantee of authenticity was not of great weight to the officials. Their decision had been based on a judgment arrived at after weeks of study and hours of careful x-ray, ultraviolet, and infrared photographing, as well as microscopic examination of paint particles, in their own laboratories.

So the painting was duly hung in the permanent collection with the usual fanfare due an important new acquisition and was much admired by the public. Two or three months later, however, a visiting connoisseur expressed his doubt about the authorship of the painting. He did not question its period or its country of origin; but he did believe the painting to be by the hand of a pupil and not by the master himself. Consternation in the ranks; the authorities examined the painting anew, consulted further scholars, made further comparisons, and finally concurred in the new opinion. The painting was definitely by the hand of a pupil. Whereupon the museum officials returned to the dealer, requested him to take back his painting and to refund the purchase price. The dealer refused, and the museum promptly instituted suit. Now for the crux of my question: upon what grounds could the museum base its suit. Was there a fraud, a misrepresentation of facts? If so, what facts? These were the questions I posed to Guiffrey, asking him what he would have done in a similar situation. His answer was immediate and categoric—he would sue.

Then, I pursued, would it not be normal to infer that you endow the dealer with a certain omniscience? To say the least, you credit him with knowing more about this artist than the officials of the museum, that "the best of his knowledge" is better than the supposedly best knowledge of the specialists in the artist's work? Then upon whom are you going to call as final authority to decide in a court of justice who is right and who painted the picture?

I did not get the answer from Guiffrey, nor have I had a satisfactory one from anyone else. The case itself did not give it to me, for the war came along and I never knew whether it came to trial or whether the museum saw the possible traps involved and dropped the whole thing.

The fact that I could talk so freely and frankly with an official of the Louvre marked a considerable change in the climate of the art world. In earlier days a certain distance was always maintained between the French museum men and the trade, and dealers did not feel as free to consult with them as with the Germans or the Italians.

There has always been a sort of unwritten code, more or less strict and more or less official according to the country concerned, governing the actions of museum staff members toward the lay world, particularly toward the dealer. The basic idea is a sound one; the museum official, like Caesar's wife, must be above reproach and so regulate his behavior that at no time can he be charged with acting for personal profit or interest. In the past, however, especially in France, this sometimes reaches ridiculous proportions.

It is elementary that men in public positions should not put themselves under obligation, yet they should be credited with sufficient good sense and intelligence to dispense with an awkward convention. The mere fact that a man chooses a museum or scholarly career would seem to indicate a lack of preoccupation with money-making. Conversely, friendly relations with the trade may be of considerable benefit to a museum. A dealer often has advance information about collections which are to be sold, or knows of a collector who is in the mood to make a donation, or, more practically, is himself willing to assist in making possible an expensive purchase. For the dealer feels a personal pride in a museum collection which he is instrumental in augmenting. Art dealing is based on good faith and reputation, values which cannot be translated into dollars and cents. It would never occur to a reputable dealer to jeopardize these assets for the sake of one possible sale. The museum official who is as good a judge of men as he is of works of art knows this.

Quite aside from this strictly ethical problem, however, the general attitude of the scholarly world in France during the days of my youth was a somewhat stuffy one. Curators knew thoroughly the permanent collections of their own museums and knew the leading private collections throughout France almost as well. Therefore, they reasoned, or so it seemed, that they were already acquainted with all the capital works of art. If the dealers' discoveries were not already on their lists of known works, they could be of little importance. Italian and German scholars, on the other hand, were always eager to see what the art market had to offer and, in general, were more objective in their relationships with the trade.

To be strictly fair to the older generation in France, however, I must acknowledge that as far as the firm of Seligmann was concerned, there had also been a degree of animosity between my father and the museum officials. It stemmed from the fact that Jacques Seligmann was one of J. P. Morgan's most active agents, and it was held against him that he was thus helping to remove from France some of her greatest art treasures. It would have been more sporting of them, perhaps, to have tempered this resentment by recognizing that a number of Morgan's generous gestures toward the French museums were made directly at my father's suggestion, but it would also perhaps have been less human.

On the other hand, these same men were unfailingly helpful and kind to me during my student days at the Louvre, going out of their way to answer my questions and resolve my perplexities. None of them ever allowed any resentment they may have felt to color the professor-student relationship, and I owe much of my direct artistic education to them. Later, when the relation changed to dealer-museum official, I made every effort to maintain this rapport by always notifying the proper curator of any great work I acquired, whether in France itself or elsewhere, so that he might have first chance at it. Likewise, I abstained from bidding at public auctions if any indication were given me that the museum was interested in the same object I sought.

Happily, time has created a climate more propitious for personal relationships between French museum officials and the art dealers. The present generation of scholars and museum men (and women, itself a new development) has been through experiences which make the ivory tower seem less precious, teaching has become less rigid, and there is altogether a better understanding of the assistance which responsible art firms can give to scholarship.

CHAPTER XVIII

The European Scene

In time, as the United States demanded more of my attention, it became impossible for me to see personally all the clients who came to the Palais de Sagan. I did try to call on them as I traveled about Europe on the necessary buying trips. Purchasing was one function of the business which always remained strictly under my control, as in my father's day it had remained under his, and the travel afforded me an opportunity to see clients whom I might miss in Paris. In the course of the years, I made nearly as many circuits of the big European cities as I made trips across the Atlantic. There were few journeys at that time which could be made comfortably by plane (an exception was the Paris-London service, on which I could fly over in the morning and return the same day), so my trips were made by train or, more often, by car.

If I am still remembered by the older personnel of European hotels where I stopped frequently, chances are I am identified as the boss of Emmanuel, my chauffeur. Shortly after my discharge from the army, my father gave me an American army-surplus Cadillac. For some reason, war nerves, perhaps, I found myself quite incapable of driving again, though I had had a license since I was eighteen, and it was decided that I should hire a chauffeur. I specified that the applicants should be ex-soldiers and the first person to answer my advertisement turned out to be the tallest, broadest, blackest, handsomest Martiniquan I had ever seen. That was Emmanuel. I liked him on sight and, since his war record was excellent, I hired him at once, much to the annoyance of my father who was sure that we should all be murdered in our beds. There was never a more devoted employee. He drove the car as though it were a part of him and cared for it meticulously. He was a fine athlete, enormously strong, and when he appeared on the beach at some Riviera resort where I might be stopping, he was the cynosure of every feminine eye. He had a girl in every town we visited. I remember being a bit annoyed one morning in the south of France, when we were to make an early start for an urgent return to Paris, that Emmanuel had not come to my hotel room to fetch the bags. Upon descending, I found Emmanuel in the courtyard surrounded by four giggling girls, all of whom had arisen at five o'clock to come and bid him farewell. He eventually married an attractive and extremely nice French girl. Emmanuel, for all his superb physique, had the southerner's susceptible lungs, and he died, shortly before World War II, after a long bout with tuberculosis. During his service I owned a low-slung, very sporty Hispano, which I had bought as much to please Emmanuel as myself. I never see a dashing car of that kind without being reminded of him.

Whether by plane, train, or car, at least once each year I visited Berlin, Vienna, the Italian cities, and occasionally Spain, to buy and to call upon clients. It was my father's belief that it was indispensable to call upon a client in his own home surroundings if one is to understand him and eventually be of help to him, and my own experience has borne this out. It is particularly true in the beginning of a dealer-collector relationship and has advantages for both. It is easier to talk of art matters and exchange views outside the gallery where comments are less likely to be interpreted as arguments to effectuate a sale. In a business establishment, the new client may feel somewhat on the defensive (an attitude which gradually disappears as he gains confidence), but at home he is relaxed and better able to assess the knowledge and character of the dealer. The dealer, in turn, has a comprehensive view of his client's taste, what periods are apt to interest him or stimulate his curiosity; whether he is susceptible of being introduced to new periods which will augment and diversify his collection or is simply interested in what is fashionably in vogue at the moment.

The dealer may also find that he has the ungrateful task of re-educating the collector about what he already owns. To take an extreme example, one may find that the "masterpieces" which the collector has described are actually over-restored, embellished, or even out-and-out frauds, and one must tactfully disillusion him and show him where his mistake is, usually in the dangerous and costly game

193

of bargain hunting. With collectors of knowledge and long experience, a home call affords a more leisurely atmosphere for discussing new developments in collecting, exchanging views about what the collector owns, giving or asking an opinion.

Quite aside from business, my trips about Europe and the calls upon collectors were a liberal education in the sui-generis character of the collections of various nationalities. It has been to me one of the most interesting revelations of the art world. There are certain painters, certain types of sculpture, which will be found only in German collections, others which will appear only in French cabinets. Each collector will arbitrarily exclude other schools and artists, refusing stubbornly to recognize their merits.

One class of works of art always had an international appeal. The precious little objets d'art of the Middle Ages and the Renaissance— early ivories and enamels, small primitive paintings, jewels and painted enamels, majolicas, and miniature bronzes—were collected almost everywhere. Perfect examples are the Guelph Treasure and the Hesse-Darmstadt Collections of Germany and the Chalandon, Spitzer, Dormeuil, Rothschild, and a half-dozen other collections in France.

However, if one eliminates this common link it is often sufficient to read an old catalogue list to identify the nationality of its owner, with the possible exception of the English. England's amateurs have seldom been limited in their tastes, a trait engendered perhaps by their essentially international business interests. Were there not portraits of Napoleon in great English houses even when his name was anathema? The artistry of Jacques Louis David and Baron Gros outweighed the opprobrium of the subject. The collectors of the United States, too, have escaped narrow confines, due possibly to variety of background and a desire to escape from the constricting frontiers of old Europe.

France being the one country where every century has been blessed with the full bloom of artistic creation, it is surprising that no Frenchman, at least to my knowledge, has ever thought of building a collection which would reflect this constantly renewed evolution. Paintings earlier than the 15th century are perforce rare, but what aesthetic, intellectual, and didactic importance there would be in a series including panels or illuminated manuscript pages from that period, portraits of the 16th century and canvases from the sophisticated Fontainebleau school, great classic compositions of the 17th century, and so on to our own time. Instead—and I speak now in generalities for certainly there were brilliant exceptions—the average French collector preferred the productions of his own 18th century, with a tendency to include the less meritorious along with the best. He might add a sprinkling of earlier objects, and there might be paintings and drawings of the early 19th century, but these were often inherited rather than acquired.

The celebrated Camille Groult Collection is a good case in point. He was a collector who almost never strayed from the French 18th century and when he did, went only as far as England. Though English 18th-century paintings occupied an impressive amount of space in his home, not all of them had been chosen with the discrimination of their French counterparts. It is, of course, for his French drawings that his collection is best known, but his La Tour and Perronneau portraits, his Fragonards, his Moreau gouaches, and his splendid group of Hubert Robert panels were all first quality.

Camille Groult was of my father's day, and if I ever met him, I have no remembrance of it, but I did know the son, Jean Groult, who inherited his father's fortune and his collection. Though he genuinely enjoyed the inherited treasures, I believe he hardly ever added to them and even from time to time has parted with some. Groult was a strange man, pleasant and courteous, but jealous of his privacy to an almost absurd degree. The Groult house, at the corner of the Avenue Malakoff and the Avenue Foch just opposite Boni de Castellane's pink palace, was a Paris landmark, with lovely gardens extending the width of the block. He once told me of a threatened lawsuit by his immediate neighbors because he wished to raise his already high walls by a trellis so there would be no direct view of his house and garden. Curiously enough, he allowed the quiet and peace which he sought to be challenged by the raucous voices and the rutilant feathers of the parrots and peacocks which he kept about both house and gardens. He was fastidious in his person and extremely meticulous about many things. It was thus a real surprise to find his most precious Fragonard and Watteau drawings "displayed" on the floor, leaning against chairs and other pieces of furniture. He had a strong streak of economy which occasionally manifested itself in peculiar ways. One day I arrived at his home in a pouring rain, and was ushered into the large gallery where most of the English paintings hung. There in the middle of the floor was a huge pail collecting the water which dripped from the ceiling. It did not seem to affect him particularly. His only comment was to turn to the butler who had shown me in and say, in the mild tone of one who has repeated it often, that something really should be done about the roof.

In contrast to his attitude of seeming aloofness, he was always well-posted on the many rumors that circulated in the art world and took considerable pleasure in repeating them with a charming wit and an unexpected sense of humor. His desire for quiet and for anonymity was perhaps also inherited from his father. Camille Groult was one of the organizers of a scheme to furnish the Château de Bagatelle when it became an artistic monument. One of the ideas advanced was to solicit gifts of works of art and to name a room for the more generous donors. Groult is supposed to have said that if he knew his name would be given to a room where he had left his works of art, he would rather they were burned, and then added, "after my death."

German collections were strong in the so-called Little Masters of Holland, not always the best, and the Germans were the first outside Italy itself, England again excepted, to stress the Italian seicento and the mannerist artists. I remember my surprise at seeing paintings by Magnasco in Austrian private collections some forty years ago when his identity had barely been revealed. There was also among the Germans a wide and rather indiscriminate love for the more provincial primitive Teutonic paintings and wood sculptures. Strange that collectors otherwise showing great refinement should become engulfed in nationalistic feeling at the expense of quality. If there is a parallel in the emotional motivation of American collectors toward the cruder types of Americana, these are at least regarded more objectively, aesthetically speaking.

On the other hand, the Germans were among the first to recognize the importance of 19th century French painting, and their interest was not limited to the Impressionists and Post-Impressionists; it went back to Courbet and Delacroix. This German appreciation for the romanticist-realist phase of French painting undoubtedly had multiple roots reaching into the soil of romantic literature, philosophy, and social evolution. The mutual admiration of writers and artists of the romantic period—Goethe, Schiller, Hugo, Byron, Delacroix—is too

196

well known to require enlargement here. Courbet, of course, belongs to a younger generation, but his "realism" certainly owes much to the earlier romanticism.

I remember going with my father to call upon Dr. Georg Swarzenski, then director of the Staedelinstitut in Frankfurt, one of Germany's greatest museums, and how impressed I was to find that he, a foremost medievalist, also had an intense interest in modern art. In fact, he was also director of the Municipal Gallery and, as such, responsible for building Frankfurt's rich collection of Impressionist and Post-Impressionist paintings and sculpture at a time when this was almost pioneering. There was probably no greater scholar of the medieval period and the Dark Ages which preceded it than Dr. Swarzenski. Like many great thinkers, he had humility, and one of his most endearing traits was a complete absence of the professorial attitude. When Hitler's excesses drove him from his post in Frankfurt to the friendly shelter of a research fellowship at the Boston Museum, the late Dr. Harold Edgell declared him "the finest acquisition" he had ever made for the museum.

In Belgium and Holland, collectors have largely preferred their national art. I do not say this to belittle their collections, only to define them. Who could doubt, for instance, the value of the remarkable Flemish paintings of Emile Renders? There have been notable exceptions, however, of collectors whose interests were truly universal. The Adolphe Stoclets of Brussels, friends and clients of my father before me, reacted to a lovely object of no matter what period with instinctive recognition of the indefinables which make one work a masterpiece and another a mere artifact. Quality may sometimes express itself by what is left out, again by the inclusion of the tiniest accent; to convey it, the artist must be endowed with a God-given sensitivity; to recognize it the beholder must possess an equal God-given receptivity. The Stoclets had this.

I have known few people who knew as much about works of art, who reacted so electrically to quality, and to whom collecting was so much a part of their lives. It would be hard to say which of the two Stoclets was the more perceptive. They were always together at exhibitions, in the galleries, or traveling. At home one was as eager as the other to show their treasures to a sympathetic audience.

There was in the Stoclets a focusing of learning and empiricism; it was the tactile value of a work of art, be it sculptured or painted, to which they reacted first; even if one cannot stroke a painting, the highly sensitive eye transmits the sensation to the tips of the fingers. The obvious did not interest them; an object must leave something unsaid, must appeal to the imagination, which may explain their special love of Oriental art, and of the very early periods of the West. Theirs was a unique collection, encompassing all forms of aesthetic creation from the elemental to the sophisticated, irrespective of national origin. To house this highly diversified collection, they wisely built, around 1905, not a traditional house, but a beautifully designed contemporary one, carefully planned to provide a rich but simple background. Joseph Hoffmann of Vienna was the architect and the house is as perfect in its way as Camondo's Petit Trianon.

I had visited Mr. and Mrs. Stoclet in the course of my European travels before World War II but did not see them again until 1949. That summer I had no excuse for visiting Brussels, but so persistently did the thought of the Stoclets recur to me, that I telephoned one day and hastened to their home. The meeting proved all I had anticipated. They seemed as happy to see me and my wife, whom they had not met, as I was to see them. Although Aldolphe Stoclet was confined to a wheel chair, they were as eagerly interested as ever in the doings of the art world. The great exhibition of German treasures of the Middle Ages at the Musée des Beaux Arts was then in progress, and, despite Adolphe Stoclet's infirmity, the two had visited it several times and planned to go again. Their lovely home, except for the addition of a few more fine objects, remained unchanged, but one visit could afford only a fleeting glimpse of the beauties within immediate reach. I was afraid, too, of tiring them by an overlong stay, so plans were made to call again the following year.

When that same autumn I had occasion to write to their son concerning some books I had promised to send from New York, he replied with the sad news that his father had died two weeks after our visit, and that Mrs. Stoclet had followed him only a few days later.

As in the Low Countries, there have always been a few collectors of international repute among the Italians and Spaniards. José Lazaro de Galanda of Madrid, for instance, was a client and friend of my father, and his son spent his student days in Paris, often as a guest in our home. During the troubled years of the thirties, Lazaro himself occupied a large apartment in Paris and later came to New York where his distinguished figure, wrapped in the large cape which he

198

Plate 97
Roger de La Fresnaye (1885–1925). "Le Quatorze Juillet," 1914, 29" x 36¼". From the
Marcel Kapferer Collection, Paris. Acquired by J. Jerome Hill, Soda Springs, California, 1950.

Plate 98

Bartholomé Murillo (1618-1680) "Christ after the Flagellation," 44" x 58". From the collections of

Plate 99
Jacopo Tintoretto (1518–1594). "The Baptism of Christ," 5′ 8½″ x 8′ 3″. From the Arthur Sachs Collection, New York. Acquired by the Cleveland Museum of Art. Gift of Hanna Fund, 1950.

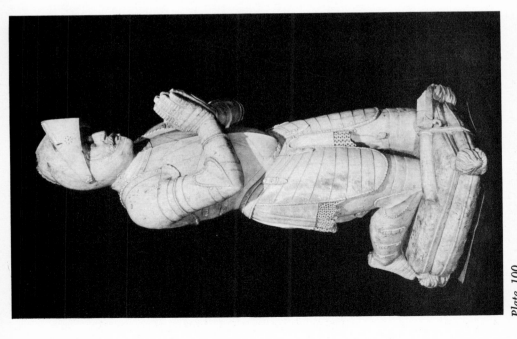

Plate 100
Pompeo Leoni (1533–1608). "Juan de Cardenas, Duke of Maqueda, and His Wife," marble, life-size. From the Church of San Juan Bautista, Maqueda. Purchased jointly with Raphael Stora, New York. Acquired by the Albright Art Gallery, Buffalo, 1948.

Plate 101
Germain Pilon (c. 1535–1590). "Saint Barbara," marble, 5′ 10½″. From the collections of Eugène Kraemer, Paris, and Baron R. de Gunzburg, Paris. Acquired by the Nelson Gallery-Atkins Museum, Kansas City, Missouri, Nelson Fund, 1949.

Plate 102
Jean-Honoré Fragonard (1732–1806). "Portrait of Hubert Robert," 25½″ x 21¼″. From the collections of Félix Doistau and Doctor Tuffier. Exhibited: "Chardin-Fragonard," Paris, 1907, #102; "Fragonard," Paris, Musée des Arts Decoratifs, 1921, #20; "Art Français," Amsterdam, Rijksmuseum, 1926, #51; "Portraits français," Paris, 1945, #44. Acquired by the Samuel H. Kress Foundation, 1952. Present collection: National Gallery of Art, Washington, D.C., Samuel H. Kress Collection, loan.

Plate 104b
Martin Schaffner (c. 1478/79–1549). "A Lady of the Schad von Mittelbiberach Family of Ulm," 1529, 38½″ x 29″. From the Rodolphe Kann Collection, Paris. Acquired by the Samuel H. Kress Foundation, 1957. Present collection: The Samuel H. Kress Collection in the Denver Art Museum.

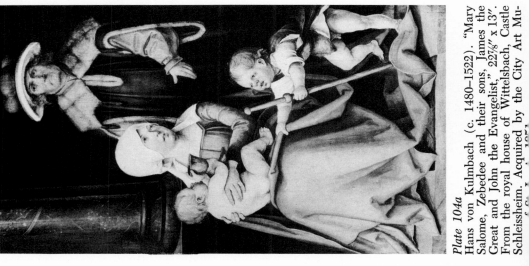

Plate 104a
Hans von Kulmbach (c. 1480–1522). "Mary Salome, Zebedee and their sons, James the Great and John the Evangelist," 22⅞″ x 13″. From the royal house of Wittelsbach, Castle Schleissheim. Acquired by the City Art Mu-

Andrea Mantegna (1431–1506). "Portrait of a Man," 9½″ x 7½″, possibly representing the Hungarian humanist Janus Pannonius. Acquired by the Samuel H. Kress Foundation, 1950. Present collection: National Gallery of Art, Washington, D.C., Samuel H. Kress Collection.

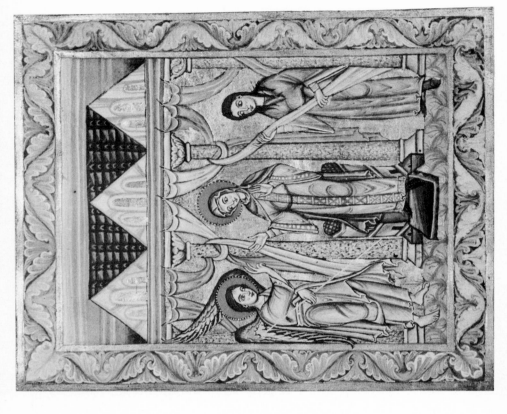

Plate 106a, b

German (Mainz), 11th century. "Three Marys at the Sepulcher" and "Annunciation," 10⅜" x 7½", two illuminations from a Missal. From the collection of the Dukes d'Arenberg, Brussels. Acquired by the Martin Bodmer Library, Geneva, 1952.

Plate 107
English, c. 1000. "St. John the Evangelist," 12″ x 7½″, illumination from a Manuscript of the Four
Gospels. From the collection of the Dukes d'Arenberg, Brussels. Acquired by the Pierpont Morgan
Library, New York, 1954 (M. 869).

Plate 108
J. A. D. Ingres (1780–1867). "Portrait of Dr. de France," 1811, 24″ x 19¾″. From the collections of Lucien Bonaparte, Prince de Canino, and the Duc de Trévise, Paris. Acquired by Emil Bührle, Zurich, 1955.

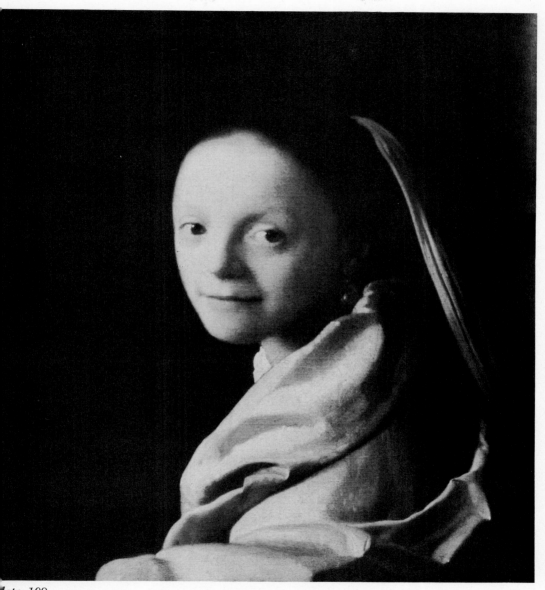

Plate 109

Jan Vermeer (1632–1675). "Portrait of a Young Girl," 17¾" x 15¾". From the collection of the Dukes d'Arenberg, Brussels. Acquired by Mr. and Mrs. Charles B. Wrightsman, New York, 1955.

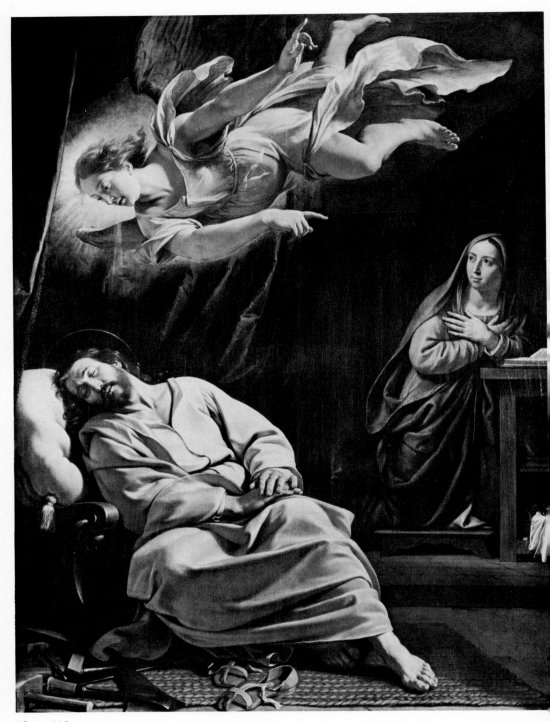

Plate 110
Philippe de Champaigne (1602–1674). "The Vision of Saint Joseph," 6′ 10″ x 5′ 1¾″. From th
Église des Minîmes, Paris, Cardinal Fesch, and Princess Ney de la Moskowa. Acquired by the N
tional Gallery, London, 1957. (Reproduced by courtesy of the Trustees.)

Plate 111
Camille Corot (1796–1875). "Judith," 1872, 41½" x 24½".
Collection: Mr. and Mrs. Germain Seligman, New York, 1943.

Plate 112
Kahlil Gibran (1922–   ). "The Voice in the Wilderness," welded iron, height 7'. Acquired by the Episcopal Academy, Philadelphia, 1958.

Plate 113
Rico Lebrun (1900–   ). "Crucifixion Triptych," central panel, 1950, overall dimensions
16′ x 26′. Acquired by Syracuse University, Syracuse, New York. Gift of the William C.
Whitney Foundation, Michael Straight, President, 1957.

Plate 114
Giovanni da Bologna (1524–1608). "Cupid," marble, height 29″. From the collection of the Ambassador G. Auriti, Rome. Acquired by the Samuel H. Kress Foundation, 1952. Present collection: The Samuel H. Kress Collection in the Seattle Art Museum.

Plate 115
Benedetto da Maiano (1442–1497). "Madonna and Child," marble, 22⅞" x 15¼". From the collection of the Prince of Liechtenstein, Vaduz. Acquired by the Samuel H. Kress Foundation, 1954. Present collection: National Gallery of Art, Washington, D.C., Samuel H. Kress Collection, loan.

Plate 116

Gustave Courbet (1819–1877). "La Grotte de la Loue," 3' 2½" x 4' 2½". Acquired by General Charles L. Lindemann, Washington, D.C., 1957. Present collection: National Gallery of Art, Washington, D.C. Gift of Charles L. Lindemann.

Eugène Delacroix (1798–1863). "Apollo Conquering the Serpent Python," first oil study for the ceiling of the Apollo Gallery of the Louvre, 1850, 21¾″ x 18″. From the collections of J. B. Faure, Duc de Trévise, and Marquis de Gramont. Collection: Mr. and Mrs. Germain Seligman, New York, 1957.

Plate 118b
Odilon Redon (1840–1916). "Saint Georges," pastel, 21¼" x 14¾".
From the collection of Mme André Bonger, Amsterdam. Ac-
quired by Dr. and Mrs. George F. Murphy, New York, 1957.

Plate 118a
Odilon Redon (1840–1916). "Le Calvaire," pastel, 27¼" x 20½".
From the collection of Mme André Bonger, Amsterdam. Acquired

Plate 119
Edgar Degas (1834–1917). "Danseuses au Foyer," 24″ x 19¾″. From the collection of Robert Treat Paine II, Boston. Acquired by Emil Bührle, Zurich, 1951.

Plate 120
Giovanni Battista Tiepolo (1696–1770). "The Meeting of Abraham and Melchizedek," drawing, 14⁹/₁₆" x 20¹/₁₆". Acquired by the Art Institute of Chicago, Carl O. Schniewind Memorial Fund, 1959.

Plate 121b
Emil Bührle (1890–1956), Zurich

Plate 121a
Leonard C. Hanna, Jr. (1890–1957), Cleveland

Plate 122
Bonino da Campione (1335?–1397). "Prudentia" (detail), marble, total height 26½". From th
collection of the Prince of Liechtenstein, Vaduz. Acquired by the Samuel H. Kress Foundatio
1954. Present collection: National Gallery of Art, Washington, D.C., Samuel H. Kress Collectio
loan.

Plate 123
Andrea Orcagna (active 1344–1368). "Angel with Tambourine," marble, height
21″. From the collection of the Prince of Liechtenstein, Vaduz. Acquired by the
Samuel H. Kress Foundation, 1954. Present collection: National Gallery of Art,
Washington, D.C., Samuel H. Kress Collection, loan.

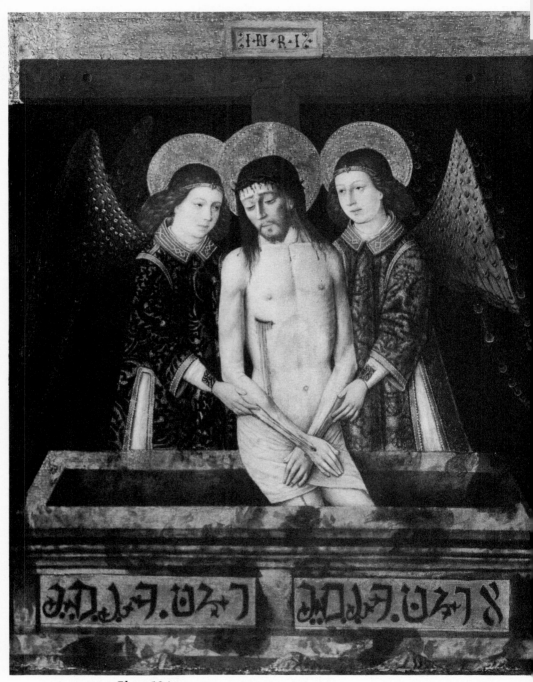

Plate 124
Franco-Spanish, 15th century. "Pieté Nostre Seigneur,"
c. 1425–1440, 24½″ x 17″. From the James W. Barney Collection, New York. Acquired by the Louvre, Paris, 1950.

Plate 125
French, 15th century. "Holy Trinity," c. 1475, 3′ 4½″ x 3′ 10½″. From the
collection of the Ambassador Camille Barrère, Rome. Acquired by the Cleveland Museum of Art, Mr. and Mrs. William H. Marlatt Collection, 1960.

Plate 126
French (Ile de France), c. 1300. "The Holy Trinity," marble, 28½″ x 13½″. Acquired by the Samuel H. Kress Foundation, 1953. Present collection: The Samuel H. Kress Collection in the Portland Art Museum.

Plate 127
French, c. 1530–1540. "Autumn," hard stone, height 4' 5½". From the Theodore Schiff Collection, Paris, with pendant, "Winter." Acquired by the Victoria and Albert Museum, London, 1959.

Plate 128
Simon Vouet (1590–1649). "Allegory of Peace," 7′ 9″ x 5′ 9″. From the Galerie du Régent (D d'Orléans), Palais-Royal. Acquired by the Société des Amis du Louvre, 1961. Present collectio The Louvre, Paris.

sometimes affected, became a familiar sight in the art galleries. He was interested primarily in the Gothic and Renaissance periods and had a remarkable perspicacity. But he also had that corollary trait of many intuitive collectors—a certain blindness to the merit of even important objects which were not his own finds. Nevertheless, he gathered a beautiful collection which has now gone back to Spain and graces the museum in Madrid which bears his name.

In Barcelona there were two interesting collectors, Luis Plandiura and Francisco Cambó. When I first met Plandiura, he had eyes for few things later than the 14th century, but within that somewhat limited scope, his taste was impressive. He had already acquired several Gothic sculptures from me when I had the good luck to discover three Spanish altar frontals of the 12th and 13th centuries, rare items indeed. In fact, I have never seen their like again outside a public collection and they are now, thanks to Plandiura, in the Barcelona Museum. I lost touch with Plandiura in the years before his death, but I understand that he later extended the scope of his collecting to include the works of contemporary artists, particularly those of his countryman, Picasso.

Francisco Cambo was a successful financier of wide interests whom I saw more often in Paris or, later, in New York enroute to Buenos Aires where he lived during the last years of his life. He was a highly cultivated man whose Spanish intensity gave a warmth and sparkle to his always interesting conversation. His collecting efforts were devoted to assembling a few diversified and carefully chosen paintings by leading masters. My firm's contribution to that effort was a capital work by Quentin de La Tour, the rare 18th century portrait painter who is still too little appreciated in this country. It represents one *Monsieur de Laideguive, Notaire,* and, strangely enough, I acquired it here in the United States. It had been in the family of William Tilden Blodgett, one of the founders and benefactors of the Metropolitan Museum since 1874, as attested by the original bill of sale and the inventory of the Blodgett Collection.

England, from the standpoint of numbers the richest collecting country for many generations, can also boast the highest average of quality, as well as the widest coverage of country and period. In the medieval field, one need only examine the bequests to the Victoria and Albert Museum—the Salting, for one—or such catalogues as those of the Taylor sales to realize the grandeur and quality of local collections. French primitives, Italian paintings of all periods, Spanish paintings, French canvases of the 17th and 18th centuries, some of the greatest masterpieces were, and still are, to be found in England. The aggregation of Poussins and Claude Lorrains is still the largest outside the Louvre, though 17th century France is represented almost entirely by those two artists except for the Philippe de Champaignes in the Wallace Collection and the National Gallery.

English collections have always been particularly rich in sculpture, a medium which few collectors have truly understood. Again one must except such men as Gustave Dreyfus in France, James Simon and Oscar Huldschinsky in Berlin, Benda, Stefan von Auspitz and Camillo Castiglioni in Austria, from whose collections came many of the great Italian Renaissance marbles today adorning American museums. One need only visit the Victoria and Albert or the British Museum or look at the catalogues of still existing private collections to realize the outstanding taste of the English amateur.

One of the firm's most charming English clients was Mrs. A. Chester Beatty, wife of the diamond and copper king, who was furnishing her London house in the French 18th century manner and covering its walls with the superb collection of Impressionist and Post-Impressionist paintings which made her famous in the art world. Her beautiful Seurat, *Le Phare de Honfleur,* and a handsome Toulouse-Lautrec, *La Femme se faisant les mains,* came from us. Chester Beatty (he is now Sir Chester), though generally in sympathy with his wife's acquisitions, was more attracted by some of the neglected French artists of the end of the 19th century. His real love, however, was, and is, his celebrated library of medieval and Oriental illuminated manuscripts.

One of the most interesting of our English clients was Sir William Burrell, the Scottish shipping magnate to whom I made one of my earliest personal sales. My father was still alive and we were together at Sagan one day when Mr. William Burrell (not yet knighted) was announced; the name meant nothing to either of us. It was my father's custom to meet everybody who came, though he might afterward leave me or someone else in charge. On this occasion we both went out to greet the visitor. After the usual amenities, the three of us went together through the different Gothic and Renaissance rooms, the periods in which Burrell had expressed an interest. Then

200

my father left us, not that he had something of immediate import to do, but he had not been impressed by Burrell's comments and thought he was wasting his time. Burrell did not strike me as a collector or as having a collector's potentialities, financially or in taste. At that time he was perhaps fifty years of age, of the lean wiry type that changes little in appearance in the middle years, and he spoke with a Scotch burr so marked that at times I had considerable difficulty understanding him.

I was left to cope with the rest of the visit as well as I could. We had been walking about for more than two hours (it was possible to spend as many more at Sagan without seeing everything), and I was at my wit's end. Nothing seemed to retain his attention and he asked for few prices. On the other hand, I reasoned that since this man had already stayed this long, it must be proof of his desire to purchase something. Finally, in desperation, I took him to one of the lateral wings of Sagan where there were stored, without much order, a lot of items of lesser interest, left-overs, so to speak, from a collection which my father had bought several years before solely for the sake of acquiring three Gothic sculptures of great beauty. It was an inspiration, for at last he found there two Flemish wood sculptures, angels of strictly decorative character, which took his fancy. Now I thought the matter would be quickly settled, but I was quite mistaken. With true Scotch canniness, he bargained, and another half-hour went by before the deal was closed. Happily, the objects were of little importance and he could get them almost at his own price.

This first visit of Sir William to Sagan brings to mind my first encounter with Jacob Epstein of Baltimore, not so much for any similarity between the two men, as for the reminder which both incidents brought me, that judgments must never be based on appearances or on a cursory acquaintance.

The scene this time was New York when the firm was occupying the house at the corner of 55th Street and Fifth Avenue with direct access to the street. It was late afternoon, and we were about to close for the day. I by chance was just at the entrance when the door opened and an elderly man walked in. From his unprepossessing aspect and rather despondent expression, I suspected a "touch" (shades of the Baroness de Rothschild), but to my surprise he asked to see Mr. Seligmann. The reception clerk evidently shared my impression and instead of turning to me, inquired what he wished to see Mr. Seligmann about. Somewhat testily, the older man replied that he would like to see some paintings.

Upon this I introduced myself, but this was only the beginning of the surprises, for without further preliminary, he demanded,

"How many Rembrandts can you show me?"

Now I decided I was facing a jester. One did not usually ask how many Rembrandts, but "have you a Rembrandt." Out of courtesy to his age, if nothing more, I showed him into the large first floor gallery, which served as a sort of reception room, and answered that I was very pleased and proud to own *one* painting by Rembrandt, and an important one. In no way daunted, he then said, "Oh, is that all? I've just been visiting several of your competitors, where I've seen at least a dozen!"

I was somewhat baffled, but I showed the one and only Rembrandt we owned at the moment, a portrait of Joris de Caullery from the Yerkes Collection. He examined it carefully and noncommittally, explaining that he was anxious to own several Rembrandts of different types and periods. When he left he gave me his name and address, with the request that I let him know should I acquire any others.

He did not buy the Rembrandt, but how wrong it would have been to base a lasting judgment on either of these first visits. Jacob Epstein assembled an excellent collection, largely of Old Masters, which he bequeathed to the Baltimore Museum. Sir William Burrell eventually built up, in his castle at Berwick-on-Tweed near the Scottish-English border, one of the greatest collections of Gothic tapestries in Britian, several of which he acquired from my firm. An especially interesting one was from the so-called Quo Vadis series and depicted Saint Peter being released from the Mamertine Prison. Woven in France in the 15th century, it had once hung in the church of St. Peter in Vienne, France, and we had acquired it, along with one of its companions (Simon the Magician, now in the Sidney Ehrman Collection in San Francisco) from the Paul Blanchet de Rives Collection.

When I knew Sir William better I found his a most sympathetic personality, modest and unassuming. I rather lost touch with him in the late thirties and forties and was surprised to learn recently that he later turned to paintings, gathering a large and diversified collection of 19th century French works, as well as a small group of Old Masters. In 1944, Sir William and Lady Burrell presented their entire collection, more than four thousand items, to the city of Glasgow, provided a building to house it, and continued to add to the Gothic section, his first love, until his death a few years ago.

My frequent visits to England were more often for the purpose of buying than for calling on clients. That country has always been, with France, one of the two great reservoirs which supply the art market. Neither Germany, Italy, nor Spain has ever been as rich a source except in certain special categories. Not only have there been great English collectors since medieval times, but the political fortunes of Europe have often directed exiles, notably during the French Revolution, from the continent toward England, carrying with them their goods and chattels.

It was doubtless as the result of such an emigration that one of my most important finds made its way to England—a set of fourteen portrait drawings representing personages of and around the court of France in the late 16th century. None was signed, but all carried, in an old script, notations of the sitter's names and what appeared to be record or inventory numbers.

For this period, the great authority was Louis Dimier, whose monumental *Histoire de la Peinture de Portrait en France au XVIe Siècle* had just appeared. I knew Dimier largely by reputation, which represented him as a hard-working scholar, somewhat grouchy, and decidedly a recluse. I felt that my find was worthy of his attention, so, since he had no telephone, I sent him a carefully worded note, asking permission to call. Several days went by before I received his polite but hardly cordial reply which, though it indicated a time for the appointment, did not hide the fact that he was extremely busy and did not welcome such interruptions. He kept me waiting some minutes in the little salon of his dark and gloomy apartment. When, after a few words of explanation, I handed him the drawings I had brought, he glanced quickly at the top one, looked at me over his glasses, and said, "I suppose you expect me to say that they are all by Clouet."

I hastened to disabuse him of this idea, adding that in my opinion if one or two showed affinities to the master, there was definitely more than one hand involved. Somewhat mollified by this, Dimier examined several more in silence and then there began to be a perceptible change in his manner, almost an excitement, as he studied more attentively the record numbers and the names written in old script on the face of the drawings. Suddenly, he jumped up and exclaimed, "But this is highly interesting. I really believe you have made an extraordinary discovery. I'll have to check, of course, but it looks to me as though some of these drawings are the missing portraits from the Fevret de Fontette Collection."

The Fevret de Fontette Collection was one of those fabulous accumulations of historical documentation—letters, engravings, drawings—which the erudite of the 18th century were so fond of gathering. Fontette himself was a member of the Parliament of Dijon and of the Academy there, and a correspondent of the Academy of Paris. In the 1760's, he sold some twenty thousand documents to Louis XV for the Bibliothèque Royale, including the careful catalogue which he had made. Thus it was known that the collection had once contained a large group of 16th century French portrait drawings but, for some unrecorded reason, these were apparently not included in the sale. No one knew what happened to them. In the 19th century some of them turned up in the Ashmolean Museum in England, via an English collector, and it was considered a possibility that more might have gone to England during the troubled years of the Revolution. Fontette had carefully marked all the documents of his collection with a special mark and a number; both Fontette's script and the marking were well known to Dimier, thus his immediate recognition. Moreover, one of the drawings was dated, presumably by the hand of the artist, and all of them carried very early notations in pencil—carefully retraced in ink—identifying the sitters.

No wonder Dimier was moved to excitement. Not only would such a find add fourteen more beautiful drawings to the slim roster of French 16th century portraits, but it would be of considerable historical interest, as all represented personages closely connected with the court of Henri III.

I gladly acceded to Dimier's request to keep the drawings for a while. From the way he spoke, I thought it would be at least a week or two before I heard from him. Not so, however. Evidently the old gentleman could not restrain his scholarly curiosity, for a day or two later I received a special delivery note, this time couched in quite cordial terms, asking me to call again. Naturally, I dropped everything and went. His hunch had been right; they were the Fontette marks. Further, he had identified twelve of them as by François

Quesnel, favorite painter of Henri III, whose works and importance are still being explored.

The atmosphere was entirely changed and Dimier was as pleasant as his misanthropic nature would allow. There is nothing like the rediscovery of a long lost work of art to put the crustiest scholar in a good mood, and here were fourteen of them. It was almost with deference that he congratulated me and asked permission to publish the drawings in a small book to appear as an addendum to his three volumes. Of course, I was only too happy to comply and to tell him, when he suggested that they should be exhibited, that I was already planning such a showing at Sagan.

The exhibition took place in April, 1927, inaugurated by a former president of the Republic, Etienne Alexandre Millerand. Before it closed, all of the drawings had been sold, not to a French museum as one might have expected, but to two charming young American collectors whom I had recently met, Mr. and Mrs. Herbert N. Straus.

All the Straus brothers, of Macy fame, were collectors. Jesse, the eldest, who later became Ambassador to France, and Percy, whose beautiful collection is now the nucleus of the museum in Houston, Texas, often visited Sagan during my father's lifetime. I did not meet Herbert, the youngest, and his lovely wife, Therese, until one of my early trips to New York after the war. Eugene Glaenzer took me to call at their small but attractive Park Avenue house and I have seldom seen a handsomer couple—he tall, slender and erect, she vivid, alive, and carrying proudly a magnificent crown of burnished gold hair. There began the friendships which are among my most treasured possessions.

The purchase of the Quesnel portraits was an almost inevitable acquisition in view of Herbert's passion for drawings, a feeling which his wife shared, for there seemed to be between them a perfect communion of thought and feeling. Always together, to what extent Therese was responsible for the choices they made is a question I shall not try to answer. When they purchased the idealized portrait of Alexander the Great, a magnificent marble bas-relief of the Florentine Renaissance, it was still an anonymous masterpiece without a story. Later, it was identified as from the hand of Andrea Verrocchio and has since been widely reproduced, but then it was only a moving and virile sculpture which said, "Here I am in all my glory"—a message which Therese and Herbert Straus understood.

For several years they had been working on a cherished project for a new home, and they had gone into it with the whole-hearted enthusiasm of amateurs and the thoroughness of scholars. They had learned enough about the intricacies of 18th century French architecture and decoration to shame a professional: the height of the ceilings, the breadth of the windows and panels, the orientation of the axes, the varieties of parquets. Either of them could have reproduced from memory the architectural style of Victor Louis of Bordeaux or the details of the Petit Trianon. But there was nothing pedantic about their approach; it was all for sheer love of the beautiful, and to love fully, one must understand. When one reaches a certain degree of culture and maturity of intellect, one wants more than that first sensuous reaction of eye or hand; though one trusts it, one needs reason, too.

Most of the lovely things they were now acquiring were chosen with this project in mind—furniture, rugs, screens, decorative bibelots. I recall particularly a set of four exquisite Beauvais tapestries, known as *The Education* or the *Four Ages of Man,* which were commissioned by Louis XVI in 1778 as a gift to Count Louis Bertier de Sauvigny, Intendant of Paris, upon his marriage to Mademoiselle Foullon. The original sketches for these charming family scenes were probably made by Fragonard, although the cartoons for the actual weaving were by François Casanova, artistic director at Beauvais. They were executed only once, an uncommon circumstance in 18th century tapestry weaving.

The site for the new Straus home, just opposite the entrance to the Frick Library on 71st Street, had been acquired, the walls were up, the floors completed, and the sumptuous *boiseries* which were to give this home its exceptional atmosphere were about to be installed, when Herbert Straus died. The dream house was never finished. Herbert Straus' life was so short that the world, even the art world, had no time to appraise him at his full stature. He was truly an exceptional man. An excellent musician, versed in literature, a discriminating collector, no branch of the fine arts was alien to him, for he reacted spontaneously to them all; yet he was an energetic businessman and an enlightened philanthropist. Herbert Straus was a man who possessed great spiritual as well as material gifts, and he used his good fortune to the full. He always showed a real concern for the welfare of his alma mater, Harvard, and, with his brothers, gave it the dormitory known as Straus Hall. He was a generous patron of the Fogg Museum, presenting, among other things, a rare early Chinese wall-painting and an important painting by Degas, *The Cotton Merchant*. Few people are aware that for many years he supplied the salary of one of the museum's curators.

Therese Straus is no less an exceptional woman, one of the most vitally alive human beings I have ever known. Her love of the beautiful has increased with the years and, following her husband's generosity, she continues to express her interest in the arts concretely. Soon after Herbert's death, she offered to present the new house, complete with the boiseries which were not yet installed, to the Metropolitan Museum to be used as an annex devoted to French art. When this appeared impractical because of maintenance problems, she instead presented the five complete rooms to the museum. Two of them, a salon from the Hotel de Tessé in Paris and a charming small round boudoir from Bordeaux, were installed during the postwar rearrangement of the museum.

For a number of years she served as a devoted and conscientious member of the Visiting Committee of the Fogg Museum and in 1938 presented twenty drawings to that collection. I understand, too, that Therese continued for some time the curator's salary. One of her most beloved treasures, the marble bas-relief by Verrocchio, has been presented to the nation and hangs in the National Gallery in Washington.

The Herbert Strauses were perfectionists in everything they did— and Therese is still so today—in their collecting, in their surroundings, above all in themselves, their manner of writing and speaking, their instinct for what should or should not be done. This is a perfectionism that has nothing to do with form for form's sake, but which springs naturally from ideals absorbed in youth and nurtured by intelligence and sensitivity. Without sensitivity, perfectionism becomes a burden to self and a bore to others, something neither of the Strauses could ever be.

CHAPTER XIX

If One Sells One Must Buy

There used to live in Paris, near the Place du Trocadéro, a most pleasant member of the diplomatic corps, M. Eugene Pelletier, who was also an ardent collector of early panel paintings, a rare predilection for a Parisian of his age and his time. He was constantly on the lookout for new acquisitions of quality, but his means were limited. In order to pay for a new acquisition, he would often have to give others in part payment or sell one outright. On one of these occasions, he invited me to call, which I did with pleasure. Quite aside from the prospects of doing business, he was a delightful conversationalist, and it was always a joy to see his truly lovely paintings.

Pelletier showed me a painting he was about to purchase, a *Circumcision* by a French master of the 15th century, a most attractive picture, in a good state of preservation and, in fact, it was one which I would gladly have purchased myself. (It has since gone to an American museum.) He explained that he could only buy it if he sold some drawings and paintings which he already owned, and asked me if I could be tempted. I had no difficulty in selecting at once a fine gouache of the school of Clouet representing King Henri II in full length (now in a private collection in New York). Then, walking over to a wall near his bed where he kept his most precious possessions, I pointed to a small, round, 16th century portrait which I thought I had recognized as a Holbein. Somewhat hesitantly I asked if he would consider parting with it. To my amazement, Pelletier replied, "Yes, I would, but in all fairness I must warn you. It is not what you think. Dr. Max Friedländer visited me a short time ago, and he does not consider it a Holbein."

This was a blow to my pride of connoisseurship, but I did appreciate indeed the gentleman's straightforwardness. Upon examining it carefully in the daylight from the window, I realized that a heavy varnish obscured some of the details and distorted the colors. Nevertheless, what was visible convinced me that if it were not by the master, it was certainly from his period and by an excellent artist, whoever he might be. So I told Pelletier that despite the negative opinion of the great expert, the picture interested me, and I would gladly buy it at a price in keeping with the circumstances. The deal was concluded and I left with my two small paintings.

Once back in my office, I called my restorer who, in my presence, removed the layers of grimy, yellow varnish. There gradually emerged a perfectly preserved portrait against the typical Holbein blue background. I was completely at a loss to understand the situation, and immediately wired Dr. Friedländer in Berlin for an appointment. If not by Holbein, who was the artist?

I handed the little portrait to Friedländer in his office at the Kaiser Friederich Museum, explaining that I knew he had seen it before, but since I now owned it, I wanted to hear about it from him personally. For a few moments he examined it with great interest and then said, that indeed, it did look like the real thing, but he did not recall ever having seen it before. "What is the opinion I am supposed to have given?" he queried.

Taken aback, I asked if I might delay the story until he had had time to examine the picture more fully. He agreed amiably, and we made an appointment for the next day. When I returned, the portrait was on his table. Dr. Friedländer at once said that there was no doubt in his mind; the painting was an original by Holbein. Further, he would be quite willing to state this in writing on the back of a photograph. Then I gave him the promised details about the source of the painting and my acquisition of it. Dr. Friedländer recalled his visit to Pelletier perfectly well, but he had no recollection of seeing the little portrait. Undoubtedly the yellow varnish, the poor light in the bedroom, and perhaps a preoccupied mind were responsible for this lapse, one I am sure which must have been rare in his full life of research and discovery. Then, with the humility of the truly learned, Friedländer added, "But I'm not the expert on Holbein. You should also consult Professor Ganz of Basel."

Ganz not only concurred in the opinion but confirmed the identity of the sitter as Sir Henry Guildford. It is now in the Detroit Institute of Arts.

Another trait of Dr. Friedländer which I found admirable, and all too rare, was his willingness to recognize the abilities of his younger assistants and his deference to their knowledge in their own fields of specialization. I once took to him a well-known group of drawings from the collections of the Princes of Anhalt-Dessau which had traditionally been labeled Holbein, but which obviously were not. Friedländer immediately referred me to one of his aides who was concentrating upon the circle of this great master, and it was thanks to him that the drawings were later established as by Peter Gaertner.

In 1924, Max Friedländer had just finished his monumental corpus of Flemish painting. When one considers how few corrections have had to be made in his early classifications and attributions, despite the quantity of documentation which has since come to light, one appreciates indeed the quality of his judgment and the surgeon-like precision of his working methods. Calm, lucid, with no rhetorical display of knowledge, he could seem almost cold when he examined a work of art. Yet one knew with certainty that he had reacted to it at once, and strongly. When the Hitler regime drove Friedländer from Germany, he continued his studies in Holland and Switzerland. Until his death in 1958 at well past ninety he was still actively writing and pursuing his researches, beloved of all who were fortunate enough to know him. I regret that my always over-charged life did not allow me to enjoy more often the real stimulation which a visit to him brought, but I am grateful for a number of delightful recollections.

Another important find of mine also involved a leading scholar, Bernard Berenson. In an Austrian house I had seen an Italian 15th century portrait of a man which struck me with great force. The painting was not recorded in any of the books, the name of the collector carried no weight—in fact, this was the only painting he owned —and he wanted a high price for it. There was no one on the spot whom I could consult. It was up to me to buy it, or leave it. Twice I went to examine the painting, and between visits dreamed about it, for it bore in every brush-stroke the hallmark of a great master. The more I thought of it, the greater was my desire to own it and the more convinced I was that my first impression was correct. The name that had immediately come to my mind was Andrea Mantegna, the rare and magnificent 15th century Paduan whose paintings in the Louvre

210

and the Museum of Tours had captivated me from my early years. I tried to tell myself that enthusiasm was clouding my judgment; to discover a Mantegna was beyond the realm of possibility. I bought it.

The next step was to take it to Berenson, the only authority who could decide whether I had been the victim of a too vivid imagination. Without hesitation and with considerable excitement, B. B. pronounced it the work of the master, and one of the great discoveries of our time. It added another portrait to the three or four already recognized as unquestionably by Mantegna. It is now in the National Gallery of Art in Washington as part of the Samuel H. Kress Collection.

Moments like these are the really great thrills of our business: to know that one can count upon one's knowledge and instinct, can trust the euphoria created by the sight of a masterpiece. However, neither conceit nor delusion of infallibility can be allowed to follow them; for then objectivity flees. Fortunately, perhaps, such finds are rare enough to keep one humble; for the most part the dealer must rely upon hard work and research.

Despite newspaper stories and word-of-mouth legend, real discoveries become rarer with every dawn. Today's public is generally aware of what it owns and the time when a precious tapestry might be found in a French cowshed or a Fragonard in an attic is long since gone. But if one sells one must buy, and one of the most practical ways of acquiring works of art is to buy a whole collection outright. It is also the most difficult financially, for it requires the immediate outlay of a considerable amount of capital. Ideally, a collection, to be a worthwhile purchase, must have a number of really outstanding objects which will find an immediate sale and realize enough to cover the lion's share of the price. There are advantages to the seller also in such an arrangement, for he receives a large sum at once and avoids the trouble of offering each item separately.

The competition between the art galleries and the art auctioneers for whole collections is keen, however, and the dealer is usually the loser. His estimate must be backed by a check, while the auctioneer has no financial commitment, and if his estimate is too high, the overoptimism will be shown only after the sale has taken place. We lost the collection of the late Parisian expert, Marius Paulme, in just that way in 1929. I was interested to come across my figures in the old files not long ago. The Paulme collection was particularly rich in drawings, and in view of the increasing interest in this province of art, my firm made a very high offer—ten million francs. Madame Paulme turned it down. I went to eleven million, my last bid—another firm had already given up—but the widow remained obdurate. "No," she said, "an auction will bring much more, I have been assured of it." An assurance, however, which committed the auctioneer to no financial responsibility. The entire collection went on the block in three sales in May, 1929, and brought roughly 13,110,000 francs. After deducting sales expenses, which must have amounted to more than the usual percentage because of the extensive publicity, I am sure she received less than I offered her. I heard that she was keenly disappointed because she had anticipated something like twenty million francs. My regrets were somewhat tempered by the sharp drop in prices which came that fall with the beginning of the depression.

The collection of the late Philippe Wiener which we acquired in Paris in 1928 was extraordinarily high in quality. It was a typically Parisian collection, with all that implies of merit and limitation, accumulated over a lifetime by a charming and cultivated man. The beautiful rooms of Sagan made a fitting background for the paintings, exquisite furniture, and bibelots. Opening day drew a brilliant audience, for the collection was well-known and was exactly the type to attract such fastidious collectors as the Baron and Baroness Edouard de Rothschild and David-Weill, whose collections already left little to be desired in either quality or quantity, but who could always be tempted by some delicately beautiful object. Henry Walters acquired, among other things, two delightful Hubert Robert paintings, *Le Portique* and *La Pièce d'Eau;* Percy Straus bought a rare small bronze head attributed to Vittorio Ghiberti, now in the Houston Museum; and George Blumenthal a charming gouache by one of the 18th century petits-maîtres, Dugourc, as well as a fine Louis XV screen of painted silk signed by Michel Gourdain. A number of pieces of exceptional merit were bought by generous benefactors for the Musée des Arts Decoratifs and for the Louvre. Within two weeks the collection was virtually sold.

In this day of increasingly high general expenses, however, there are few firms who are willing to tie up the capital demanded by an outright purchase of a great collection. If it is a diversified one, with a wide range of media, country, and period, there are also not many dealers who are equipped, physically or by experience, to handle it

212

in its entirety. Thus the dealer may act simply as selling agent for all, or part, of a collection. Sometimes a collector, or his heirs, not pressed for time or money, feel that a gradual dispersal will be more advantageous than either an auction or a sale en bloc. In that case, the only sound plan, from the viewpoint of both seller and dealer, is to appoint a sole agent to act as representative of the owner under an exclusive contract covering a specific period of time. Yet, it is amazing how many owners of works of art believe that they will obtain better prices by opening the field to every dealer, broker, or intermediary who wants a try at it. Actually, the only person to whom this type of competition brings a better price is the ultimate purchaser. When a painting, for instance, is offered to a potential buyer at one figure by a dealer, and the next day an intermediary feels sure he can obtain it at a lower price, the potential buyer is very apt to sit back and wait for a third proposition. Meantime, the painting is being offered hither and yon, and should this go on long enough, the result is not only a lowering of price, but also a loss of prestige as the reputation of the object becomes a little shopworn. I have heard many a fine painting dismissed with a casual, "Oh, yes, it's been hanging around the market for months now. Every dealer in town has offered it to me."

An exclusive contract, on the other hand, assures the collector-seller that his agent's interests are his own, for there is an agreed basis of sales commission, and a fixed minimum of acceptable price on each work to be offered. Thus the agent strives to obtain the best possible figure for every item, since he also benefits, and the possibility of conflict between the contracting parties is eliminated from the start. Patently the prospective seller must choose his agent wisely. In the case of trustees or executors of an estate, it is doubly important, for the agent must be an expert who can evaluate the collection, advise upon the best method of liquidating it, and then execute the plan. It may seem at first blush that the evaluation of a collection should be left to someone outside the business world of art, an art historian or a scholar. But the scholar has little time to keep abreast of prices, or to know the condition of markets, and is often a specialist in one particular area, with a limited grasp of others. Within the business art world, too, there are specialists; one firm may be known for its modern paintings and impressionists; another may be expert in Dutch 17th century paintings; and another in classical objects. If the collection

213

to be appraised and sold is a diversified one, encompassing all phases of Western art, the field of choice is a restricted one.

Every such collection presents its own peculiar challenge. One of the most interesting I ever handled, in view of its magnitude and the problems involved, was the Clarence H. Mackay Collection. Clarence H. Mackay, of cable and telegraph fortune, belonged to the second generation of moguls, having inherited largely from his father, John W. Mackay, a pioneer of the Montana and Nevada silver mining days. But he collected with all the fervor and prodigality of his great predecessors. He was for many years a Trustee of the Metropolitan Museum and was always a generous patron of the arts, both with his money and with loans from his collection. His estate at Roslyn, with its beautiful grounds landscaped in the French manner by Jacques Greber, was one of the loveliest on Long Island, and one of the most hospitable, for he entertained lavishly and often. He had been a good client of my father, and the firm's New York partner, Eugene Glaenzer, had become one of Mackay's close friends, going frequently to Roslyn for weekends. While I never reached this degree of intimacy, I often saw Mackay in the years before his death and gained a firsthand acquaintance with his magnificent collection. His Italian Renaissance and primitive paintings were of superlative quality; the sculptures and bronzes were equally fine; his Gothic tapestries were famous; and his arms and armor collection was renowned for its size and its beauty.

Soon after Mackay's death in November, 1938, it became apparent that this once extremely wealthy man had been hard hit by the depression. In addition, his resources were so tied up in financial operations that the only immediately available liquid assets were the real estate at Roslyn and his collection. Mackay, himself, had sold several important works of art and others were privately sold shortly after his death—the celebrated series of paintings by Sassetta, the Mantegna, the King Arthur tapestry, and a famous suit of armor—but the balance was still extremely valuable. Nevertheless, the trustees of the estate, Frank L. Polk, a former Under Secretary of State, and his associates, none of whom were collectors, found themselves faced with several complex problems. It is unusual for works of art to constitute so large a portion of a wealthy man's estate. It is still more unusual for a collection to be so top-heavy with objects of a particu-

214

larly difficult-to-sell type, purchased at the abnormally high prices of the twenties. Now, in the late thirties, the once popular and expensive Renaissance and 18th century decorative arts, the tapestries, the arms and armor had lost their appeal to the buying public.

My firm had acted as advisor and agent for the dispersal of part of the lovely Mortimer L. Schiff collection, and it was in part due to John M. Schiff's recommendation that the Trustees of the Mackay estate asked me to act for them. My role was to be a dual one; to sell, of course, but mainly and immediately, to advise on a procedure which would be the most advantageous to the estate. To complicate matters, only certain categories of objects had been catalogued. The vast collection of arms and armor, the hundreds of lesser items of a decorative character, and quantities of fine furniture and hangings were not even on an inventory list. It was not the first time that I had been struck by this singular lack of order on the part of businessmen collectors who must certainly have had method and precision in their commercial dealings.

My first task, then, was to familiarize myself with the contents of the huge Roslyn house. Before committing them to paper, I had to try to classify the items in my mind so that I could suggest an over-all plan flexible enough to be modified or enlarged as circumstances might dictate. I felt an urgency, because I was convinced, despite disagreement from Mr. Polk, who made light of my pessimism, that war was inevitable. It seemed imperative to me to take advantage of the European market to dispose of the objects for which the United States demand was limited. I had also heard that the Nazis, especially Goering and Hitler, were buying heavily of arms and armor.

Not only was there a prodigious number of these items, but the lack of a proper inventory meant that we had no information about previous collections, names of makers, country or date of origin. Armor is a very special study, and while training and experience enabled me to recognize easily the quality and relative merit of one item as compared with another, I am no expert. I made this clear to Mr. Polk at the beginning, but he assured me that no better man had been suggested and I would just have to go ahead as best I could. Fortunately, we were able to enlist the invaluable assistance of Stephen S. Grancsay, Curator of Arms and Armor at the Metroplitan, and New York's most astute amateur, Otto von Kienbusch. I cannot recall ever having had more willing collaborators, and I am happy to have this opportunity to express again my personal thanks for their time and patience.

The big question was how much to put up at auction and how much to reserve for private sale. An auction has certain advantages in the liquidation of an estate, in that the prices attained are accepted at law as final and indisputable valuations. But an auction is not always the best way to dispose of exceptional and high-priced works of art. There is a risk even in fixing the date of an auction; for any unforeseeable reason, political, social, or even personal, that date may turn out to be exactly the wrong one. It is both expensive and bad psychology to postpone an announced sale, and if the handful of leading collectors and museum representatives are not present, the expensive works of art may sell far below their estimated valuations. Furthermore, an auction allows no way to feel out public reactions and to adjust estimates on objects for which there is no recent basis of pricing.

My recommendations, then, were to hold an immediate auction in London of arms and armor, thus trimming down the collection to a certain degree, follow up with a sale of the lesser items in New York, and reserve the capital pieces for private sale. The Trustees were favorably disposed toward the London auction, and it was duly held. But they rejected the idea of a New York public sale, even of the lesser objects. In view of the great number of these and the necessity to vacate the Roslyn house, it was fortunate that my firm was still occupying the house at 3 East 51st Street where many of them could be stored and where the more important items could be properly shown.

Meanwhile, negotiations were going forward with museums, foundations, and collectors for the sale of the major pieces. There is in our business, as I presume there is in others, an understanding that preferential treatment, a first view, is offered to regular clients of a firm. The choice items in a collection are often sold before the doors are opened to the public, and may never even be exhibited at all. Thus, the 11th century German baptismal font and Germain Pilon's bronze fountain went to the Boston Museum of Fine Arts; the Cleveland Museum acquired the two marble *Pleurants* from the tombs of the Dukes of Burgundy; and the Samuel H. Kress Foundation carried off the rare *Madonna and Child* of Verrocchio. The Metropolitan Museum added to their already considerable list the superb 15th

216

century *Hector* tapestry, the exquisite 14th century staghorn saddle from the collection of Prince Trivulzio of Milan, and a famous suit of armor made for Henri II of France.

During the months that my firm handled the collection, nearly one hundred full suits of armor and uncounted miscellaneous weapons and accoutrements were sold. All in all, when I relinquished my duties with the estate, the total of sales was approaching the million dollar mark. It is perhaps a small figure compared to the total of the prices originally paid, but a satisfactory one considering that changing taste had had its effect on the American market for many of the items and that the European markets were closed to us before the end of 1939.

CHAPTER XX

The Rise of the American Museum

An art dealer derives a singular satisfaction from seeing his objects placed in a museum, for this constitutes an official recognition, so to speak, of his knowledge and taste. With most dealers, museums and public institutions enjoy a measure of priority, even though special terms are often necessary and the transaction is rarely as profitable as a private sale. Perhaps this is short-sighted— after all, an art dealer is not a philanthropist; why not sell to the highest bidder? True enough, but that leaves out certain very human considerations.

Consider the older museums of Europe with their immensity of riches—the collections of the Louvre or the National Gallery of London. It is a challenge to find another painting or sculpture of fitting quality and condition to grace these halls. Once acquired, the object must then run the gauntlet of a team of curators and museum officials who are experts in their fields. Because they are public or quasi-public officials, they are open to criticism from public and press alike if they make a mistake. Once the object meets the aesthetic standards, it must then be considered in the light of the always limited budgets, which means it is carefully weighed in relation to the whole collection before being recommended. If at last a work of art passes all these obstacles, the dealer feels an unequaled satisfaction in seeing his treasure hung on the walls of the museum for the public to admire.

Thus in London when I see in the National Gallery "my" great Ingres *Portrait of Madame Moitessier* and "my" Philippe de Champaigne *Vision of Saint Joseph,* or at the Courtauld Institute the stunning *Jane Avril* of Toulouse-Lautrec; when I visit the Musée Royal in Brussels and find once again the big 15th century panel of

218

the *Saint Barbara Legend;* or pause in the Louvre before the impressive unfinished portrait of Bonaparte by J. L. David or the recently discovered, monumental Simon Vouet, there comes a special thrill which has nothing to do with price or profit.

In the United States, the years between the two world wars witnessed the rise of the American museum as a new and formidable buying power in the art market. If, occasionally, the art dealer is nostalgic for the days of the millionaire private collector who could, and did, buy any rare item which took his fancy, regardless of price and without lengthy consultations with experts and trustees, those moments are quickly forgotten in his pride and pleasure in the role he has played in the enrichment of American museums. Their astonishing growth, in both size and number, in the last forty years is a phenomenon unique in the world and in history; unique because it has come about almost entirely through the generosity of private citizens. If Jacques Seligmann could repeat today the circuit of the eastern half of the United States which we made in 1913, he would find the storerooms of the "empty shells" about which he complained crowded with works of art for which they have no exhibition space.

Just for contrast, let us look at the first important purchase made by the Metropolitan Museum in its beginning year of 1871, incidentally a transaction which has proved well worth the efforts it took. John Taylor Johnston, its President, and William Tilden Blodgett, Vice-President, had heard of a group of excellent paintings available for purchase. So determined were they to have them that, no funds being available, Blodgett gave his personal guarantee for a bank loan of a hundred thousand dollars to hold the paintings until they could pass the hat. The list of donors is impressive. In addition to Blodgett and Johnston, a banker and railroad magnate, there was Rutherfurd Stuyvesant, F. W. Rhinelander, A. T. Stewart, Lucius Tuckerman, John Jacob Astor, and Theodore Roosevelt. With the possible exception of Stewart, who had just paid an exorbitant price for a huge canvas by Meissonnier, *Friedland 1807*, none of these men could be considered a collector. They were simply conscientious citizens discharging a civic duty. Since then, successive generations of public-minded citizens have continued to discharge their duties toward the aesthetic needs of New York and the country with overwhelming largess. To enumerate the gifts and bequests which have come to the Metropolitan since that time would require a chapter—the Harkness,

Havemeyer, Altman, Morgan, Friedsam, Bache, Wentworth, and Blumenthal collections; spectacular items from the Vanderbilts, Whitneys, Kresses, Mrs. Herbert N. Straus; the endowment funds, the Fletcher, Munsey, Harkness, Baker, Hearn, and, capping them all, the stupendous gift of John D. Rockefeller, Jr., which made possible the building and installing of the Cloisters. It is breathtaking when one realizes that almost all of this has happened within the last four decades.

A vast majority of the great collections amassed in the opening decades of the century are now in public museums. One of the most recent is the Walter Arensberg Collection of contemporary art, presented to the Philadelphia Museum, and that museum is, in fact, a good case in point. It has benefited to an astonishing degree from bequests. The basis of Philadelphia's permanent collection was laid by the gift of the famous John G. Johnson Collection which, not so many years ago, still hung in the small, dark house where I called with my father on my first visit to the United States. Then followed the McFadden, the Wilstach, the Hamilton Rice, the Stotesbury Collections and, in the contemporary field, the A. E. Gallatin paintings. Not only must the value of all this go far beyond the amounts spent by the museum for independent purchases, but how could one today even attempt to put a value in dollars on the Johnson Collection? Many of its masterpieces are unique examples, not to be found elsewhere.

Boston, Philadelphia, Chicago, and St. Louis have all been recipients of collections or endowments, but like New York, they are older cities whose museums go back many years. More exciting as social phenomena are the newer museums in the younger cities which, if less rich in inherited private collections, have been freer, for this very reason, to develop along less traditional lines. The Cleveland Museum, for instance, which opened its doors in 1916, has a character all its own in the supreme quality of its acquisitions. In less than fifty years it has taken its place among the great museums of the world. This brilliant record is the result of a sound initial policy, consistently applied, thanks to the presence for many years of a highly learned and cultivated man, William M. Milliken, as director, and to trustees who not only understood their responsibilities, but were willing to follow the advice of the director and his able assistants in expending the income of the museum's endowments. Moreover, the city of Cleve-

220

land has concurrently produced a number of collectors who have helped to create and encourage public appreciation by supporting and lending to exhibitions, and who have enriched the museum by bequests and gifts. It is not just coincidence, however, that the beautiful collections left to the museum in recent years—the Prentiss, Severance, Rogers, and Hanna—complement each other and supplement the holdings of the museum so happily. It is the result of an effective working agreement between the citizens of Cleveland, the museum staff, and the Board of Trustees.

The art of being a museum trustee is rather special. I do not know anyone who understood it better than Leonard C. Hanna, Jr., of Cleveland. He gave the museum forty-four years of lively and personal interest as well as endowments of almost unprecedented generosity. When he became a member of the Advisory Council of the still-unopened museum, he was not himself a collector. Even in 1920, when he became a trustee and a member of the Accession Committee, his interest in art per se was still an academic one. When I first met Len Hanna, some thirty-odd years ago, he had but one picture on the walls of his New York apartment. As I recall, it was a large white flower by Georgia O'Keeffe, graceful and delicate in its sweep of line, and striking in its decorative elegance. There are depths in this artist's paintings which go beyond the merely decorative; the sensuous curves, the rich almost monochromatic tonalities, seem to have a mysterious life and inner pulsation which can be translated into the actual movement of an unfolding petal. There was a parallel between this canvas and the man who owned it, for Len Hanna, too, did not reveal himself easily.

He was charming of manner and cordial in his approach, fastidious in his dress and about the appointments of his home. In casual conversation he appeared to be a man whose interests were limited to the pleasanter aspects of life—art, literature, the theater, and music. He did derive great pleasure from these, but Len Hanna was no grand seigneur of leisure. Heir to one of the great industrial empires of the Middle West, with headquarters in his native Cleveland, he took an active part in its affairs and all the time-consuming responsibilities it entailed. Even here, however, one never found him in the spotlight or in the press; that he left to others. Like many another son of wealth, he undoubtedly found it necessary over the years to build up a certain defense, for he was by nature generous and sympathetic,

221

but his reserve only dissolved in the intimacy of a small chosen company. Just as reserved was he in his role of Maecenas—a name which he would have been the last to apply to himself. I feel sure that in setting up the fabulous Hanna Fund, for many years one of the main sources of revenue of the Cleveland Museum, he would have preferred to disguise the trust under some anonymous title, except that he also wished to honor the past generations of his illustrious family, particularly his mother, by this memorial.

When Len purchased his first painting, I feel sure that he had no real thought of becoming a collector. But once begun, like many another before him, he found collecting had become a vital part of his life and he devoted hours of time and study to it. He also had a nature to which works of art were a necessary nutriment, to be enjoyed intuitively as well as intellectually. As a Trustee of the Museum, however, he believed that his proper function was simply to pass on and endorse the choices proposed by the two remarkably talented men of his staff, William Milliken and Henry S. Francis, and quite correctly so. Nevertheless, I know that certain acquisitions were initiated because he had the taste and the knowledge to recognize the value to the museum of objects which the executive staff had not yet had an opportunity to see.

Hanna's lavish gestures toward the Cleveland Museum reflected not only his civic pride and his love for his native city, but also his own passionate interest in works of art. As his exquisite collection grew, he was often at a loss to know where to place a new treasure. I was more than once reminded of Henry Walters when Hanna bought another beautiful object; I was never certain whether he was motivated by his personal desire or the needs of the museum.

The development of Len Hanna's taste was swift, and followed an exceptional course. Hardly was he started in one direction when his eclecticism drew him in another, but never in a current vogue. If he had a favorite school or period, it was probably the Impressionists and Post-Impressionists. Yet, his early appreciation of Picasso, for the beginner that he then was, constituted an unusual step into the unconventional, and he developed an interest in Degas and Gothic marble sculpture at almost the same time. Collectors willing and eager in so short a time to cross the intellectual boundaries of period and aesthetic expression, gathering the best and enjoying their very diversity,

222

are exceedingly rare. Hanna's searching mind and his response to tactile beauty were bound to lead him into constantly wider horizons.

The Toledo Museum, supported mainly by the bequest of Edward Drummond Libbey, opened its doors in 1911. Since then it has had to enlarge its building twice, in 1925 and again in 1933. The Minneapolis Museum, under the leadership of such cultured citizens as the John R. Vanderlips and Alfred F. Pillsbury, inaugurated its museum building in 1915 and added to it in 1927. The Detroit Institute of Arts was chartered as a municipal project in 1918 but owes its present beautiful building, opened in 1927, more to private funds than to municipal taxation. Here, too, the personalities of its directors, the late Dr. William R. Valentiner and Edgar P. Richardson, were influencing factors in the growth of private collections destined to augment and enrich the museum.

This special role of the museum director is certainly one of his most important. His task should not be confined to the direct development of the collection in his charge; he should strive to group about the institution interested citizens susceptible of being stirred to collect for their own pleasure, and subtly guide them toward purchases which may some day serve the needs of the museum. The position has been reversed: yesterday, the collector made the museum; today, the museum must make the collector.

Wilhelm von Bode, director of the Kaiser Friedrich Museum for many years, understood this role to perfection. He is said to have told James Simon, who indicated his intention of leaving his collection to the museum, that he must buy a certain painting just submitted by a dealer.

"But I don't like it," Mr. Simon protested, "and I don't want it in my collection."

"That is not the question," replied Bode. "The museum needs it; we cannot let it go, and we cannot afford to buy it. Meanwhile you might just as well have it and you'll probably learn to like it."

Simon is alleged to have bought it. No one knows whether he ever learned to like it.

I once saw Bode in action as he spun a Machiavellian plot to play collector against dealer and enrich the museum from both. I had gone to Berlin to purchase several paintings and decided to take two portraits to Bode for his opinion, as one of them had been attributed by one critic to Scorel and by another to Mabuse. He knew the painting well and considered it definitely by Scorel. He was so taken with it that he immediately told me he would like a collector friend to purchase it, for it would be a noteworthy eventual addition to the museum.

"If he buys the Scorel," Bode said, "I think you should present the smaller portrait to the Kaiser Friedrich!"

I was not averse to the proposition, since the smaller portrait, although by Cranach, was not of considerable value. However, Bode's plan did not work, as the prospective buyer was out of town for several weeks, and I was reluctant to be separated for so long a time from my most recent important purchase without greater certainty of a sale. Nevertheless, Bode's principle is a good one, although it might be exercised in a more subtle and elegant manner.

During the second quarter of the 20th century, American museums have continued to multiply in Oklahoma, Texas, Colorado, Washington, Oregon, and California. In Kansas City, Missouri, a single bequest made possible the almost magical inauguration in 1933 of a magnificent building and a collection of considerable merit, neither of which existed five years earlier. William Rockhill Nelson, the dynamic Kansas City newspaper publisher, belonged to the same breed and generation of pioneering businessmen as the big collectors of my father's day, but he started too late to form a personal art gallery worthy of the city to which he was so devoted. Instead, he chose to endow it with the fortune he had amassed, and today the collections of the William Rockhill Nelson Gallery vie in quality with those of cities twice Kansas City's size and museums twice as old. No other country would be capable of such a tour de force.

The fabulous National Gallery in Washington was not yet even a dream in my father's time, and Andrew Mellon had scarcely begun to collect. If the patrons of American culture have been popularly accused of inordinate pride in wishing to perpetuate their names upon the façades of public institutions, here was one to refute the charge. Andrew Mellon specifically directed that the handsome marble structure he gave to the nation should be known simply as the National Gallery of Art in order, as he wrote, that it might "attract gifts from other citizens who may in the future desire to contribute works of art . . . to form a great national collection." Mellon himself set the criterion for those future donors in the hundred and fifty or more paintings and sculptures which he had so carefully chosen over the years. His hopes have been amply fulfilled. Before the museum building was completed, Samuel H. Kress had presented the greater part of his collection of several hundred Italian paintings. Within a year after its opening in 1939, Joseph E. Widener had added the truly princely collection which his father had started and he had perfected. Andrew Mellon's dream of establishing in Washington a national gallery comparable to its European prototypes was well on its way to realization.

The Widener Collection was started by Peter A. B. Widener, and it was presented to the nation in his memory, but it was the son, Joseph, who played the active role in its development and improvement. He gradually eliminated paintings he considered less worthy and added others, the great Van Dycks, the Grecos, the exquisite Mantegna, the powerful Castagno. He had a keen sense of quality and an eclectic taste; thus he was capable of acquiring old masters with one hand and, with the other, the *Dead Toreador* of Manet or the small but exquisite *Race Course* of Degas. The Degas must also have had appeal because of its subject, since Widener's stables were as well known as his collection, although not always to the same people. I learned of this side of his life only through a chance mention of the Widener collection to a horse-fancying friend, who in turn knew nothing of his art interests. We were each equally shocked at the other's abysmal ignorance.

Joseph Widener was an exceptional man and I always regretted that I knew him so late in his collecting career. He had made several important acquisitions from my father, among them the previously mentioned Houdon busts of the Brongniard children, and I had called on him with my father in 1913. But when I settled down in New York more than ten years later, his collection, except for a few spectacular paintings, was already complete. He was a difficult man to approach and his outward attitude of aloofness, quasi-indifference, always made me feel that I should be as brief as possible lest he grow bored. I was wrong. Once the ice was broken, he could be extremely affable, and he was amazingly well-informed on affairs in the art world. On one occasion I made an appointment to meet him at his office in Philadelphia and motor with him to Elkins Park for luncheon. In the car, he told me of unexpected visitors at the house; hence the drive out would be our only chance to talk privately. Did I have anything to show him? I brought out certain catalogues and photographs of items which I believed might interest him, and which I also thought would be news. Not so. As soon as the collection from which they came was mentioned, he interrupted me to say that he had already heard about them but the prices were out of line. What did I think they could be bought for? My figures were evidently the same as those he had been quoted, and so the matter was dropped. With every visit Widener later made to my gallery, I sensed a closer relationship, but by that time it was extremely difficult to find anything to tempt a collector of his caliber, and the only purchase he ever made from me was a superb Louis XVI table, attributed to Riesener.

I first met Samuel H. Kress, who personally and through the Foundation which bears his name has so enriched the National Gallery, toward the end of 1924 when he purchased from me two small 16th century enamels and a little French 18th century table. I feel sure that then he had no thought of forming a great art foundation. Many of America's great philanthropic funds have contributed to the advancement of artists and of museums, but the Samuel H. Kress Foundation is unique. It buys works of art solely for the purpose of giving them away. The National Gallery in Washington has always, since the initial gift in 1939, been its first concern, but in addition, the Foundation has been of invaluable assistance in rounding out the existing collections of some twenty other institutions. In some cases it has actually served as the impetus for the creation of a museum where none existed.

If the primary purpose of an art museum is to preserve the beauty of the past for the inspiration of artists and the spiritual pleasure of the sensitive layman, it has a corollary function in education. A child's earliest conceptions are often founded on familiar paintings or reproductions. Mention of George Washington immediately calls up an image of the statesman of Stuart, the soldier of Peale, or the valiant figure standing perilously in a small boat on the Delaware. The pioneering west is graven on the mind's eye by *Custer's Last Stand*. The Napoleonic era is summed up by David's *Coronation*. For the adult, as well as the child, the walls of a museum offer a never exhausted source of material for a study of the humanities and social evolution. Representational art has had perhaps its most far-reaching influence in the area of the world's religions. Those of us fortunate

226

enough to have had early access to an art museum learned there the stories of the Old and New Testaments as surely as from Sunday-school teaching or Bible reading. Great art scholars are often better versed in hagiography, iconology, the symbolism of early Christianity, and the problems of comparative religion than many a churchman. The Roman Catholic Church has been for many centuries aware of the proselytizing value of works of art and the emotional effect of sacred paintings and sculptures set in an environment of stained glass and incense.

These spiritual and didactic values may have played a considerable role in the formative stages of the projects of the brothers Samuel H. and Rush H. Kress. Both had a fundamentally religious background, not in any narrow sense of ritual and dogma, but in the wider concept which distinguishes good from bad, right from wrong, for love of one's fellow men rather than from fear of eternal damnation. The gradual evolution of the aesthetic interests of the two men has been a fascinating one; the longing for beauty in its timid beginnings; the conflicting scepticism of businessmen who have come up the long, hard way; their entrance into a rarefied atmosphere where they believed merchandising methods could be applied; and a final realization that their progress was blocked by these methods.

Many men would have been so disillusioned as to give up at this point, but not the brothers Kress; temporary reverses were not new in their lives. They simply started anew, opened their buying operations to competition, and welcomed criticism, in a reaffirmation of their determination to secure the finest examples of man's artistic achievement. New methods of acquisition and of ultimate distribution were worked out and the Foundation was reorganized into a comprehensive and efficient organization.

Rush, the younger of the two Kress brothers, succeeded to the duties of the presidency during the long illness of Samuel. If, as head of the Foundation, he has made the more important and final decisions, he has been actively seconded in the executive field by two exceptional men, the late Dr. Herbert L. Spencer and Guy Emerson. The latter is in charge of the operations involved in the purchase and distribution of the works of art.

Guy Emerson is by training a banker and by avocation an ornithologist. But it is obvious that his wide cultural background, his innate refinement, and his sense of delicate values have developed in him a very sound art judgment. Nevertheless, he maintains an attitude of complete aloofness toward the final purchase, leaving the expression of artistic opinion and ultimate recommendation to his able technical advisors, John Walker, director of the National Gallery of Art in Washington, Mario Modestini, connoisseur and technician, whose province includes the scientific art laboratory, and until recently, the late noted art historian Dr. William Suida.

In the early years of the Kress Foundation, definite stress was laid on the primitive schools of Italy, and for quite a number of years the collection was restricted to this field. However, as the Kress's own interests broadened, so did the collection. French paintings of all periods up to the Davidian reaction (but including Ingres) were added, as were German paintings, but since little of merit was created there after the 16th century, they offer a limited scope. The addition of the Spanish school opened a whole new vista, particularly in the early years when the problems of Flemish and Portuguese influence are still too obscure to delineate definite boundaries. More unusual, a superb collection of sculpture was gradually built, particularly among the great creations of France and Italy.

Obviously, the broad museum and scholarly background of Dr. Suida was of inestimable value in the execution of this program. He was for many years Director of the Museum at Gratz, Austria, and a member of the faculty of the University of Gratz. Earlier in his career he had held posts both at Vienna University and in the German Institute for Italian Studies in Florence. Though no school or period left him indifferent and he reacted instantly to the qualities inherent in each, Italian art was his first love. Within that broad field, it was the seicento which captured his special attention. He was one of the first to appreciate the interest of this still little explored area, and his studies of its varying influences, from Naples to Bologna and Genoa, are of supreme importance. Dr. Suida had a fantastic memory for the involved details of Italian history—a particularly valuable talent for an art historian working in seicento studies, a period when aesthetic development is strongly marked by political and social events.

During the early days of my own career in Paris, Dr. Suida came from time to time to see my father at Sagan, but I only came to know him well as my interest in paintings developed and I had occasion to consult him either at his museum or on his trips to Paris. He was an unfailing source of perceptive knowledge. One of the few good things which came out of the miseries of World War II was that it brought such men to our American museums and universities. In these past years I never ceased to marvel at the inexhaustible capacity for work of this frail, scholarly man of almost eighty, who not only performed exacting duties as advisor to the Kress Foundation, but made lengthy annual pilgrimages to a dozen European countries, found time to pursue his own researches in an ever widening area and to publish them.

CHAPTER XXI

The Second World War

In Paris, a few years before the outbreak of the second world war, we began reluctantly to think of selling the Palais de Sagan, which was still a part of my father's estate. It was not an easy decision to make, because Sagan held associations dear to all of us. But there were many practical considerations to urge it. The building was huge, and with the prevailing trends in collecting, the firm had less and less need for so lavish and expensive an establishment; the quarters on rue de la Paix were sufficiently spacious. Europe was exceedingly uneasy politically, as well as economically, and it seemed wise to take steps with an eye to the future. We had made no real efforts toward selling, though we had been approached by several of the foreign embassies in Paris—Sagan was admirably suited, and situated, for embassy purposes—when one day the decision was practically made for us by the City of Paris.

The great Paris Exposition of 1937 was well beyond the planning stage. The handsome modern buildings which replaced the old Trocadéro and the two large exhibition halls on the avenue du President Wilson, one the Museum of Modern Art, were actually under construction. Other land was being cleared for the grounds and the gardens of the fair. Among the older buildings which occupied some of the needed ground was the Polish Embassy which, obviously, could not simply be condemned in the usual manner. To induce the Poles to move, in principle not difficult as their building was too small and not particularly elegant, the City of Paris offered an even trade of a more suitable house. Somewhat to the dismay of the city fathers, the Poles chose the Palais de Sagan, a rather grander gesture than the City of Paris had been prepared to make. The Poles

230

insisted that it was Sagan or nothing, until the city gave in, and it looked as though the deal was all set. There then intervened a contre-temps which threatened to break off negotiations but which afforded the only light touch to the passing of Sagan from Seligmann hands. The problem was solved through a masterpiece of French wit and diplomatic ingenuity.

The difficulty lay in a short, narrow driveway, just wide enough for a single vehicle, which went from the entrance on the rue St. Dominique back to the main courtyard of Sagan. The land on either side of the passageway had long since been built up with houses which faced upon the street and which, in the 18th century, had been granted "right of light and sight" in perpetuity upon this narrow strip of the grounds of Sagan. There was the catch; the Polish Ambassador did not see how he could allow the neighbors to trespass upon the sanctity of Polish territory. Impasse. French law was French law. The architect for the City of Paris finally resolved the dilemma. He suggested that the city retain the passageway, nationalize it, and grant the Poles right of access to their courtyard. In short, he created a new "Polish corridor." The Poles were happy, the city officials were happy, and the firm of Seligmann moved out of the Palais de Sagan, to establish headquarters at 9 rue de la Paix.

Shortly after this I took another step which I had contemplated for some time; I made the New York office my personal headquarters and the United States my legal residence. My young half-brother, François-Gerard, had finished his military service and had already taken his place in the Paris firm. I had fewer obligations in Europe, and I now felt free to establish myself in the country which had so long been my real home. It was in no sense, however, a severing of the two firms, and I continued to commute between Paris and New York until the summer of 1939.

That was the summer of the New York World's Fair. The art section, covering European painting from 1300 to 1800, was one of its outstanding achievements. Directed by Dr. William R. Valentiner, it was particularly rich in the so-called primitive periods and the Dutch 17th century, with important loans of such precious and seldom-seen paintings as the *Ince Hall Madonna* of Van Eyck, lent by the National Gallery of Australia in Melbourne. The Marquis de Cuevas was largely responsible for the financing of the art building, and when despite the menace of a new European war, it was decided to continue the fair for another year, he generously agreed to guarantee the very considerable additional expense. But he made certain conditions —he was to approve, first, the membership of the organizing committee and, second, the works of art exhibited, specifying further that a large place be reserved for Spanish paintings.

The new exhibition was planned to begin with the High Renaissance in Italy and extend through the 19th century, including American paintings. Dr. A. Hamilton Rice and Walter Pach headed the committee, and among its members were Charles Henschel, President of Knoedler & Company, and Hans Waegen, formerly of my own organization. I had been a member of the Honorary Committee of 1939, and when the Marquis asked that I take a more active part in the new one, I was happy to agree. But I, in turn, stipulated for the inclusion of French works of certain epochs and by certain artists who were little known in the United States and unjustly neglected. Thus the planning of the French section was largely accorded to me.

I had several aims. The art of 18th century France was a favorite with American collectors at the beginning of the century, but it had undergone a marked decline among the younger generation, due to a total misconception of what it really represented. Dismissed as "rococo," a term against which French art historians do battle and which properly applies only to the pastiches created outside France, the French 18th century was popularly regarded as a frivolous art of the boudoir. The Château of Versailles and the Grand Trianon— even the Petit Trianon, so precious yet so pure in form—certainly do not lend themselves to frivolity or give an impression of boudoir. As light as may have been the private lives of certain monarchs, the etiquette of the Court imposed a very strict discipline. For the fair, then, it seemed important to try to overcome this misunderstanding by exhibiting the more austere side of the French 18th century—its elegance, proportion, and restrained dignity. To this end special emphasis was laid upon the great portraits which personify the civilization that was the envy of all Europe.

Little had been seen here, too, of the French 17th century, and even among the great 19th century masters certain key figures were still too little known and appreciated. I therefore submitted to the French Ambassador a list of capital paintings in the Louvre and provincial museums which seemed to me necessary if we were to make an ideal exhibition, the Watteaus of the Louvre, for instance, and at least one monumental canvas of Delacroix, *Liberté sur les Barricades* or the *Massacres at Scio*, for canvases of this caliber just do not exist in American collections. Courbet, on the other hand, and to a certain extent Seurat and Redon, still in 1939 not widely known, could be more or less adequately represented here.

Grover Whalen, director general of the fair, was struck by the publicity value of important loans from the museums of France in those uncertain days of the summer of 1939 and conceived the idea of asking for an American battleship to take delivery of them. But events were moving too fast for us. The second world war descended before the arrangements could be completed, and France had more pressing matters on hand than aid to the World's Fair Committee of New York. The war also ended any hope of securing other European loans; that we succeeded in getting together a representative ensemble, including a Spanish section to meet the approval of the Marquis de Cuevas, speaks for the richness of American collections. The fair reopened in May of 1940, one day after the Nazis overran Belgium and the Netherlands. The so-called phony war of the winter of 1939–1940 had now become all too real.

France, of course, had been at war since September, and my young brother, François-Gerard, was called up immediately. He made the weary trek to Dunkirk and then joined the Resistance, where he made a brilliant record in extremely dangerous work. By some miracle, my sisters and their families escaped the awful fates of so many Jews, though they lived through terrible years of wandering and hiding. My brother André managed to get to this country with his family in 1940 and opened a gallery in New York. He was among the first to rush back to France in 1945 but died of a heart attack soon after his homecoming. My cousin René, ill in a New York hospital, completely lost his will to live when France fell in June, 1940, and died within a week of that most awful of days. Jean Seligmann, son of my Uncle Arnold, was captured and shot at Vincennes. Albert Meyer, my father's and my longtime associate in the Paris firm, died in a concentration camp under atrocious conditions.

Almost the entire stock of the Paris firm was confiscated as Jewish property and sold at public auction by order of the Vichy government. The family house on the rue de Constantine and its entire contents suffered the same fate, as did my private collection, much of which

233

was still in my Paris apartment. At this time, the Paris records were burned to keep them from falling into Nazi hands.

There was distressingly little that I could do to help here in New York. Though I was no longer of age to be called to the French army there was still the possibility that the American army might find me of use when the United States got into the conflict, as seemed to me inevitable. Encouraged by several of my old comrades of the First Division, many of whom occupied high ranks in Washington, I applied for a post to which my knowledge of the two countries would have particularly fitted me. Unfortunately, age was against me and I had to content myself with what all American civilians were doing—everything we personally could to aid and abet. I had little heart for the art business.

The news of the lootings of works of art, and of the vast collections which Hitler and Goering were assembling, began to spread almost immediately after the fall of France. This was of such moment to me that I felt it imperative to take certain protective steps to assist in the reclamation of looted property after the war. I drew up a memorandum containing my ideas which was duly forwarded to Washington through Francis Henry Taylor of the Metropolitan Museum, who was also working on the problem. I suggested that all works of art identifiable as property which had been looted or sold through coercion, or was so suspected because a satisfactory provenance could not be furnished, be "neutralized" for a period of twenty-five years and that descriptions of such works of art be given wide circulation. I had several conferences with Baron Edouard of Rothschild on the topic; he and the Baroness had fled France to New York and were living in a modest apartment. He was much concerned about the fate of the Rothschild collections, and I thought if I could get a few influential collectors such as he to set an example by preparing their lists, it would encourage others to do the same. He approved the idea for others, but, with typical Rothschild reluctance to draw public attention, refused for himself. Baron Robert, who also spent some time in New York during the war, had taken the precaution of scattering the most precious items from his collection among friends. While he, of course, wondered whether he would ever see them again, he was much too worried over the fate of his sons, Alain and Elie, officers in tank corps and at that time prisoners of the Germans, to give much thought to the lesser problem. Fortunately, most of us did recover

234

the greater portion of our art properties, but this was due to the methodical temperament of the Germans, who kept such careful records of their pseudo-purchases, rather than to any official lists registered with the government. Ironically, the addition of "Chosen for the private collection of Goering," as the Paris exhibition catalogue of recovered works of art so euphemistically put it, will doubtless add interest to the provenance for future art historians.

I still feel that there should be some sort of international agreement for the protection of owners of works of art and potential buyers. Museum collections, of course, are well known, but if private collectors had had their possessions registered with some central bureau, there would have been much less chicanery after the war. By no means all the looted objects found their way home, and several museums would have been spared the onus of receiving stolen property.

When it was finally all over and we could begin to think of getting back to the business of living again and of selling works of art, I went to France as soon as possible to see my family, what could be done to help them, and whether we could pick up the pieces of the Paris firm. It had always been my wish that the two firms of Seligmann, separated when my father and my Uncle Arnold quarreled in 1912, be reunited. Over the years, I had made several attempts to effect this reconciliation, but without concrete results. The war, in a sad way accomplished this. Jean, who was executed by the Nazis, had been at the head of Arnold Seligmann & Cie. since the death of his father; his brother, Armand, a successful attorney, had no desire to run an art business, and the firm was thus without a leader. They still had the old quarters, the original Seligmann Galleries, on the Place Vendôme. We were anxious to dispose of the rue de la Paix building, which rent ceilings had made an economic burden. To consolidate the two firms, now that old enmities had been washed out by mutual hardships, seemed the reasonable thing. It was not a complete merger, however. It really substituted one split, this time an amicable one, for another. It was agreed to make separate financial and administrative entities of the Paris and New York houses. Thus today, François-Gerard has the combined Paris firms at Place Vendôme and I the New York business, affiliated only by ties of affection.

In New York the art market remained reasonably active during the war years, but at least as far as my own gallery was concerned, exhibitions were practically discontinued. This was partially due to the fact that the firm decided to give up the big house on 51st Street and move to our present smaller quarters at 5 East 57th Street, a process which considerably disrupted normal gallery activities. Our first showing of note in the new galleries was an exhibition of the paintings of the *Plongeurs* series by Fernand Léger, who was then living in this country, in the spring of 1944.

One of the first postwar concerns was to reactivate the Contemporary American Department, with Theresa Parker, of course, at its head. She organized one of the most remarkable series of exhibitions the firm ever held, entitled "Twenty-five and Under." The purpose was to make it possible for young artists from Seattle or Butte, Santa Fe or Dallas, to exhibit in New York, and they created a tremendous stimulus, not only for the artists, but for us. The participants were mainly youngsters just out of military service, and all of us were touched by their eagerness to turn once again from an atmosphere of destruction to one of creation. The out-of-town artists were selected from those recommended by colleges or art centers throughout the country, and those from the New York area by direct contact. Those shows were so warmly received by both newspapers and periodicals that many invitations resulted and a traveling schedule kept the series on tour for a year. There were other exhibitions with the same purpose in mind, "Paintings from Cold Water Flats," "Six by Six, Paintings by Printmakers," etc. Among the artists introduced in that postwar period were such names as Roger Anliker, now Associate Professor at Carnegie Tech.; Kahlil Gibran, who since has turned very successfully to sculpture; Robert Goodnough, whose name one hears more often each year; Sam Hunter, writer and museum director; Harry Jackson whose paintings at that time were quite abstract; Wolf Kahn and his brother Peter, presently on the art staff at Cornell; Arthur Kraft of Kansas City and creator of many sculptures at the Northland Shopping Center outside of Detroit, of which Victor Gruen was the architect; Seong Moy, the lyrical printmaker and painter, who now has his own summer school in Provincetown; the sculptor David Newman; and Larry Rivers, then concerned with abstraction.

Ultimately we settled down to the sponsorship of a small group, with exhibitions spaced in a measure more commensurate with our limited quarters. Rico Lebrun became our first "name" artist, and two years before his great *Crucifixion* exhibition at the Los Angeles

236

County Museum opened, we held his first one-man painting show. Cleve Gray, who had recently returned from overseas, became the second on our roster, with his dramatic impressions of war-torn buildings. As time went on other names were added and the inevitable changes took place, with the American Department continuing in its policy of showing works of quality regardless of direction.

Not the least stimulating aspect of presenting contemporary exhibitions is the contact it brings with young collectors and students. Exhibitions of whatever period also attract both the student artist and the student art historian, and we have always striven to make the gallery hospitable to them, whether it be for loans or to study periods and artists of which the firm may have examples. Furthermore, it has always been our policy to allow payments over a given time to the young collector with a limited income. Years ago I realized how discouraging it must be for a would-be collector to read of the astronomic prices brought by paintings fashionable at the moment, yet a drawing, if available, might prove a foreseeable acquisition.

The aesthetic and emotional appeal of drawings is infinite, for here one shares the artist's first thoughts, personal and intimate, often fleeting, quickly recorded like notes of a melody which haunt the musician. Certain drawings of Seurat, for instance, reveal a lyricism which never reached his paintings, excluded by the strict scientific laws the artist set for himself. What limited knowledge we would have of the universality of Leonardo's vision were it not for his drawings, or of artists whose output in paint was small, like Dürer and Mantegna, or of those who died very young, like Gericault, Bonington, and Seurat.

An artist's graphic production is indispensable to an understanding of the evolution of his technique and of his style. It is almost an obsessive point with me (perhaps an evidence of conservatism) that before an artist can be called great he must be a capable draftsman. Artists who try to dispense with this basic skill, dismissing it as an old-fashioned method, are headed toward creative sterility. It is easy to argue that thoughts and inspirations may be projected directly on canvas without preliminary drawings or water-color sketches; but oil is not a sufficiently supple medium to lend itself to spontaneous essays. More practically, it is too expensive for the trials and errors of the novice or for recording the hundreds of ideas which come crowding to the creative mind. I find it extremely difficult to take seriously an artist who cannot show me pencil or wash sketches, so much more revealing of his inner personality and his progressive evolution than a series of finished oils.

There is no doubt that drawings have been attracting an ever-wider public, and one man has probably had more to do with this than almost anyone else, Paul J. Sachs of the Fogg Art Museum. His own collection, much of it now presented to his beloved Fogg, is a remarkable one, but it was his eloquence as a teacher of future museum curators, art historians, and collectors which gave impetus to the renaissance of drawings among American amateurs.

CHAPTER XXII

The Postwar Scene

World War II closed the European art market to American buyers for almost six years. As soon as travel was again feasible there was naturally a great rush of dealers to replenish diminished stocks and collectors to see what American dollars would buy. The postwar market was further enlivened by the fact that both France and England, always the reservoirs par excellence which supply the world, were on a closed economy. That is, they could export, within certain limits imposed by the national museums, but they would not import. Perforce any French or English capital available for such luxuries had to be spent within the boundaries of the respective countries. European collectors, to whom works of art are capital assets, spurred by fear of inflation and currency devaluation, bid against one another and against the foreign collectors and dealers. The natural result was an increase in prices.

The art market had already experienced the effect of this kind of closed economy during the Nazi regime in Germany, where prices were roughly one-third higher than on the free markets of France and England or in the United States. The postwar years saw this repeated in France and England. It should be emphasized, however, that this economic phenomenon applies only to works of international importance; the price of objects of purely local interest is governed by local demand. This is an important point which few collectors understand. A good example is Americana, a field in which certain collectors have invested lavishly. In the United States, Americana has historical, cultural, and sentimental value, hence it brings good prices. But even a fine collection would bring little on the Paris market, unless someone should decide to speculate with an eye to the American trade. The comparatively high prices paid in New York a few years ago for paintings by certain Swedish artists were due to this arbitrage; they were bought solely for export. No lack of aesthetic merit is implied in either case; it is simply that each plays only a tributary role in the over-all pageant of art history. A collection of paintings by the French petits-maîtres, despite shipping costs, could certainly bring a better return in Paris than in New York; likewise a collection reflecting the German aesthetic might find a readier market in Berlin or Frankfurt. The prices of great international leaders may drop under economic or social stress, but they always have a market whether at home or abroad.

The possibility of acquiring a great work of art diminishes each year, however, in proportion to shrinkage of the market supply. Laws controlling their export from Western Europe grow ever more stringent. Supply from the Iron Curtain countries has been almost entirely cut off. Each year a certain number of paintings enter public museums; barring exceedingly unusual circumstance, these are out of the market forever. All of these factors contribute to the prices which must be paid today for great paintings. What valuation is to be put on a Van Eyck, an important Watteau, or a Vermeer? Rarity places them beyond the normal laws of supply and demand; it becomes a question of the available means of a private collector or a public institution.

Nevertheless there are still great collections of superior quality which will eventually reach the market again. This is particularly true in Europe where laws of inheritance and the tax structure do not encourage the lavish benefactions which have channeled American collections into museums. It also happens, both in this country and abroad, that a collector's heirs have little interest in his treasures, preferring cash to aesthetic satisfaction.

There are fewer than forty fully acknowledged and recognized paintings by Vermeer. Only four are in private hands and may reasonably be expected ever to reach the market. The most exciting moment of my career came when one of these was turned over to me to sell. Some of the people who made this possible must remain anonymous and some of the details omitted, but it began like this.

Soon after the war, in Florence, I was surprised on the street by a familiar voice urgently calling my name. The caller was an old friend who had been trying to catch up with me all day. He knew I was scheduled to leave the city that night, but could I, he asked somewhat breathlessly, take time to talk with him. He had some photographs from the Arenberg Collection which he thought would interest me.

The name was enough. To any historian or art specialist, Arenberg means one of the oldest ducal and princely families of Europe, connected directly or indirectly with past and present crowned heads. It goes back to before the 11th century, with Everard IV de la Marck, Sire d'Arenberg, the first to receive the title of Comte de la Marck et d'Arenberg. In 1547, the Emperor Charles V, then sovereign of the Low Countries, reaffirmed to the descendants the privilege of bearing the arms and the name of Arenberg. In Brussels today, the Palais d'Arenberg, a national monument, recalls their illustrious past. To me, the name of Arenberg meant even more. My father had visited the late Engelbert-Marie, Duc d'Arenberg, fifteenth Duc d'Arschot et de Croy, fourth Prince de Recklinghausen et Comte de la Marck, in Brussels on a few occasions. He had told me of the great connoisseurship of that much titled gentleman, as well as of the difficulties he encountered in approaching him, for the Prince received few visitors and those with reluctance. The Marquis de Biron, who was connected with the Arenbergs through his sister's marriage, and whom I had often seen in my earlier years, frequently mentioned the Duke. The name also signified to me once vast holdings of land, large coal mining interests, castles in Belgium and Germany, but above all, it meant a great collection of works of art of the first importance. I did not know what had become of this collection following the death of the Duc Engelbert-Marie in 1949, except that since 1914 it was no longer in Brussels. For forty-odd years it had remained entirely hidden. No one knew what was still in it.

Most persistent of all the thoughts that ran through my head as I walked to my hotel with my friend was, "What of the lovely Vermeer *Portrait of a Young Girl?*" It had become a legend to art historians. It had even been said that the painting no longer existed. Members of the Arenberg family had found it convenient to be unaware of its present whereabouts, thus evading inquiry and an immense amount of correspondence. I was almost afraid to ask my friend about it. When he assured me that the Vermeer did indeed still exist, but was not for sale, I must have shown mixed feelings of relief and disappointment, for he hastened to spread before me a group of photographs, saying, "But what do you know about the Arenberg library of manuscripts?" Then he sat back with a satisfied smile to watch my reactions. For a moment I was speechless. One would expect a collection of the age and renown of the Arenberg to include manuscripts, but I was not prepared for their quality, for the apparently exceptional state of their preservation, or for their sumptuous beauty. For the moment I even forgot Vermeer.

Manuscripts are a specialist's province, and I am not an expert in the field, but later when I was able to examine these beautiful volumes, I knew once more that quality has no bounds; it is a universal property which unites all great works of art, be they manuscripts, armor, paintings, or sculpture. Even to the nonspecialist, manuscripts of this quality need little explanation. The periods and countries of their origin, their remarkable state of preservation, the crispness of the parchment, the exquisite freshness of the illuminations were at once apparent, while a lingering knowledge of Latin, Old French and German, gave me a further clue to their importance.

The task of handling these ancient and beautiful books during the weeks they were in my firm's care was to afford me the unexpected delight of delving into a new branch of knowledge, of acquiring a small library on the subject, and in some measure gaining the technical knowledge required. When it came to establishing a scientific catalogue, however, I realized that these manuscripts deserved the attention of a specialist, one with both knowledge and sensitivity. We appealed to Professor Meyer Schapiro of Columbia University. The physical details of exhibiting the delicate and precious books also called for professional advice, which was enthusiastically given by Frederick B. Adams and Miss Meta Harrsen of the Morgan Library and Miss Dorothy Miner of the Walters Gallery in Baltimore.

When the manuscripts were at last exhibited at my gallery in the fall of 1952, it was truly a revelation. Most of them were unknown, even to scholars. Of the thirty-three books shown, four had last been seen publicly in 1904 and the others were not even mentioned in the literature. During the final week of the showing, special guards had to be installed, so large was the crowd the manuscripts drew to my gallery. On the opening day, an exceedingly rare 11th century German Missal of the School of Mainz, still in its original binding, was purchased by cable by Martin Bodmer, a Swiss connoisseur whose library at Geneva is a landmark of science and beauty. A Netherland-ish Book of Hours of the Utrecht School (about 1415) went to the Morgan Library, which also later acquired a superb English Gospel of great rarity, dating from around the year 1000. The exquisitely rich and refined Book of Hours attributed to the Master of Boucicaut, a document of tremendous interest for the development of French primitive painting, a South Netherlandish Psalter of extraordinary character, and the Guillebert de Metz Book of Hours with seventeen delicately beautiful full-page miniatures went to a Parisian collector.

But all this was in the future as I looked at the photographs in Florence. I was still entranced with the idea of the Vermeer. Though I had been told it was not for sale, I was given the great treat of seeing it, and I shall never forget the emotion of the moment when it was at last placed in my hands—just to look at. Here was one of the world's most precious paintings, not just because it is rare and costly, but because its sheer beauty and its moving subject exude a mysteri-ous power that is unforgettable. The painting represents, with the utmost simplicity, a tender young girl, wearing a pale blue shawl about her thin, childish shoulders; a creamy yellow scarf flows from her hair, and an incredibly delicate pearl adorns her ear. She is not a beautiful girl, but in her eyes is concentrated an amazing vitality, as she looks wonderingly out at the world, a mysterious near-smile upon her lips; she seems actually to breathe and to move. Much has already been written of her, and much more will be, but no descrip-tion and no photograph can do her justice; she must be seen.

Since 1829, when it was first known to be in the Arenberg Collec-tion, few people had seen this painting which I held in my hands. Today, when the name of Vermeer is familiar even to the layman, it is easy to forget that his discovery by the modern world goes back only to the mid-19th century when W. Thoré-Burger, a French poli-tician, critic and journalist, became entranced by the beauty of the great *View of Delft* in the Mauritshuis at the Hague, and set out to learn more about this unknown Dutchman who signed his canvas with the monogram IVM. The Arenberg portrait was the fourth paint-ing in the oeuvre of the master to be identified by Thoré-Burger, who discovered it when he was called upon to catalogue the paintings of the ducal collection in 1859. This unassuming little volume, apparently the only catalogue ever made of the collection, is important in many ways. Not only does it give us an insight into the Arenberg Collection as it existed then, but since it was written at the beginning of Thoré-Burger's researches on Vermeer, it is of great interest in the study of that master. Even in the staid words of the catalogue, one senses the excitement of the exiled Frenchman, on the threshold of one of art history's great discoveries, as he records the painting found in the Galerie d'Arenberg. After recounting something of the history of this unknown Jan Vermeer of Delft, he continues:

"And his works? By his works one knows the master. Very well, his works, which, in fact, indicate a workman of the first rank, his works number. . . . Count them: one landscape in the museum of the Hague. Two pictures in the collection of M. Six van Hillegom of Amsterdam, *perhaps* a picture which is attributed to him in the Van der Hoop Museum in Amsterdam, and . . . a portrait in the Galerie d'Arenberg!" Not abandoning his objectivity or his natural scepticism, he follows this statement with a note to the effect that he has just been told of a fifth, in the collection of Count Czernin of Vienna, representing an artist in his studio with a map in the background, but, he adds, "I have not yet seen it."

Since this first recording in the Arenberg inventory, the painting has been listed among the incontestable Vermeers in all the books devoted to the artist, beginning with Thoré-Burger's own published in 1866. It had been exhibited, to my knowledge, only once, in Düsseldorf in 1904. And now after my one tantalizing glimpse, back it had to go, into seclusion once more.

In time, the painting's owner decided that this exquisite canvas should be put in my custody, but it was not to be offered for sale, nor could it be shown. It could undergo a light cleaning—which was done at my gallery under my personal supervision—and, for purposes of identification and study, the various scientific photographs, x-ray, ultraviolet, and infrared, could be made. A frame was also to be chosen, with a glass to protect the canvas against air pollution, and a special chamois-lined case, like a great jewel-box, was ordered for it.

Finally, the day came when I was authorized to arrange its sale. The news created a sensation. Connoisseurs, collectors, and museum officials from all over the United States and, presently, from Europe came to see the "prodigal daughter." All of them, particularly the museum directors and their trustees, coveted it, and made plans for its acquisition. None of these were to materialize. Within a few hours after Mr. and Mrs. Charles B. Wrightsman, discriminating collectors and generous donors to the Metropolitan Museum, saw and fell in love with the lovely little girl, this unique masterpiece had found a new home.

If Europe remains the prime source of rare works—though not always a Vermeer—Europe also continues to nourish exceptional collectors. In my experience there is no better evidence of the vitality of the tradition than the example of the late Emil Bührle.

A collector like Bührle is a joy and a challenge to a dealer. He not only set himself a very definite plan, but had great knowledge in his chosen areas and a wholly justified pride in his achievements. Bührle's first thought was to bring together a collection which would present a picture of the evolution of art from roughly the beginning of impressionism to our day. While such a group would have a tremendous pedagogical quality, it would impose an aesthetic and intellectual limit. Art, after all, involves other enjoyments besides that of teaching. It was strange to me that a man endowed with so real a love of the beautiful as Bührle should be so categorical and determined about his collecting, one of the few fields where escape into time and space is still possible. It was also difficult to imagine that a man so thoroughly immersed in international questions and in constant communication with men from all over the world, could limit his aesthetic enjoyment to so short a span, say 1870 to 1950.

Then he did step over this self-imposed boundary when he recognized the importance of Courbet, an artist still too much neglected. When he began to take an interest in Ingres and Fragonard and then in drawings and water colors, to which he had so far given little heed, I realized how quickly Bührle was evolving. As further evidence that my first instinct was right, he explained, shortly after he had acquired several 18th century Italian paintings, that he had discovered the close link between these artists and the French Impressionists. It sounded almost as though, having originally set a doctrinal program, he needed to justify to himself, and perhaps to others, this enlargement of his circle of interest, as if enjoyment alone were not a good enough reason. The intellectual pleasure of knowing that Renoir is indebted to Fragonard, who in turn had been impressed by Tiepolo, or that Cezanne via Courbet continues the austere tradition of the French classicists of the 17th century is not necessary to the emotional enjoyment of their works.

245

Emil Bührle, a tall, slender man, was elegant in a reserved way and evidently fastidious about his appearance. His determined features were softened by his smile, and his long, sensitive fingers were perhaps a clue to his love for art and the beautiful. In an address in June, 1954, at the University of Zurich, he said that "a real collector is a thwarted artist." This may be true, but it is not quite convincing in his case; I doubt that Emil Bührle would ever have had the patience or tranquility of mind to become a painter. He was essentially a man of action whose vitality and dynamism surpassed that of most people. He was as willing to start a chat at midnight as at eight o'clock breakfast. His methods of working, in fact, reminded me of American business titans of the past. Unlike many of the Americans, however, Bührle, in spite of his fortune, lived very simply with democratic Swiss dislike of ostentation. The real luxury of his home, besides his collection, is its magnificent site overlooking the Lake of Zurich. But Bührle's achievements seemed more American than European, probably because we have believed that the Old World no longer offered such possibilities.

He was born in Pforzheim, in Baden, South Germany, in 1890 and the double pattern of his life, science and art, seems to have been set in his formative years. As a boy of sixteen, his lively interest in scientific problems earned him the nickname of "Electric Jacob"; yet, his college career was essentially devoted to literature and the arts. Perhaps it was his responsibilities as an artillery officer in World War I, and later the necessity of gaining a livelihood, which turned his thoughts once again to industrial science.

He was working for a great Magdeburg machine works when that company acquired, in 1923, a relatively small machine tool plant in Oerlikon, just outside Zurich. Bührle, then thirty-four years old, was appointed its director. By 1929, he owned a controlling interest in the Oerlikon Werkzeugmaschinenfabrik and by 1937, Bührle, now a Swiss citizen, was the sole stockholder. This swift rise was largely due to his foresight in purchasing the patents for the twenty-millimeter Becker cannon which, with improvements and changes, became the famous Oerlikon gun. When World War II erupted, production was extended to England and after 1941, the gun was manufactured on a tremendous scale in the United States. The original purpose of the Oerlikon factory, however, was never superseded—the manufacture of industrial machine tools for peaceful purposes. Today it ranges from locomotive parts to spinners for cotton and nylon thread, and includes vast researches and production in electronics.

As for his art collection, Bührle once compared its growth to successive waves reaching a beach. It started, he told me, as a mild hobby with the early purchase of two water colors by Heckel which he always kept on his walls for sentimental reasons. This first enthusiasm, encouraged and fostered by his friend, Hugo von Tschudi, then Director of the National Gallery in Berlin, Bührle transformed into a definite program to which he devoted the same determination, pride, and love that he gave to his business. I doubt that Emil Bührle ever undertook anything which he did not see through, and in this same purposeful manner, he pursued his ambition to build a collection worthy of the name he had made for himself.

Though he always referred to his "collection," it was actually already a museum, one which many a city would indeed envy. The representation of Van Gogh is unique outside those owned by the heirs of the artist himself. The number and quality of paintings by Cezanne is more than impressive. There is a room devoted to Degas, another filled with paintings by Renoir. He was fortunate in having the encouragement and cooperation of Mrs. Bührle and his charming daughter, for a close relationship of both affection and understanding of works of art is rare indeed among families of collectors. His family also shared his interest in the generous prizes he established in Paris for young artists and in the public spirit which prompted him to lend freely from his collection.

If Emil Bührle could find the time, he was always willing to listen to new ideas and theories, but time was the asset with which he was least willing to part. He was more lavish with money than with minutes. To him money represented time already spent, whereas present time represented future success. Perhaps with the years—he was still a comparatively young man when he died in 1956—he might have granted himself more hours for the enjoyment of the aesthetic treasure he was storing up and which he truly loved.

CHAPTER XXIII

Sculpture

The neglect of sculpture in recent years, and my own special love for it, has led me to ponder the reasons for this lack of public appreciation. Certainly it was not always so; is it, then, just another inexplicable change in public taste, or are there deeper reasons?

Perhaps the explanation goes back to the elemental reactions of infancy, when the first response is to motion and color. Yet, the child's first creative instinct is undeniably to build or to model. Left to his own devices in proximity to sand and water, he creates forms which his imagination endows with the attributes of a fortress, a man, a horse. Modeling with any element at hand is an aptitude which man acquires before the hand has sufficient coordination to guide pencil or crayon.

Evidently, however, this instinct to mold with the hands is shoved aside by environment. Should the child be attracted by the charms of art, as he grows older, it will be to two-dimensional representation in color; and appreciation of black and white comes only with a later evolution. When interest (and I speak now of the layman, not the creative artist) develops to the sophistication of black and white, why does it not simultaneously reach out to sculpture which has the added element of three-dimensionalism?

The explanation escapes me. With the development of the tactile sense, it seems to me that to caress, even visually, a sensitive and beautifully realized sculpture yields great rewards; it actually calls for a lesser effort of the imagination than a similar tactile reaction to a two-dimensional representation. My wife tells me of having once conducted a party of blind youngsters through the museum in Kansas

248

City, where she was a staff member. In the painting galleries one could only try with the feeble means of words to convey by description what a painting looked like, but they were allowed to "see" the sculpture with their hands. It was fascinating to watch their reactions. One teen-aged girl actually recoiled when her probing fingers ran over the hideous grimace of a Chinese demon-guardian. She definitely felt the menace of his expression and cried out, "Oh, he is ugly." But she smiled and allowed her hands to linger lovingly upon the velvety planes of a marble Madonna.

The blind girl was undoubtedly an unusually perceptive child, and her hands had developed a sensitivity to compensate for her lack of sight. But if the hands are able to convey such vivid images to the mind, why is it more difficult for the eye to do so? One can only conclude that a person is born with this faculty, or he lacks it. If it exists in essence, it may be developed; but if nature has left it out, it cannot be acquired. I have observed that some people are instantaneously affected by the sight of great sculpture while others, however hard they may try, remain cold and untouched. It is true, however, that the full measure of enjoyment comes only with an imagination able to understand the purpose of the artist who created each sculpture, to place it mentally in its proper environment, so that its height, its distance from the beholder, its background are implicitly understood. To do this requires knowledge as well as love.

Personally I would go so far as to say that sculpture is the highest form of art, and the sculptor, creative capacities being equal, is a greater artist than the painter. This opinion will doubtless be challenged, but it is one which I am little apt, at this point in my age and experience, to change. It derives directly from the sheer enjoyment I receive from a great plastic form. This predilection, which I may have inherited from my father, also an ardent admirer of sculpture, explains the emphasis our firm has always put on this particular field. It is instinctive, not a result of a premeditated decision or of business acumen. In fact, the reluctance of the public, and even of many museums, to collect sculpture makes it one of the least profitable fields for the dealer.

Let there be no misunderstanding. I speak only in terms of works of superior quality. First among the requisites is the material. Marble is to me the medium par excellence. Always the most costly, it is also the most difficult to work; an inadvertent stroke of the chisel cannot be made good. The greatest artists ever since the Greeks have chosen it for their masterpieces. Next comes bronze, which up to the 16th and even the 17th centuries was a difficult technique to master, at least in a monumental work. In the 18th century, with a few exceptions, bronze was again abandoned in favor of marble; but in the 19th it regained its prominence through such artists as Rodin and Degas.

There are exceptions, of course. One of my proudest finds of many years back was a wonderful pink stone angel of the 13th century which had turned up among the debris of a demolition in the old city of Strasbourg. It was actually Robert Forrer, connoisseur, collector, and Professor at the University of Strasbourg who discovered it, but it was too big to be shown to advantage in his small house; over five feet in height, it needed perspective. He could not hide his chagrin that he must let it go. How ideally beautiful, how moving is this angel, yet how simple its lines. The slight *dehanchement,* the inclination of the head, and, above all, the divine smile give it an intense life, warmed by the delicate glow of the pink stone. Certainly there is no more magnificent achievement in all art than the stone sculptures of the Middle Ages. Stone was also marvelously used in the Renaissance, nor can one overlook the delightful boxwood figures and ivory carvings of these periods.

This feeling for materials has led me to disregard certain media which in my earlier years I was willing to consider—sculptures made in molds or by similar techniques, terra cottas, stuccos, plasters, which allow reproduction ad infinitum. Houdon, for example, reminds us in his notes that he delivered twenty-one plaster busts made after his famous marble portrait of Sophie Arnould. Evidently they were passed around to her admirers much as photographs would be today. Again, however, I must make exception of the charming productions of the 18th century in France, when artists like Clodion and Marin achieved such delicacy in terra cotta. On the other hand, one knows all too many monotonous and dull polychromed stuccos of the Renaissance, "inspired" by Donatello or Rossellino.

This does not imply that they are necessarily fakes, though there have been plenty, for molded media lend themselves easily to the hand of the faker. Not even the difficulties of marble, however, have been proof against the master forger, the classic example being the great, for he was great in his twisted way, Alceo Dossena. It was thanks to the timely warnings of Dr. Leo Planiscig, then Curator of the Kunsthistorisches Museum in Vienna, that I never joined the ranks of Dossena's victims. During one of my visits to Planiscig in the early twenties, he showed me photographs he had gathered over the past several years of Italian sculptures, all of which were forgeries. They were pieces which had been widely extolled in Italy, and Planiscig, knowing my partiality to marbles, suggested that I be on my guard. Sooner or later one would undoubtedly be offered to me.

Planiscig did not then know the name of the forger, but he was making every effort to trace each piece back to its origin. He was already convinced that all of them had come from the same Italian city. A year or so later, I again saw his files, now grown to considerable proportions, and by that time he had learned the identity of the forger-craftsman. Seen together they revealed their common characteristics; particularly striking was a similarity of vacuousness which became more and more noticeable as it was multiplied by numerous examples. Meanwhile, I had seen and studied one of these spurious sculptures, which was so attractive that had I not been forewarned, I should probably have been another victim. Had Dossena been content to make only one or two statues, it would doubtless have taken much longer to expose him; fortunately, overproduction is the common mistake of most forgers, and the greedy intermediaries who exploit them.

It was Planiscig's intention to make his discoveries known first to his colleagues and then to publish his documents. When the Dossena affair was made public in 1928, Planiscig's photographs were used in an article appearing in the *Illustrated London News,* one of them carrying the notation that the sculpture had been offered to the Kunsthistorisches Museum in 1922 and refused. Although many people have since claimed to have been the first to recognize the work of the perverted Italian genius, I do not believe that Dossena would have been exposed as early as he was without the pioneering detective work of Leo Planiscig.

Planiscig was a great scholar of the whole field of Italian sculpture, but bronzes were particularly dear to him. Though Bode had already devoted some study to them, it was the authoritative works of Planiscig which demonstrated their real importance. Many of the greatest artists of the 15th and 16th centuries worked in this medium, and our knowledge of such men as Giovanni da Bologna and the Leoni would

251

be indeed incomplete without a study of the bronzes. One of my most cherished finds in bronze, a small thing as precious objects often are, was not really my find, but Leo Planiscig's.

He had seen, in an obscure Viennese antique shop, a little bronze Venus with an Amor, mounted on the same base with a quite ordinary equestrian Marcus Aurelius or some such Roman, with which it had nothing whatever to do. His discerning eye had detected at once that they were completely different in period, treatment, and patina. If he were not greatly mistaken, the Venus was certainly by the hand of one of the masters of Italian Renaissance sculpture. I chanced to be in Vienna at the time and Planiscig told me about it. He was well known to the shop owner, he said, and had been there several times. He did not want to go back again for fear of arousing too much interest, but would I go? "I won't mention an artist," he said, "but if you get it, I'd like a chance to study it for a few days; then I'll tell you if I'm right or wrong."

Dr. Planiscig's word on bronze sculpture was law to me. Even without it, had I seen the little Venus first, I would have bought it, so immediate was its appeal. In spite of its size, small enough to fit in one's pocket, it evoked a tactile reaction of tantalizing proportions. Shed of its encumbrances of base and Marcus Aurelius, dusted and polished, the soft, mellowness of the extraordinary patina gave it the "feel" of gold, and every facet of its modeling revealed the fingers of a master. Obviously cast from a wax model, it had been carefully chiseled and hammered in every minute detail; the hair, the nails on hands and feet, all were exquisitely delineated, but with a mastery that gave the whole an intense vitality and an amazing monumentality.

Planiscig kept it in his office for several days, studying it and comparing it with other bronzes in the Kunsthistorische Collection. At last he told me what he had not dared express earlier for fear that his imagination had run away with him. Dramatically, placing it side by side with the great *Tellus and Neptune* saltcellar of the museum's collection (the same one exhibited in the United States with the Vienna Treasures in 1949–1950), he pointed out what was then to me, as to him, the only answer. It could only be from the hand of that fabulous genius of the jewel-like and the monumental, Benvenuto Cellini.

Naturally, Planiscig wanted it desperately for his museum, but no funds were available. So, in the hope that it might some day find its way into the institution he so loved, he suggested that we offer it to a Viennese collector and benefactor of the museum. At this moment, Dr. William Valentiner also happened to be in Vienna. He immediately concurred in the attribution to Cellini and he, too, would have liked to acquire it for the Detroit Museum. However, I was committed to Planiscig's collector friend, August Lederer. Lederer and his son, Eric, collected together in a rare partnership; if Eric had the greater taste and knowledge, his father was willing and pleased to be guided by him. But the Vienna Museum did not get the small bronze, either. The superb Lederer Collection of Renaissance paintings and objets d'art, including the Cellini, was looted during the last war so I was told. I have never known its fate.

I encountered Leo Planiscig once in Venice when he was devoting his holiday to a search for unrecorded sculptures among the churches, palaces, and public buildings of that lovely old city. Until that time I had met him only in his official capacity of Curator in Vienna, and it was the hours I spent in his company in Venice which developed a real friendship and led me to a full appreciation of one of the most charming men I have ever known. His gaiety, his sharp wit, his brilliantly quick mind made him a delightful companion, as well as a learned mentor. He was then gathering documents on the Lombardi dynasty—Pietro, Antonio, and the great Tullio—and he initiated me into the difficulties of scaffoldings as we climbed about lofty churches, I gleaning precious bits of knowledge as he chatted about the works he was examining. When I saw him last, a few summers ago, at the villa in Florence to which he had retired after the Nazi invasion of Austria, he showed me the large, carefully labeled and documented file of photographs for his book on the Lombardi. An untimely death unfortunately prevented the publication of this work to which he had given so much time and effort. It also prevented the fulfillment of one of his dearest wishes, a visit to the United States.

Mutual interest also drew me to Paul Vitry, for many years Chief Curator of Sculpture at the Louvre, but I am afraid it was a somewhat frustrating friendship for both of us. Upon three different occasions we had numerous conversations and lengthy correspondence about French sculptures which both of us would have liked to see remain in France, but which could not for lack of funds.

One of these was a marble bas-relief, a *Descent from the Cross,* by the rare 16th century French sculptor, Jean Goujon. I hastened to call it to Vitry's attention, not solely because he was a Curator of the Louvre, but also because he was a connoisseur who reacted to beauty with sensitivity and intuition as well as assured judgment. He needed no documentation to attest its historical existence before allowing himself to admire a work of art. If documents were available, well and good, but their lack never caused him to deny a lovely object its very identity, as too frequently happened in the Chartist tradition of scholarship.

Vitry was highly interested by the bas-relief, brought his colleagues to see it, and asked me if I would be willing to reserve it while he endeavored to raise the funds for its purchase. When the Louvre itself could not finance it, he asked for an extension of time while he negotiated with the Institut de France in the hope that they might buy it for the Musée Jacquemart-André. Since I had found the sculpture in England and re-imported it into France, I needed no authorization to export it again, and I was under no obligation to present it first to the French museums; but the dearth of French Renaissance sculptures in their homeland gave me a double moral responsibility, and I was happy to grant his request for more time. That the bas-relief eventually found its way to the Metropolitan Museum in New York is surely America's gain, but France's loss cannot be laid to any lack of effort on the part of Paul Vitry.

Another series of interviews with Vitry concerned a life-sized marble statue of Saint Barbara by another 16th century French sculptor, Germain Pilon. In this case he found himself in an embarrassing dilemma. He wanted the statue, but apparently the Louvre had not bid for it at the Kraemer auction in 1913 (Vitry was not yet Chief Curator at that time), and now it was difficult for him to propose it at a considerably higher price. This handsome marble, now in Kansas City, must surely have been part of a monumental architectural composition, still unidentified. However, I feel certain that a keen eye will some day detect the clue to this mystery in some neglected document in the prodigious archives of France. If Vitry were still alive, it would in all probability be he who would dig it up, for with true scholarly objectivity, he never lost interest in the problems of a sculpture which he admired, even though it might have passed from his official province.

254

I saw this intellectual tenacity well demonstrated in connection with another work which the firm owned, this time a marble bust by Jean-Antoine Houdon of the charlatan Cagliostro, who played an important, if not very savory role in the annals of the 18th century. The bust had come from the Wallace-Bagatelle Collection, and Vitry, who was an authority on Houdon, had written of it as far back as 1908, when it was lent to an exhibition by Sir John Murray Scott. I am sure Vitry must have coveted it for the Louvre even then, and now that it was available, it was the same old story no funds and no interested donor in sight. Apparently, Vitry never forgot the piece or the problem which it had posed to him as a student of Houdon's work. The problem was that there were two nearly identical marbles of Cagliostro, both signed and dated the same year. A most unusual circumstance, for while Houdon frequently made a whole series of plasters, he seldom repeated himself in marble; the Voltaire series is an exception. They had come to light at about the same time in the 1860's, after having been lost to public knowledge, one going to Lord Hertford, and the other eventually to the museum at Aix-en-Provence. Who had commissioned them, and why had Houdon found it necessary to make two?

When the Cagliostro bust went to London, at Paul Vitry's request, for the great exhibition of French art in 1932, I sent the meager historical data I had. Upon receiving the catalogue, I was amazed to find that Vitry had added not only to the bibliography but to the history. (The Cagliostro appears only in the later editions of the 1932 catalogue, as the bust was in New York at the time and I hesitated to send it on account of the fragility of the marble until too late for the early printing.) He had discovered that the Cardinal de Rohan, a great admirer of the mercurial Cagliostro, had once owned a marble portrait of him. Further, Vitry found that another had at one time been in the Temple of Freemasonry in Lyon. When I saw Vitry, he told me he had concluded that my portrait must surely be the one originally commissioned by Rohan, his reasoning being that so important a personage and so great a connoisseur as Rohan would never have accepted the Aix bust because of blemishes in the marble itself. Vitry had hoped to have both at the London exhibition in order to compare them in detail. I am sorry this was not done, as I have always believed that they differ in subtle ways that photographs, made in different places under different conditions, are not precise enough to reveal.

It was my personal love of sculpture which led me to persist in the pursuit of what appeared for a time to be a figment of my imagination—a group of Italian marble sculptures of the 14th and 15th centuries from the collection of His Highness the Prince of Liechtenstein.

The justly celebrated collection of the House of Liechtenstein was begun in the 15th century, with at least one Prince in each generation a devoted gatherer of works of art. In the 19th century, Johann II put the final touches on its greatness, published catalogues and guide books, and opened the galleries of the Liechtenstein Palace in Vienna to the public. Just before World War II, the works of art were removed to the tiny principality of Liechtenstein where, with the exception of a part which has been exhibited in various European museums, it had remained.

When rumors began to circulate, several years ago, about possible sales from this princely group, I realized that the most important paintings would be sold at extremely high prices, high enough to preclude the possibility of outright purchase by dealers. This impression was confirmed when several paintings were consigned for sale to certain galleries, but without exclusive contract. I was not interested in this kind of procedure, nor in the paintings of lesser merit which might admit of outright purchase. My thoughts turned in the direction of sculpture, for it seemed to me that this collection, built up over several centuries when paintings were not the sole interest of the amateur, should include exceptional sculptures.

I had a vague recollection of having seen marbles in the Vienna Gallery years ago, but the only object I could recall with any clarity was a well-known bas-relief of a Madonna and Child, then attributed to Rossellino. I consulted catalogues and old guide books, the latest of an exhibition in 1952 in Lucerne of part of the collection. It mentioned only a few small bronzes and no larger works. The old guide books were of little assistance for they contained vague references and no reproductions; the only work of importance prominently mentioned was the aforesaid Rossellino now attributed to Benedetto da Maiano.

My search seemed to lead nowhere. The obvious solution of going directly to the castle in Vaduz where the Prince now resided hardly seemed the proper method. At that point it occurred to me that my best source of information was, again, Leo Planiscig, whose knowledge of Austrian collections was encyclopedic. Accordingly, on my next trip to Europe, I called on him in Florence, where he had taken refuge after the Nazi invasion of Austria. He was able to confirm my belief that a group of exceptional trecento and quattrocento Italian marbles had been in the Liechtenstein Collection. Most valuable, however, was his recollection that photographs existed in a certain library, difficult of access but possible.

After lengthy correspondence, the reproductions at last reached my hands. Then came a process of elimination. Finally, photographs of seven Italian sculptures of the 14th and 15th centuries, all in marble, were selected. Provided reality bore out the reproductions, it was these that my firm would try to purchase. There would be no consignment and no third parties involved.

It is only just and proper that due credit be given here to the late Dr. William R. Valentiner for the distinterested help and guidance he gave me in making my choice. Italian sculpture was also one of his most beloved areas of research. So broad was his knowledge that a glance at the photographs enabled him to identify several of them immediately, opinions which he was happy to reaffirm when he saw the originals. The catalogue which my firm published—masterpieces of this rarity call for a special publication—sums up the available data for those who care to consult it, but the mastery of Valentiner's immediate classification is worthy of comment.

He at once recognized the exquisite Angel of the Annunciation by the Master of the Mascoli Altar as belonging with three figures, a Virgin and the Saints Peter and Paul, already in the Samuel H. Kress Foundation Collection. Thus when the Foundation acquired the seven Liechtenstein sculptures for the National Gallery, the Angel Gabriel could once more greet the Virgin, and the gesture of his upraised hand regain its full significance. The Prudentia and the Justitia, briefly mentioned in the Liechtenstein catalogue as by a Naples artist of the 14th century, called to his mind the tomb of Folchino degli Schizzi in Cremona, a dated monument signed by Bonino da Campione. He was able to reinforce this attribution by the most convincing evidence when he produced from his remarkable files what apparently is the only existing photograph of the Cremona tomb. Not the least of my admiration for Valentiner was the fact that he always knew exactly where in his tiers of file cabinets to find what he wanted.

I first met William Valentiner when I accompanied my father to the United States in 1913. American museums, in those early days of their history, had few professional art historians or museum experts and it was J. Pierpont Morgan, the Metropolitan's new President, who began to recruit trained personnel both here and abroad. When Morgan appealed to Wilhelm von Bode, Director of the Kaiser Friedrich Museum in Berlin for a recommendation for the department of decorative art, Bode named his young assistant, Valentiner, as his first choice. Valentiner served in this capacity from 1908 until World War I called him back to Germany. Immediately after the war he returned to this country, became a citizen and, as head of the Detroit Institute of Arts, helped build that museum into one of the nation's finest. At the time of his death in 1959, he was consultant to Detroit and to the Los Angeles County Museum, as well as Director of the new North Carolina Museum of Art at Raleigh. His entire career was closely linked to the artistic development of the United States to which he made significant contribution.

His chief fields of interest—and he was unsurpassed in them—were Dutch painting and Italian sculpture. His studies in the latter revealed a vast amount of fascinating new material. It is amazing that so much misconception could still exist in a field already so well worked. Too often we have been satisfied with the repetition of hearsay, the printing and reprinting of legends which do not stand up under close examination and empirical study.

The amount of actual physical labor involved in the study of sculpture is far greater than in paintings, entailing as it often does on-the-spot work in old buildings or ancient churches in towns off the beaten path. Valentiner, like Planiscig, had special scaffoldings built to enable him to climb to some shadowy part of a church to study at close range a statue practically hidden in the obscurity. Getting permission to do so and finding a photographer willing to make the same climb in order to record the findings were not the least of the difficulties.

When I last saw Valentiner, in the summer of 1959, he was seventy-eight, and we spent two long sessions examining together the several rooms of French 17th century paintings then on exhibition in Paris. He was as eager to absorb new knowledge as he had been thirty years earlier, and he was as straight and as slim. He had the same trick of throwing his head backward as though looking down from a great height which gave him an air of slight condescension, even offishness. This, as I knew, was largely a shield against intrusions on the tremendous amount of work he accomplished daily. Valentiner's great quality as an art historian and expert was his instantaneous and enthusiastic reaction to beauty, an especially remarkable quality in view of his early training in the narrow and pedantic Teutonic school. He never hesitated to make an affirmative approach, unlike those who systematically choose to be negative until they have dissected a work of art to find out how and why it ticks. He had faith, and rightly, in his own judgment and in his reaction to those imponderables which create an emotional euphoria.

CHAPTER XXIV

Summing Up

In the more than forty years in which Jacques Seligmann headed his firm, he witnessed many changes in the manner of collecting, in the type of objects collected, and in the economics of the art world. But the changes which took place between 1880 and 1923 were small compared to those of the last four decades. Men who were masters of their profession in 1920 might find themselves in a completely alien world today.

The art scene must be viewed in its relation to the political, social, and economic crises which have buffeted the world. Though several American industrialists had built superb collections before 1914, prosperous Europe with its balanced economy and stores of gold was still the center of the art world. Who would have dreamed then that Russian public treasures would one day be included in a National Gallery at Washington? For that matter, who would have believed that an American National Gallery, then nonexistent, would in so short a time become one of the world's leading museums?

While Europeans by no means ceased to be interested in works of art after World War I, the might of purchasing power shifted with the mass of gold. The tempo of collecting in the United States increased, first in quantity, then in quality, as new museums and universities began to vie with one another in the advancement of culture and the acquisition of artistic wealth. New York seemed in a fair way to becoming the art capital of the world. When World War II once more plunged Europe into chaos and the postwar years raised the American dollar to new heights of desirability, the trend was accelerated. The reversal which came with the swift recovery of the European economy in the fifties, particularly as it affected the art market, is one of the amazing phenomena of our time. The art markets of London and Paris are more brilliant than ever and if European museums still are not able to compete fully with their richer American rivals, American private collectors once more must take European private competition into serious account.

In collecting itself, the rising demand for paintings, which began in the twenties with the passion for old masters, continued through the thirties with an equal passion for Impressionists and Post-Impressionists. It has reached staggering heights in the prices paid at public auction in the last few years for paintings of almost every description.

And the preoccupation with names still goes on, even though art history has come of age, and research among the derivative artists has proven that a name is often an ephemeral thing. Attributions have been revised to reduce the number of paintings firmly given to many a well-known master and, in turn, to develop a number of school painters of considerable interest. We have long known, for instance, that the larger compositions of Rubens were seldom painted by him in toto. By the same process we have discovered that El Greco had a son who was an excellent artist. The great Giambattista Tiepolo has had to move over a bit to make room for his son, Giandomenico, who was once scarcely noticed. There have been similar splittings of personalities, or, in reverse, regroupings about one artist of works which have been attributed to several. The artist whose oeuvre has remained intact is rare. As new evidence is found, these, too, may have to share their glory.

It is interesting to speculate upon the possible reaction of the owners of paintings by Pieter de Hooch had Thoré-Burger's research taken place in the 1920's or even in the 1950's, instead of the 1850's. Would these collectors or museum directors have been pleased that their finest Pieter de Hoochs, for which they had paid high prices, were now attributed, by an obscure journalist, to some unknown artist from Delft called Jan Vermeer?

If one is willing to be sufficiently objective, it must be admitted that the desire to know the name of the author of a great masterpiece is a curiosity of the intellect which often obscures the primary aim of aesthetic value. An excellent example can be found in medieval art. It would be interesting, indeed exciting, to discover the names of the creators of medieval painting and sculpture, but that knowledge would add not one whit to the superb beauty of these rare works.

261

This is not to minimize the work of research scholars; quite the contrary. It is they who have helped us to a rationalization of art, to a philosophy of understanding and appreciation. To ignore their labors would be to prefer the fog of ignorance which surrounded the infancy of art history. Moreover, the art historian needs to be a man of considerable courage; rare is the scholar who has not at one time or another been held up to criticism for his classifications or attributions. This type of criticism is a real compliment. It takes learning and enthusiasm, as well as courage, to launch into new territory where the daring scholar must take a stand and back it up with stylistic evidence. Often he has no documents on which to found his theory, but must rely entirely on his keen senses and basic knowledge; if he stumbles, his explorations at least show the way for others. The passive type of criticism which turns out volumes in tedious series, superbly illustrated with fully recorded and well-established works of art presents no problems. Neither does it add an ounce to the weight of our knowledge.

The scholar first became indispensable to the dealer for the endorsement he could give, but how much more necessary he is today for the enrichment his publications, his cooperation, and an ever-increasing personal relationship has brought to the dealer. Indeed, it is he who has put the dealer on his mettle to develop his own knowledge, to build up his own research staff and his own library, to become himself something of an art historian.

With art scholarship in constant evolution, with new discoveries and new documentation coming to light every day, it would seem that the name of an artist should mean less to the collector and bring him once more to my father's dictum, "Only quality counts. Quality is enduring, and quality can be judged." This very process—the attribution of a work of art first to one master and then, in the course of time, to another—should propel a collector to search for quality. Can we admire less the lovely profile portrait, formerly in the Mackay Collection and now in the National Gallery in Washington, because it was once called a Pisanello but now seems generally recognized as by an unknown French artist of the international style? Does it actually diminish our enjoyment of the superb youthful David—the beautiful marble of the Widener Collection—to know that John Pope-Hennessy has recently proved beyond doubt that it is the work of Rosellino rather than a capital work of Donatello? Joe Widener, were he still alive, might be disappointed, for it can be argued that, for the time being at least, a work by Donatello may have a greater financial worth. It is possible, also, that Widener might not have bought it had it been called Rossellino, and that would have been a great loss to the country's art collection.

Moreover, if a great name can sell a fine work of art, there is the dangerous possibility that it can also over-sell a less worthy one. Witness the sheeplike rush of certain of today's collectors to acquire canvases by names in the modern field. Not every painting of an artist is equally great; over-emphasis increases an already dangerous tendency to admire the mediocre with the superb because it bears the name of a master. So determined was Rouault to guard his reputation, even after the grave, that he destroyed great numbers of paintings which he considered unworthy of his talent. Renoir, unfortunately, did not take such precautions; the leavings of Renoir's studio, the sketches, the studies, the discarded canvases, are now all carefully catalogued and stamped. These indifferent little paintings can add nothing to the grandeur of the master and, what is more, can give little aesthetic satisfaction to their owners.

The dealers must certainly share the blame for this trend. The constant repetition of exhibitions of the works of the favorites of the late 19th and 20th centuries only serves to confirm a public taste already too eager to follow the leader, instead of broadening that taste to look objectively at the relative merits of periods and artists. As much as we admire Renoir and Van Gogh, it is not the function of the progressive dealer to show their works over and over again. That is the province of the museums which can keep them permanently on display. The dealer should dare to show the neglected artist, the forgotten period, if convinced they are neglected or forgotten undeservedly, not through lack of intrinsic merit.

This great inflation of prestige and price of 19th and early 20th century paintings has another unfortunate aspect—its effect upon contemporary artists. Much of the speculative buying today in the contemporary field can be described as blind buying. Choices often are made not because of any particular enjoyment of the paintings themselves or for their quality, but for purely mercenary ends. The simple of mind, knowing the golden opportunities which their fathers missed —the Cezannes, the Van Goghs, the Seurats which went begging for purchasers during the lifetimes of the artists—imagine that they are

263

assured of future profits when they invest in any painting by a young artist around whom enough publicity has been woven. In their haste to take advantage of a good thing, the speculators—dealers and collectors alike—urge the artist to produce beyond his capacity. The artist, unless he has great force of character, may allow himself to be drawn into a hot-house atmosphere, under an obligation to work at double time. Genius cannot be created by force of will, an artist's tempo of production cannot be accelerated beyond its normal pace, nor can his creative direction be set by another.

The clamor that accompanies every exhibition of the work of some much advertised young newcomer (the younger, the better, as he will have longer to live and more time to produce) creates a climate difficult to escape unless strict objectivity is guarded. Real and lasting recognition has seldom come to an artist in a single showing of a few canvasas; his talent can only be truly evaluated upon aesthetic progress. This needs time. And it is not the quality of his publicity which must stand the test of time, but the quality of his creative ability.

Of course, the dealer should encourage and promote the young unknown artist, and, of course, the public should buy his work. But the situation as we too often see it today is an affront to real artists who know that true success does not come easily; that there are bound to be setbacks along the way, and that hard work and glamor are not synonymous. Just as it takes knowledge and affection to choose a painting of, say, the 17th century which comes without a pedigree and no certification of a great master's name, so it takes knowledge and affection to choose contemporary works of art which will satisfy the aesthetic sense, and at prices in keeping with the qualities displayed.

Great private collections of international scope and importance have been comparatively few in any age, but they have all had two things in common, quality and diversity. The man who acquires ten mediocre objects because their individual prices are low, rather than one outstanding piece, defeats the purpose of the true collector, enjoyment of what he owns. The ten lesser items can yield him an emotional and aesthetic return only in terms of that lesser quality; the exceptional work of art will always be a joy. As for the material aspects, I have never found it difficult to dispose of exceptional works; it is the average item in a collection that takes time and effort, even at a low price. The former sell themselves; the latter have to be sold.

Similarly, specialization is a pitfall avoided by the true collector. Art is in essence universal, and to limit its scope, willfully or unconsciously, is contrary to its very spirit. The more one delves into any single aspect of civilization, the narrower one's outlook is apt to become, with attention focusing more and more on the particular, the details rather than the whole. Collecting then either follows the line of least resistance, easy because it is familiar, or develops into an obsessive ambition to be supreme in a narrow field. We collect for our own enjoyment, but we should be sufficiently introspective to be sure that it is enjoyment of an object and not a competition. Specialization is also demonstrably detrimental from the investment point of view. The one-line collector creates his own rise in price, as dealers vie with one another to find what they know he will covet. Should he be faced with the necessity of selling, he may create his own depression. An avalanche of works of art of a single type on a restricted market usually sends prices tumbling.

Quality and diversity, then, are the inescapable requisites of a worthwhile collection, whether it is made for aesthetic satisfaction or financial gain. And works of art are an investment. An astute Frenchman once told me that he had divided his investments into three equal parts—securities, real estate, and a well-diversified collection of works of art. "If the last pays no tangible dividends, it gives me an enjoyment for which dividends could not compensate, and it is the investment about which I worry least. I know that if the value of one painting goes down, another is surely going up." Henry Walters claimed that within a number of years the government would have paid for his collection in terms of the income tax he would have had to pay on the return from a like amount invested in income-bearing properties.

These observations on the economics of the art market are of importance only as they reflect and validate larger truths. Despite the catastrophes mankind brings on itself, art is a universal stimulus and an index of culture which remains constant. Prehistoric drawings on the walls of caves trace the aesthetic urge to roots deep in the primeval soul. Art in its infinite variations has served through the ages as an exorcism of the fears, hatreds, and the hallucinations which haunt our dreams. It expresses all the spiritual aspirations in man.

This constant longing for the spiritual values inherent in all forms of aesthetic creation is today as alive as ever. The Westerner has been fascinated for years by the beauty and variety of Oriental art and has attained some understanding of its significance. Before World War II, Japanese private and public collectors had begun to take a lively interest in Western painting, particularly the modern schools. It raises the possibility of the great civilizations of Occident and Orient, so opposed and uncomprehending, finding a common ground under the aegis of art. Must mergers of great cultures take place only by force of treaties imposed by statesmen, based on material considerations of arms and economics? Is it not possible to conceive a greater union of minds through art?

Art in all its forms has been historically the most enduring language for the mingling of souls in common enjoyment, for that is one of its paramount values—a joy to be shared by all who are willing to see and to feel, a great international tongue by which men can speak and be thrilled across the centuries and across the world.

The inventory which so fortunately was located is a copy of a legal document of one hundred and five pages, dated February 16, 1912, "*à Paris, rue Laffite* [sic] *No. 2, dans un appartement où résidait Sir John Edward Arthur* [*Jean Edouard Arthur*] *Murray-Scott. . . .*" It was established at the request of Douglas Alexander Scott (*major général de l'armée anglaise, en retraite, demeurant à Trusley Court Godalming, Surrey, Angleterre*) and Frederick William Capron, solicitor (*demeurant à Londres*), Savile Place No. 7 "*. . . agissant en qualité d'exécuteurs testamentaires, avec saisine, ainsi qu'ils l'ont déclaré dans la procuration ci-dessus énoncée, de Sir John Edward Arthur Murray Scott, en son vivant, sujet anglais Baronnet. . . .*"

The inventory, which is also an appraisal, is divided as follows: the library; the silver; racing trophies; table china, kitchen equipment, servants' furnishings, linens, carriages, and the wine cellar; ordinary household furnishings; the tapestries; the paintings, watercolors, and drawings; "*Objets d'intérêt artistique, historique et national*" (including sculpture, furniture, decorative objects, and engravings); a detailing of the silver already listed.

The library, which contained around three thousand volumes, is revealing of the characters and tastes of its successive owners. Besides the standard literary works both ancient and modern of a "gentleman's library," there was a wide range of historical works, memoires of the 18th century, Napoleonia, and books on every phase of artistic production, many of them today rare items of primary source material. Since the Seligmann firm did not deal in books, the entire library was sold to the English bookseller Bumpus.

The table silver could have served a regiment and the wine cellar with its one hundred and fifty bottles of Château Malescot, six hundred bottles of Saint Emilion, and one hundred and sixty bottles of Mouton Rothschild, to mention only a few, would make a gourmet sigh with envy. The comparative paucity of table china and linens of all sorts—only three sets of table linen are listed—attests to the years of bachelor status of the house on the rue Laffitte. Likewise the "rolling stock" seems to have fallen on bad days, for the Victoria is listed as *hors d'usage* and the other three carriages as *très usagés*.

The Tapestries

Twelve tapestries hung in the *grande galerie* and another is listed as stored there in a cupboard, while a set of four more were on loan to the Musée des Arts Décoratifs. They were as follows:

Histoire de Psyche	—after cartoons by Boucher. A set of five, Beauvais, Louis XVI period. Now in the Philadelphia Museum as a bequest of Mrs. Hamilton Rice (formerly Mrs. George Widener).
Le Repas	—after designs by Le Prince. One of the *Jeux russiens* series, Beauvais, Louis XV period. Now in the Metropolitan Museum of Art as gift of Mrs. Oliver Gould Jennings in memory of Mr. Jennings.
Four Beauvais panels	—representing animals and birds in landscape backgrounds. This is the set which was on loan to the Musée des Arts Décoratifs and may have been sold to Mr. George Kessler. Present whereabouts unknown.
Chancellerie	—or Arms of France, on red background. Gobelins, 18th century. Collection of François-Gérard Seligmann, Paris.
Arms of France	—Gobelins, 18th century. Described as "Arms of France supported by two female figures and surmounted by two *amours* holding a crown." Whereabouts unknown.
Arms of England	—Brussels, 18th century. Whereabouts unknown.
La Terre	—Set of three, Gobelins, 18th century. Whereabouts unknown.
La Toilette de Flore	
Junon et Diane	
Fleurs-de-lys	—on blue ground. Gobelins, 18th century. Whereabouts unknown.

The Paintings

Of the thirteen pages of paintings, watercolors, and drawings in the inventory, it is possible today to list fifty-odd of which the present ownership is known or at least to whom they passed from the Seligmann firm. Fortunately, the majority of the important works are in this list. The last collection named is the most recent.

Ballue, H.	Six watercolors	Collection of Mr. and Mrs. Germain Seligman.
Boilly, Louis	*La Jarretière*	Charles W. Clark (1921).
	Scène de carnaval or *Boulevard du Crime*	S. H. Golding (1925).
	La Danse des chiens	Mrs. George F. Baker, Jr. (1929).
	Le Vieillard jaloux *Poussez ferme*	Alfred Lowenstein. Messrs. Agnew & Sons (1952).
Boucher, F.	*Birth and Triumph of Venus*	Baron Eugene de Rothschild. Metropolitan Museum of Art. Gift of Henry Walters and Germain Seligman.
	Jupiter and Callisto *Angélique et Médor*	Knoedler & Co. (1914). Morton F. Plant. Mrs. William Hayward. Mrs. John E. Rovensky Sale, Parke-Bernet, Jan. 15–19, 1957, Nos. 457–58.
	Diane et Endymion	Knoedler & Co. (1914). W. R. Timken. National Gallery of Art, Washington, bequest of Mrs. W. R. Timken.
	La Musique or *La Muse Erato*	Knoedler & Co. (1914). W. R. Timken. London Art market (1950).
	Cupid and the Graces	Knoedler & Co. (1914). The Gulbenkian Collection, on loan to National Gallery of Art, Washington.

269

Boucher, F.	*La Musique* *Le Dessin* *Portrait de jeune Femme*	Knoedler & Co. (1914). The Frick Collection.
	Jupiter and Callisto *Jupiter and Léda* (pastels)	Albert Meyer. René Fribourg.
Bruchner (or Buckner)	*Femme à la Mantille* *noir*	Looted, Paris, 1940–44 from private collection of Germain Seligman.
David, J. L.	*Portrait of Napoleon I*	The Fogg Art Museum— Grenville L. Winthrop Collection.
Dumont, François	*Carnet de bal de Marie-* *Antoinette* with por- traits of the Queen, the Comtesse d'Artois, the Comtesse de Pro- vence and their two sons	Succession Arthur Veil- Picard.
French, 18th cen- tury	*Les Bains chinois*	Musée Carnavalet, Paris, gift of Jacques Selig- mann.
Guardi, Francesco	*La Campanile, Venice* *Place St. Marc, Venice*	Knoedler & Co. (1914). Madame Soucaret, Paris.
	Vue de la Place St. Marc *Vue de la Piazzetta*	Count Moise de Camondo. Musée Nissim de Camondo, Paris.
Lancret, Nicolas	Set of *demi-lune* over- doors: *Baigneuses* *Concert champêtre* *Hallali End of the Hunt* *Le Petit Déjeuner*	Knoedler & Co. (1914). Morton F. Plant. M. H. de Young Museum, San Francisco.

270

Laure, Jules	*Portrait of Lola Montez en Amazone*	Looted, Paris, 1940–44, from private collection of Germain Seligman
Lemoyne, François	*Léda et le cygne*	François-Gérard Seligmann, Paris
*Mignard, Pierre	*Portrait d'une Reine avec son fils et cupidon*	National Gallery, London, by will of Sir John Murray Scott
Nattier, J.-M.	*Madame Henriette de France en vestale*	Detroit Museum of Art
Prud'hon, P.-P.	*Académie de femme Académie d'homme* (drawings)	Baron Gourgaud, Paris
Raffet	*La Retraite*	Looted, Paris, 1940–44.
Taunay	*Scène de chasse Bergers à la ruine*	Clarence H. Geist, Philadelphia
Tocqué, Louis	*Portrait du duc de Chartres*	Germain Seligman
Van Loo, Amadée	*La Déclaration La Rupture*	Sold in Paris, 1925. Whereabouts unknown.
Vernet, Carle	*Le Poulain* (watercolor)	Looted, Paris, 1940–44 from collection of Germain Seligman
	Chevaux dans la prairie	Collection of Mr. and Mrs. Germain Seligman
*Vernet, Horace	*The Battle of Hanau The Battle of Montmirail The Battle of Valmy The Battle of Jemmapes*	National Gallery, London, by will of Sir John Murray Scott
Vestier, Antoine	*Mlle Duthé at the bath*	Arthur Veil-Picard, Paris

* Watteau (attr.)   *L'Accord parfait*   National Gallery, London, by will of Sir John Murray Scott

* These paintings are listed on the inventory as *"les tableaux . . . qui seraient légués à la National Gallery de Londres,"* but according to the public press, the will of John Murray Scott had not been found at the time of the taking of the inventory. Both the Watteau and the Mignard are listed in the catalogue of French paintings (1950) of the National Gallery, the latter as *La Marquise de Seignelay and two of her children.*

Among the more interesting paintings of which all trace has been lost are the following:

Boilly, Louis   *L'Etreinte* (Possibly *La douce Resistance* mentioned by Harisse, No. 172, as "Wallace Collection, Paris")
                 La Marche incroyable
                 Les Galants surpris
                 Villageois dans un interior jouant avec un oiseau
Boucher, F.   *Pastorale*—gouache, oval
                 La Cible des amours
Lami, Eugene   *Le Bal de l'Opéra*

Others by Moreau, Schall, Le Prince, Baron Gérard, Gavarni, the Vernets, Isabey, Hondecoeter, Courbet, quantities of drawings without names or by many lesser known artists, make up the balance.

Not appearing on the inventory, but reproduced in the *Connoisseur* of May, 1914, as "in the Sir John Murray Scott Collection in Paris" is a curious full-length portrait purportedly representing Louis XI. The notice continues:

"It hung formerly in the Palais Royal . . . the artist's name has been lost sight of, but that it is an authentic contemporary portrait of the cruel king is undisputed. During the revolution of 1848 one of the mob shot a bullet through the region where the heart is popularly supposed to exist in the human body as evidence of his protest against kings. The damage has since been repaired and in the general distribution of State possessions the portrait eventually passed into the hands of Lord Hertford and so to Sir John Murray Scott."

From the reproduction it seems doubtful that it is a 15th century original, but it may well be one of the 17th century copies of historic portraits which are known to have hung in the Palais Royal. Its whereabouts has not been discovered.

The Sculpture

All the sculpture is listed under the heading of *Objets d'intérêt artistique, historique, et national* and the following pieces can be placed more or less definitely:

Bouchardon, Edmé	*Amour taillant son arc dans la massue d'Hercule*—marble	Lord Wimborne. Mortimer Schiff. Samuel H. Kress Collection, National Gallery, Washington.
Clodion	*Satyresse tenant deux enfants*—terra cotta	The Walters Gallery, Baltimore
Coysevox, Antoine	*Louis XIV* (now known as *Le Grand Dauphin*)—marble	The Samuel H. Kress Collection, National Gallery, Washington
	Le duc d'Orléans—marble	
Girardon, F.	*Louis XIV à cheval*—bronze	Looted, 1940–44, from the Seligmann home in Paris
Houdon, J.-A.	*Portrait of Cagliostro*—marble	The Samuel H. Kress Collection, National Gallery, Washington
	Portrait of Sophie Arnould—marble	Musée du Louvre, gift of Edgar Stern, 1947
	La Frileuse—bronze	Mrs. H. P. Davison, New York
	Seated Voltaire—marble maquette	Mortimer L. Schiff Collection until 1938
Lemoyne, J.-B.	*Baigneuse debout*—marble. Presumed portrait of Madame de Pompadour.	Formerly collection of Baron Edmond de Rothschild
Pigalle	*Cupid*—bronze	The Walters Gallery, Baltimore
Rousseau	*Ulysse bendant son arc*	The Corcoran Art Gallery Washington, gift of Senator W. A. Clark
French, 18th century	*Louis XV à cheval*—bronze	Fernand Javal, Paris
	Two groups of children —bronze *doré*	George Blumenthal
	Pair of bust portraits of women—bronze	The Walters Collection, Baltimore

Again a number of items remain untraced, among them a marble bust of la Dubarry after Pajou, a bather in white marble by Falconet, and a marble bust portrait of a man in armor of the style of Louis XVI. This last item is possibly of little interest, as many statues of largely decorative character had been used in the garden at Bagatelle and this may be one of those, as it is listed as having been stored in the carriage house.

The Furniture and Ornamental Objects

The furniture and ornamental objects which filled the house to over-flowing are, of course, the most difficult to trace, for such works of art are not as carefully recorded as are paintings and sculpture. The task is further complicated, as pointed out earlier, by the fact that many other items which bear the Wallace pedigree reached the market through the various sales of Sir John Murray Scott's English holdings and thus did not pass through the hands of Jacques Seligmann. Lacking the Paris records of the firm, it becomes somewhat too great a task for the confines of this book to try to determine the fate of all the lovely pieces which once adorned the Château de Bagatelle and No. 2 rue Laffitte.

Nor does it seem necessary to attempt to describe again the appearance of the rooms, as the several articles and books cited give a very good picture of them. Suffice it here to note certain important pieces which are today in museums, or well-known collections, or have appeared in recent public sales.

Musée Nissim de Camondo, Paris

An extraordinarily fine *ameublement de salon* by Georges Jacob, ca. 1785. Of carved and gilded wood, covered in Beauvais tapestry on green background, the set consists of two *canapés*, a *marquise*, ten chairs, and a fire screen.

A pair of four-fold tapestry screens, Beauvais, ca. 1750–60

Metropolitan Museum of Art, New York

A monumental *bureau à cylindre*, late Louis XVI, style of Guillaume Beneman, also referred to as the *bureau du roi*. Presented in 1919 by Jacques Seligmann with a plaque bearing the following inscription: "In memory of Mr. J. P. Morgan and as a souvenir of the help which the Americans have given in France during the war."

The Frick Collection, New York

Among a number of items, the most important are:

A Louis XVI table by Riesener with bronzes attributed to Gouthière

A pair of rare Louis XVI consoles ornamented with Mustapha medallions
A pair of lacquer *étagères*, Louis XVI
A pair of gilt-bronze *flambeaux*, Louis XVI
A Louis XVI gilt-bronze *pendule*

Miss Helen Frick, New York

A Louis XVI secretary, *table de chevet*, and a *table de malade*

The Cleveland Museum of Art

A Louis XVI bed attributed to Georges Jacob, with original Philippe de Lasalle embroidered satin upholstery and covers. Said to have belonged to Marie Antoinette. Formerly in the collection of Arthur Veil-Picard, Paris.

A pair of bronze *doré* candelabra, signed by Clodion. Grace Rainey Rogers Collection.

A Louis XV desk. John L. Severance Collection.

The William Rockhill Nelson Gallery of Art, Kansas City

A pair of monumental red porphyry urns, French, 17th century, ornamented with ormulu and mounted on matching column bases

The George Blumenthal Collection

Contained at least seven items:
Two fine Louis XVI table-desks, one signed by Montigny
Six Jacob chairs, gilded and upholstered in tapestry
An Empire bronze and red marble *gueridon*
A rare Louis XVI mahogany and bronze music stand
Two pairs of Louis XVI bronze *doré flambeaux*

Mrs. F. Gray Griswold, New York

A Falconet clock, ca. 1775 (Lepautre)

Private Collection, London

Empire secretary in Thuya wood
Empire *meuble d'entre-deux* in Thuya wood

The late Alfred Lowenstein of Brussels

A rare Louis XVI salon set, *canapé* and eight chairs, with Beauvais tapestries after designs by François Casanova

Mrs. George Rasmussen, New York

An 18th century carved and gilded wood mirror frame with a crest of the arms of France surmounted by a crown and the Order of the Saint Esprit

The late George Rasmussen, Chicago

Louis XV upright desk in *bois de rose* and marquetry

Console by Riesener with green marble top

Louis XVI *meuble d'entre-deux* with flanking *étagères* attributed to Pafrat

A Louis XV chaise longue upholstered with Beauvais tapestry in floral pattern on rose background. One of the finest pieces in the Wallace collection.

The Mortimer L. Schiff Collection

A Louis XVI console ornamented with Sèvres plaques

François-Gérard Seligmann, Paris

A pair of Louis XVI green marble vases ornamented with female heads in bronze *doré*

A pair of Louis XV *microscopes variés* mounted in bronze *doré*

Arthur Veil-Picard Collection, Paris

Régence ormolu and blue enamel luster of rare and exquisite quality. Recently presented to the Louvre, Paris.

A pair of superb Riesener commodes

A *bureau de dame* and several small tables, all French 18th century

The Henry Walters Collection

A number of decorative items and a notable *bureau à cylindre* and commode of the Louis XVI period

Mr. and Mrs. Charles B. Wrightsman, New York

Commode, French, 18th century, style of Cressent.

Bureau-plat, French, 18th century, style of Cressent.

Gilt-wood screen, French, Louis XVI, by Georges Jacob, originally made for Marie Antoinette and coming from the Château de Saint-Cloud. Formerly in the Dutasta Collection, Paris.

Collection of the author

A pair of late 18th century gilt bronze and silver candlesticks representing *amours* riding on crocodiles

In addition, a number of items which had been retained by the Seligmann family were lost by looting in the late war, including a handsome Louis XVI clock, a pair of Empire gilt bronze candelabra, and a fine Louis XVI *bergère* upholstered in Beauvais tapestry of Boucher subject.

A number of pieces which are either signed, or attributed on good authority to a particular cabinet maker, have not been traced. Conspicuous among them is an upright Louis XVI desk attributed to Saunier, a table by Carlin, a secretary by BVRB, a lacquer cabinet by Cramer, and a table-desk by Dubois.

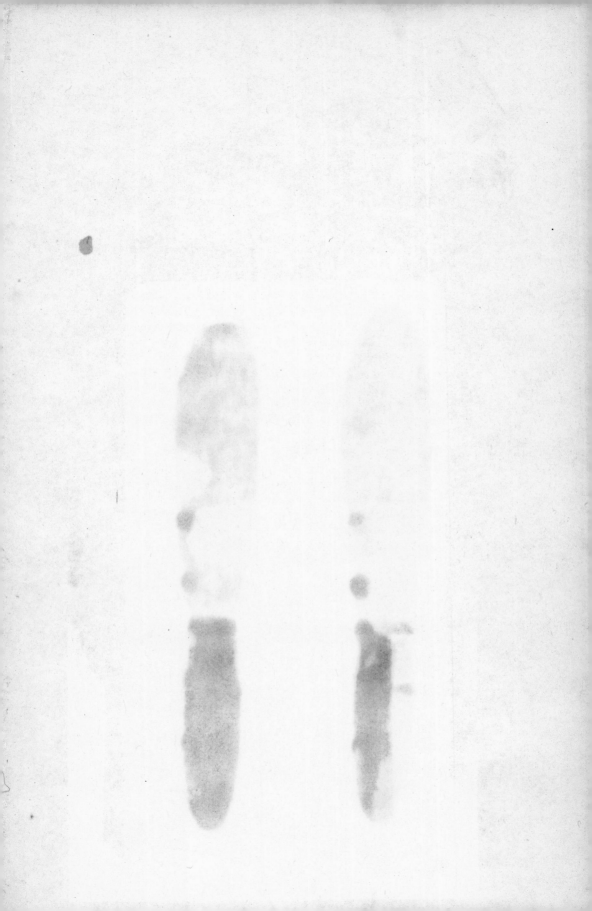